LINDELL'S LIST

Saving British and American Women at Ravensbrück

PETER HORE

First published 2016
This paperback edition published 2019

The History Press
97 St George's Place
Cheltenham, GL50 3QB
www.thehistorypress.co.uk

British Library Cataloguing in Publication Data.
A catalogue record for this book is available from the British Library.

ISBN 978 0 7509 9212 1

Typesetting and origination by The History Press
Printed and bound in Great Britain by TJ International Ltd

CONTENTS

ACKNOWLEDGEMENTS

Three people are responsible for the genesis of this book. First, Annie Hamilton, former commandant of the First Aid Nursing Yeomanry, who encouraged me to write about her girls. Annie introduced me to Yvonne Burney (née Baseden), who told me her story and that of her friend, Mary Lindell, who saved her life in wartime. Annie also introduced me to Michael Foot who, over lunches at the Special Forces Club and the Savill Club, told me about the things he had written about and some of those he had not. I am indebted to all three for their kindness, confidence and the knowledge they imparted.

This work would not have been possible without my travels and research in Belgium, Britain, Denmark, Ireland, France, Germany, Sweden and the USA. In addition to the staff of various archives and libraries in Europe and America, who have been invariably helpful and ready to assist with their knowledge, I would like to thank especially the many courteous and kindly staff at the Imperial War Museum, Kennington and the National Archives at Kew, and in Sweden at Landsarkivet i Lund, at Malmö Stadsarkivet and at Malmöhuset.

In particular, I wish to thank in alphabetical order: Colonel Edwin W. Anderson, US Army SF; Trish Anderson, senior librarian at the Law Society; Colonel Simon Bailey, Yvonne's son; Iain Ballantyne, guru; Professor Judith Barrett Litoff of Bryant University, Smithfield, RI; Yvonne Baseden, F Section SOE; France Bertram, granddaughter of Lucienne Dixon; Roger Bray, ITV; Lena Breitner; Laurence Brisé, mairie de Mauléon-Licharre; Roger Bryant, neighbour of Bruce Lindell; Suzanne Cane; Sebastian Claesson of Autoimages; Oliver Clutton-Brock, author; Phillipe Connant in Belgium; Pierre Cosaque; Martyn Cox; Kathleen Dow, University of Michigan; Pierre-Emmanuel Dufayel, *Fondation pour la Mémoire de la Déportation*; Hilding Ekelund, son of 'Elisabeth Smith'; Isabel Hore Fazan, researcher in Torquay;

Magnus Gertten of Autoimages; the late Scott Goodall, father and author of *The Freedom Trail*; Ian and Elizabeth Granville Miller, residents of Sauveterre-de-Béarn; Christer Hägg; Richard Heaune of the German Occupation Museum, Guernsey; Jonas Hedburg from the Nordiska Museet, Stockholm; Pete Jackson, Toquette's son; Keith Janes, escapelines.com; Hans-Gunther Jantzen; Jenny Kauntze, First Aid Nursing Yeomanry; Stephen Kippax, the SOE Society; Karen V. Kukil, William Allan Neilson Library, Smith College, Northampton, MA; Joël Larroque, Collège Saint François, Mauléon Soule; Michael Moores LeBlanc; Bengt Lindholm, Malmö Stadsarkiv; Diane Morgan, RAF Escaping Society; David Murphy, National University of Ireland; Janice O'Brien, researcher at Colindale; Bob O'Hara, researcher at Kew; Sandra J. Ott; Charles Owen, military obituarist at the *Daily Telegraph*; Philippa Paterson, French translator; Anne-Marie Pavillard, BDIC Service des archives; the late Sune Persson, professor and author; Charles Pinck, the OSS Society; Graham Pitchfork, RAF obituarist at the *Daily Telegraph*; Major Jo-ann Price, Historical Museum and Historians Office, the Salvation Army, Central Territory, USA; Judith Provoyeur; Edouard Renière, Belgium; Lorraine Riemer, Pete's daughter; Suzanne Rodriguez, California; Neasa Roughan, archives assistant at the Royal College of Nursing Archives; Lord Eric de Saumarez, Guernsey; Monika Schnell, Mahn- und Gedenkstätte Ravensbrück; Naomi Sharp, the Salvation Army International Heritage Centre; Penny Small, muse and French translator; Sim Smiley, National Archives and Records Administration, College Park, MD, USA; Ewen Southby-Tailyour; Anders Otte Stensager; Annika Tergius, Landsarkivet i Lund; Daniel Thuret; Robert Trembath; Stephen Tyas; Maria van der Tang; Hal Vaughan; Peter Verstraeten; Magnus Waldebron, Malmö Museum; and Pam Zimmerman.

With a special thanks to all those friends and companions who helped me in 2014 to walk the Chemin de la Liberté in the footsteps of Mary Lindell's escapers.

No work can be adequately completed without a first-class publications team, and I would like to thank Michael Leventhal, Jo de Vries, and all at The History Press, especially Chrissy McMorris, the unknown reader, Martin Latham and Jemma Cox.

AUTHOR'S FOREWORD

The title of this book is based on an actual incident in April 1945 when the SS guards at Ravensbrück denied that they held any American or British women prisoners, and Mary Lindell produced her list from her pinafore pocket. Prior to this incident, through the black night of despair that fell on France in 1940 and the years of German occupation and oppression which followed, Mary's passionate opposition to tyranny was turned into practical deeds. The flame of her patriotism could not be dimmed, she was fearless to the point of foolhardiness, and she continued her resistance to the Nazis even when thrown into Ravensbrück, a concentration camp which was known as the 'Women's Hell', where tens of thousands were murdered.

Mary held strong opinions and she defied the British, French, German and Swedish authorities in pursuit of what she believed to be right, and when tested in the horrors of war, and life in the concentration camp, she showed herself to be patriotic, determined, careless of her own life and convinced of the right-eousness of her cause. She was not young and beautiful like some of the agents who, after the war, stood in the limelight. Her bravery was sustained through more than five years of war, under the most difficult of conditions and personal danger to her and to her family.

The best-known version of Mary Lindell's life is Barry Wynne's 1961 book, *No Drums … No Trumpets*, which has since been republished under different titles. This was written after Wynne and Mary had been closeted in a hotel in England for several weeks, at the end of which Mary was sick and tired of the whole process of interview and re-interview. 'The book was a mess,' she told the American feminist Margaret L. Rossiter when interviewed by her, and when pressed by Rossiter as to whether the facts in *No Drums … No Trumpets* could be relied upon, Mary replied, coyly, 'Mostly.'[1]

Starting in 1976, Rossiter taped many interviews, now in the University of Michigan State University special collections, for her 1986 book, *Women in the Resistance*. Her interviewees included many heroes and heroines of the French Resistance, including Mary Lindell, and when her hours of interviews with Mary were synthesised into one chapter,[2] Rossiter gave possibly the best description of Mary Lindell:

> A handsome woman [she was then some 80 years old] of medium height, with chestnut hair and brown eyes, Mary Lindell has a commanding personality. She liked to give orders, and she spoke with the self-confidence of an aristocrat. However, Mary was not like a traditional lady. She was sometimes ungracious and abrupt; if she thought people were phoney, she told them so. At other times she was charming, a good mimic, and an amusing raconteur. She did not like humdrum routine, and enjoyed the challenge of outwitting people, particularly the Germans.[3]

Two other primary sources about Mary's life are television programmes. The first, *It Happened to Me – Mary Lindell: the Escapers*, was made in 1960 by the BBC and presented by Alan Whicker, and is a re-enactment of some of Mary's wartime exploits, concentrating on the part of the Marie-Claire escape line that ran out of France over the Pyrenees into Spain, and involving some of the original participants.[4] No copy survives in any archive but a rare copy has been preserved in France by Scott Goodall MBE. The second was made in 1980 as part of a series by Yorkshire TV and presented by Robert Morley,[5] with the accompanying book by Kevin Sim.[6] Mary also gave oral evidence to the Hamburg War Crimes Tribunal.

These oral and filmic accounts allow us to hear Mary's memories of her experiences in her own words, and are the source of the dialogues in this book. Where Mary recounted similar events on different occasions, the dialogue is synthesised.

Two much more recent female authors have been dismissive of Mary Lindell. Sarah Helm trivialised her as 'a bossy Englishwoman', but Helm was focussed on events inside the camp at Ravensbrück, and she overlooked the breadth of Mary's achievements, the complex shades of her personality, and that it was her strength of character which kept her and others alive in the camp.[7]

As to Mary's character, she was every Englishman's nightmare of a mother superior, mother-in-law, stepmother and lady master of foxhounds. Or, as her brother put it, 'she was not just difficult with the Gestapo, she was difficult with everyone!'[8] She also had the raconteur's capacity for embroidering her stories.

However, the actual achievements of 'selfless, stubborn, arrogant Mary' are well catalogued in the official record and well summarised by Oliver Clutton-Brock in his encyclopaedic study of escape lines in the Second World War.[9]

The French journalist Marie-Laure le Foulon has also trashed Mary's reputation.[10] However, she has relied overly on the witness of one other woman, and has interpreted a small number of documents in the French archives in the blackest possible way. In a range of accusations, le Foulon has suggested that Mary's lovers included the impeccable British captain, Jimmy Windsor Lewis of the Welsh Guards, in 1940 and Obersturmführer Percy Treite, camp doctor at Ravensbrück in 1944 (two 'boys' who were a generation younger than her) and that in the years between she was a stooge, if not an agent, of the Germans. There is no evidence for any of this except old-fashioned French revolutionary-style denunciation, but in her attempt to find evidence where none exists for these allegations, le Foulon has even submitted Mary to an examination after her death by a French *psychiatre-psychanalyste*.

It is moot to ask why anyone writing about the Resistance in France should choose to attack a British heroine when there are so many others whose roles in the Resistance might not bear the same scrutiny to which le Foulon has subjected Mary Lindell. This question lies heaviest on the RMA ('Resisters of the Month of August') and the FFS ('*Forces Françaises de Septembre*'), the men and women who stood by for four years while their country was occupied, and only answered the call to arms in late 1944 when it was clear that the Allied landings were successful and that the Allies were winning the war. The question should also weigh on the conscience of the rival parties who fought each other for the future rule of France, while on 15 August 1944 they allowed the Germans to transport thousands of Frenchmen and women prisoners through Paris to suffer horribly and die in appalling conditions in Germany.

However, it is Max Hastings who has commented that most accounts of wartime agents, particularly women agents and especially in France, contain 'large doses of romantic twaddle'.[11] If Wynne's account of Mary's life is thesis filled with romantic twaddle, and le Foulon's is antithesis, my account is synthesis. My lodestar in writing *Lindell's List* has been finding the original records written as close as possible to the events to which they refer. If I have missed any, it is my fault.

This account of Mary's life and achievements uses archives in Sweden, where the women on Lindell's list were taken by the Swedish Red Cross in April 1945, which have rarely been used by anglophone scholars, and archives in Belgium, Denmark, France, Germany and the USA, which shed more light on

Mary's career and her contemporaries and colleagues in the Second World War. They enable the claims made for her and against her to be quantified. All errors of omission and commission are mine and mine alone.

Mary was not, as le Foulon has reported, a Joan of Arc. Indeed, with her fervent sense of Englishness and contempt for many aspects of French life, Mary is unlikely to have appreciated such a comparison: rather she took the martyred Englishwoman Edith Cavell as her role model. However, nothing can detract from Mary's absolute bravery, displayed not on some occasion when the red mist of anger fell upon her and drove her to do something outlandish, but bravery sustained during two world wars against all odds, and in the most difficult of circumstances. Here, then, is her life in a time of war, wrack and wonder and it is presented 'warts and all'.

PGH
Iping Marsh
June 2016

INTRODUCTION

Hamburg, 1947

It is February 1947 in a cold, war-ravaged Hamburg. For three months a war crimes tribunal has been hearing of the sickening, dark deeds that were done at Ravensbrück, a concentration camp through which some 130,000 women passed during the Second World War and where perhaps half of them were murdered by the Germans.

There are fifteen defendants in the dock: six of them are women. They all appear to be middle class, are smartly dressed, and the women are well coiffured. They wear numbered placards round their necks. Two prisoners – Number 9, Carmen Mory, and Number 10, Vera Salvequart – wear fur coats, and in the photographs of the courtroom they alternately flirt with the cameraman and look down demurely at their laps.

Mory is a 40-year-old doctor's daughter from Switzerland. Well educated and multi-lingual but thwarted in her ambition to become a singer, she had turned to journalism, and as a reporter in Berlin had admired the Nazis. She had spied for the Germans in France and had been sentenced to death, but the German invasion of France had saved her from being shot. Her German controller and lover gave her a new mission, to pretend to be a member of the French Resistance, but when he tired of her she was sent to Ravensbrück on trumped up charges, and there she became a trustee and one of the most feared women in the camp.[1]

Prisoner Number 10 is 30-something Vera Salvequart, a Czech-born nurse sent to Ravensbrück after being accused of taking a Jewish lover. There, in the camp's medical wing, she had blithely helped to select her fellow prisoners for the gas chambers, poisoned her fellow prisoners and inspected the cadavers for gold teeth which were then ripped out.

Two other women in the dock are careful to look away from the camera. Number 11 is Elisabeth Marschall, at 61 the oldest person in the dock, and the only one who has anything of the appearance of the archetypal criminal. As *oberschwester*, or head nurse, she is accused, among other crimes, of having forced fifty mothers and their babies into a cattle wagon without food or water, and sending them to their deaths.

By contrast, the blonde 26-year-old Dorothea Binz, Number 5, looks impossibly demure and incapable of the dreadful charges which are levelled against her – that, as chief wardress at Ravensbrück, she slapped, beat, kicked, shot and abused her fellow women and killed them on a whim. Allegedly Binz went on romantic evening strolls round the camp with her lover, an SS guard, and her pet dog, and enjoyed seeing female prisoners being set upon and whipped. In the photographs it does seem that butter would not melt in her mouth.

The women sit on one side of the dock and nine men sit across the gangway. At the very end of the row, upright and staring straight ahead and dressed in what looks like a tweed jacket, is camp doctor Percy Treite, who is accused of the neglect of his patients, ghastly experiments, forced sterilisations and killings. The number on his placard is an unlucky 13.

The court consists of seven soldiers: they are inured, even bored, by the dreadful things they are hearing from a procession of witnesses. This is a court set up under military law. The senior military officer is Major General Victor Westropp, who comes from a long line of soldiers and land owners.[2] Westropp is the consummate staff officer, a bureaucrat in uniform whose greatest problem in the Second World War had been how to discipline, care for and feed 400,000 Axis prisoners in Italy who gobbled up four shiploads of food every week.

His fellow judges on the court martial are an artilleryman, a tank officer, a foot soldier and a captain of the Royal Army Service Corps, together with a Polish and French officer. Only the French officer is legally qualified. They are, however, advised by a barrister who, under the military system of justice, bears the title of Judge Advocate and in England is a King's Counsel. His foreign first names, Carl Ludwig Stirling, belie his British nationality.[3]

The prosecutor is one of the few other legally qualified officers, Stephen Stewart, who just a few years before had been Stefan Strauss. Strauss, fearing his name was on a death list, had fled Austria in 1938 just before *Anschluss*, the Nazi takeover of that country, and had been called to the bar in London under his new name.

Emphasising the inexperience of the court, the prosecutor's assistant is the 24-year-old Cambridge graduate John da Cunha.[1] During the war da Cunha had served as a tank commander in the 23rd Hussars and taken part in the Normandy invasion, landing at Sword beach on D-Day Plus 4. Three weeks later, during the siege of Caen, da Cunha was seriously wounded by shrapnel, and while convalescing he had been summoned to the War Office to be told he was being sent to Germany to help with the preparation for the war crimes tribunals. No one showed any interest in whether or not da Cunha was fit for duty or had any legal training, but he was asked if he had a stomach injury. When da Cunha replied that he had not, he was told, 'Good. You can eat the disgusting German food, then. Off you go to war crimes.'

Da Cunha recalled that, after he opened and read his first war crimes file, he vomited. He travelled throughout Europe tracing survivors and witnesses from the concentration camps, and reported directly to Group Captain Tony Somerhough, the head of the investigation team. Da Cunha recalled that when Binz was arrested, despite her reputation for evil during three years at the camp, she had to be carried into the prison, so badly were her legs shaking. 'She was so terrified that the same might be done to her as she had done to others.'

It is the twenty-seventh day of the trial. The court has fallen into a routine. A steady procession of witnesses tell of the evils of Ravensbrück. Their story is monotonous, and the keen sense of horror and revulsion which Westropp felt at the beginning has dulled. He is fretting that his military career, which might have ended with a knighthood and the governorship of some remote colony, is coming to an end in this courtroom.

Suddenly the court is woken up by a diminutive figure dressed in her blue Red Cross uniform, replete with British, French and Russian decorations from the First World War. This is Mary Lindell, Comtesse de Milleville, 50 years old, gaunt but still handsome and, despite her small stature, imperious.

Stirling, who is in a hanging mood, interrupts her evidence to demand what she is doing here. Mary has already outwitted a German general, faced a German court martial that sentenced her to nine months' imprisonment, fled through wartime France to England, returned to France to set up an escape line, been arrested, wounded while trying to flee again and thrown into the women's hell at Ravensbrück. Now, not even Stirling can overawe Mary, and she replies, 'Because I am British and I believe that justice is justice, fair is fair, and because we British and American women who were in the camp owe our lives to Dr Treite.'

I

ENOUGH FOR ONE LIFETIME

Mary Lindell was christened Gertrude Mary, but in her teenage years she began try out other identities and adopted the name of Ghita Mary. She was Ghita when, after the First World War, she married the French count Maurice de Milleville, and in the 1940s she signed herself as Ghita de Milleville. Only after the Second World War did she settle for being plain Mary, and this is the name by which we will know her. Aged 15, Mary had inherited wealth from a godfather and, as she would later tell an interviewer, 'That is why I became arrogant and independent, because from fifteen onwards I never knew what money was – do you see what I mean? It just was there.'

Riches did not save Mary from being packed off to Miss Guyer's Girton Hall Ladies' School, a minor boarding school in Torquay. Miss Guyer's school was in a large Georgian house close to the seafront, but sheltered by a hill from the prevailing winds. The 1911 census shows that for the score of pupils there were six domestic staff and four teachers, two of them French – Odette St André and Magda Gautrand. Mary's fellow pupils were a mixture of Devon locals and children of empire from as far afield as India and Australia. One of the pupils was from Hamburg and another, Denise Serge-Basset, from France. This was where Mary learned her French, which she spoke with a pronounced English schoolgirl accent until the end of her days.

Her mother, Gertrude, was a scion of the Colls family, housepainters in south London who, with their friends the Trollopes (who had started as wall-paper hangers and with whom they intermarried), had in a few generations transformed themselves to contractors and developers in booming nineteenth-century London. Their company, Trollope & Colls, built many landmark London buildings including the Haymarket Theatre and Claridge's Hotel, though neither the Trollopes nor Colls had been heard of when the Mansion

House was built two centuries before. This did not stop Mary claiming that her mother's father was the architect of that building too.

Mary recalled her mother was 'just a sweet woman who had so much money she didn't know what to do with it'. A surviving picture shows Mary's bespectacled mother in the uniform of the Young Women's Christian Association, looking rather prim and severe.

When in her old age Mary was asked what gave her the confidence and courage to achieve so much in her life, she claimed that she had blue blood, that her father's family were Czech and had come to England in the retinue of Prince Albert, and that she was a direct descendent of the kings of Bohemia. In fact, William Clement Lindell was from Yorkshire and was a lawyer, though he had no great incentive to practise law and preferred to spend his afternoons sleeping in his library. Whether Mary's claim was an ingenuous middle-class fancy or a symptom of her chronic weakness for self-deception, she certainly liked to tell a good story, and exaggeration was not unknown in Mary's telling of her life story.

Bruce, her brother, was born at Sutton in Surrey in 1894, and Mary a year later on 11 September 1895. The Lindells moved several times before settling at Marlow, on the Thames. It was there in August 1914 that, according to Mary, the family were at the table when the butler brought in a telegram for her father to read, and he exclaimed, 'My God, we're at war!' Bruce was on a grand tour which had taken him as far as Chile, and his father looked first at his wife and then pointed at Mary, 'Well, your brother's not here, this kid can go. Up tomorrow!'

Accounts of the First World War rarely mention the mobilisation of women, except as munitions workers and Land Army recruits, but as early as September 1914 a Women's Hospital Corps had been sent from London to Paris and by November British women doctors were, for the first time, working as army surgeons at a military hospital established in the Grand Hotel at Wimereux, north of Boulogne. Also in 1914, the French Flag Nursing Corps was established to provide a corps of certificated British nurses for service in French military hospitals.

Just before her 19th birthday, Mary became part of this mobilisation and was sent to London to live with her grandmother and to train to be a VAD (Voluntary Aid Detachment). The VAD had been founded in 1909: confusingly each member and each unit were called a detachment, or simply a VAD. In 1914 there were several hundred VAD units in Britain and some 40,000 individual VADs. They were mainly middle- and upper-class girls who were unaccustomed to menial work.

The Red Cross, who had helped to found the VAD, was unwilling to send them abroad and the army would not accept VADs at the front line. Further, the VADs – though well represented in romantic literature, such as in Hemingway's *Farewell to Arms* and Brittain's *Testament of Youth* – were unused to the hierarchy and discipline of hospitals, and they lacked the skills of trained nurses. However, as the scale of the war grew, there developed a shortage of nurses to tend the wounded from the slaughter on the Western Front, and reluctantly the authorities agreed that girls older than 23 and with at least three months' hospital experience would be accepted for overseas service.

In turn, many VADs were critical of the nursing profession, and Mary seems to have been one of these. Her training was brief and she soon clashed with authority. The matron was exasperated by her, or rather, according to Mary, 'The matron didn't like me. I will say I was very incompetent, but I think she must have been a bit Communist or Socialist.'[1]

Ordered to light the fires, she proved inept and her soldier patients used to leap from their sickbeds saying, 'You get out of the way, miss, we'll do it for you.' When put on to emptying bedpans she proved no more successful. Mary's idea was to rinse them under the bath tap, but she was scolded by matron, 'You call that cleaning a bed pan!'

'No,' replied Mary, 'but I tell you what, you're going to find out what cleaning a face means,' and, Mary claimed, she waved a loo brush in matron's face. It was one of her favourite stories, which sometimes ended with the embellishment that she was arrested and charged with insulting a superior officer.

VAD Mary's clash with her matron is a metaphor for the rivalry and resentment between the volunteers and the professionals. One member of the National Union of Trained Nurses, writing from a hospital in France, complained:

> [It is] now, when many of the fine ladies have returned to Paris, and others are very tired, that we English nurses are most useful … If any untrained help is employed in military hospitals abroad it certainly need not be supplied by sending untrained people from the United Kingdom, as all our Allies have Red Cross Societies which can supply untrained workers locally who are conversant both with the country and the language.[2]

Individual nurses welcomed the opportunity and the freedom that foreign service presented, one writing to the *British Journal of Nursing*, 'It is to be regretted that the intelligent action of the French Government in employing English nurses has given umbrage to certain Red Cross ladies.'[3] In fact, the profession of nursing in the USA, Britain and the British Empire was only a generation or two old, and on the Continent nursing was still dominated by nuns, who had little training. Eventually nurses from Britain, Australia, Canada, India and New Zealand (and fifteen from Japan) would serve abroad in France, Belgium, Russia, Siberia, Serbia, Montenegro, Romania, Italy, Holland and Salonika.[4] Soon there were British nurses at the Scottish Women's Hospital at Chantilly, the Glamorgan and Monmouthshire Hospital at Berck Plage, the Hospital Sophie Berthelot at Calais, the Hospital of St Paul at Cherbourg, the Hospital Militaire 38 at Deauville, the Auxiliary Hospital at Lure, and hospitals at Dieppe, Dunkirk, Aix-les-Bains, Poitiers, Rouen and many other places.[5]

Somehow, perhaps because the French were not so scrupulous in observing any age limits, Mary sidestepped all these efforts and in March 1915 she volunteered for a branch of the French Red Cross, the *Société de Secours aux Blessés Militaires*, to work in a French hospital in Dinard, a fashionable resort on the Brittany coast where the hotels and casinos were being requisitioned to become hospitals.

Mary was nursing in Brittany when, in October 1915, the news of the execution of Edith Cavell suddenly broke. Pre-war, Edith Cavell had been part of an international movement to improve the standards of nursing, and she had been recruited to be the matron of a nursing school at Ixelles in Brussels. At the war's start she had nursed Allied wounded, but when Belgium was overrun by the Germans she nursed Germans too. In defiance of German martial law Edith began also to shelter wounded British and French soldiers who had evaded capture by the invader and young Belgians of military age, and she joined the Belgian Resistance in helping them to escape into neutral Holland. Arrested in August 1915, within a very short space of weeks she was court-martialled and sentenced to death.

Despite an international outcry which included strong representations by the then neutral US government, she was executed by firing squad on 12 October 1915. The death of a woman under such circumstances caused a wave of revulsion throughout the civilised world. One newspaper, describing it as 'foul murder', said, 'the hearts of the nation will be stirred to the depths at this brave woman's martyrdom at the hands of the arch-Hun who has fouled Europe with blood.'[6] The same newspaper recorded that 'a service at St Paul's cathedral in memory of the martyred nurse Edith Cavell was one of the most striking and impressive tributes that the nation has ever paid within the walls of the national sanctuary'.[7]

Edith Cavell, who had inspired great love and respect in Belgium,[8] now became in death an internationally renowned figure. The Church of England, which does not make saints, created the unusual honour of an Edith Cavell

Day. However, her death was also used for propaganda purposes,[9] and it was 100 years before a more objective view of her life and wartime deeds emerged.[10] Nevertheless, the halo around Edith, and also Gabrielle Petit, inspired a generation of nurses and for several generations afterwards other young women have been motivated by tales of her brave conduct.

Meanwhile, Mary served on in hospitals in northern France until 1917. Little detail is known of Mary's career during this war, but one incident is agreed by all authors. One elderly, bearded soldier, seeing Mary climb down from an ambulance, declared, 'Look, it's a skirt!'

His companion replied, 'No, no, it's a baby.'

From then on she was known as '*le bébé Anglaise*'.

Also, the local newspaper at home, no doubt primed by her mother, carried news of Mary. The *Reading Mercury* reported:

> Miss Ghita Lindell who had been engaged in nursing service in France since an early period of the war has been given the gold medal of the Russian Order of St Anne for her work in nursing wounded Russian soldiers in France. Miss Lindell is a daughter of Mr and Mrs Lindell of Kensington, and formerly of Glade Road, Marlow. Miss Lindell had previously been awarded the *Medaille de Reconnaissance Françaises*.[11]

In December 1917 she was formerly recruited into the French Army and sent to a field hospital in the Château Vauxbuin, south of Soissons, where Anne-Marie Canton Bacara was the matron.

By the spring of 1918 the fighting on the Western Front was deadlocked after four years of horrendous trench warfare when, on 27 May, the Germans opened a massive attack with a heavy artillery bombardment including gas shells, followed by several divisions of crack troops. Their aim was a knockout blow against the French before thousands of fresh American troops joined in the battle on the Allied side. The Allies were taken by surprise and within a few days the Germans had advanced 40km towards Paris, their advance only halted on 6 June when the Americans arrived at the front. The French Army, falling back in disarray, lost nearly 100,000 men, the weight of the attack falling on a line between Reims and Soissons where Mary found herself behind enemy lines.

Mary seems hardly ever to have spoken about this incident, and only briefly to Barry Wynne,[12] but another local English newspaper recorded the award to 'Miss Ghita Lindell of the French Red Cross, daughter of Mr and Mrs Lindell who formerly resided at Marlow … the French Croix de Guerre for bravery and devotion to the wounded during the French retreat in May [1918]'.[13] So too did the *Daily Mirror*.[14] The citation read:

> On the 28 and 29 May [1918] while the enemy were advancing, she distinguished herself by her dedication, her sang froid, and her complete disregard of danger. After her unit had withdrawn, and despite continual bombardment, she remained at her post, where she helped to save material, cared for the wounded and succeeded in evacuating some farms where there were children and elderly who were unable to flee.[15]

Sim gives a freer translation of this, saying that the citation read, 'for days and nights without number she [had] helped to save the lives of hundreds of wounded in the face of constant bombardment',[16] while Wynne, ever keen to exaggerate Mary's achievements, wrote that she had helped to evacuate a field hospital under fire, dodging the shelling and enemy fire in no-man's-land.[17] Wynne also repeated Mary's story that she had been reported in the *Daily Mail* of London as missing and presumed dead. There was a report in the *Daily Mail* about 'Brave Nurses',[18] and under a story about the German advance around Soissons there was a report in the *Western Mail* of 'Hospital Again Bombed/ Nurses Killed: Patients Wounded',[19] and it seems likely that one of these reports was transmuted in Mary's lively mind into a report of her death.

The medal-giving ceremony tells us a little more about Mary. She was ordered to parade in a clean apron, but when a lecherous, old French general exclaimed, '*Ah, une jeune fille,*' and reached out to fumble with her dress, she seized the medal from his hands and pinned it on herself. Few other details have survived of Mary's service in the First World War, though according to Wynne she was gassed and she survived a bout of Spanish flu. Subsequently Mary feigned embarrassment that Wynne had written so much about her experience of the First World War.[20]

Post-war, both Mary and her mother were awarded campaign medals. Gertrude, her mother, got hers for her work for the YWCA.[21] Mary's record card, in the name of Ghita Lindell, shows that after four years' nursing in the most stressful conditions she had acquired some skills, and she is shown as an anaesthetist working for the French Red Cross.[22]

There are long gaps in Mary's life story in the interwar years. Somehow she found her way to Poland, and in Warsaw in about 1920 she married a French count, 'Maurice' Marie Joseph de Milleville. How she met Maurice and quite when she learned that the count already had a wife and children in Normandy is not clear, but Maurice had omitted to obtain a divorce in France. Consequently, even if the Catholic Church had allowed such a thing, her marriage was not recognised in French law.

She was an innocent teenager from a Victorian family background when the war started, and she had grown to maturity under extraordinary conditions working as a nurse in a field hospital. Nevertheless, it must have been a shock to her middle-class values when she realised that her marriage was invalid. However, her use in the interwar years of the title Comtesse de Milleville does not appear to have been challenged by any member of Maurice's family, not even his first wife. And even if in law marriage to a Frenchman gave her French nationality, Mary kept her British passport and always maintained that she was British.

She settled in Paris and the 1920s and 1930s appear to have been years of contentment. There is no hint, in anything that Mary has left to posterity, as to when she found out that her marriage was bigamous, but in August 1942 when she had escaped from France and was being debriefed by Neave, he noted, 'Marriage not considered valid. Has lived in France since last war.'[23]

By 1939 she was living in a handsome Paris apartment in the rue Erlanger in the 16th arrondisement. As the Comtesse de Milleville, she raised three children – Maurice, Octave (or Oky) and Marie, who was also called Barbé. Mary also maintained her contact with the *Société de Secours aux Blessés Militaires*, and on occasions wore her Croix de Guerre and a row of British, French and Russian medal ribbons on her uniform.

In the interwar years, the rising German menace made little difference to the pace of life in Paris, and not until 1940, when the German Army and Air Force turned from their conquests in the east and Scandinavia to blitzkrieg in the west, did the atmosphere change. Mary's life had not been much affected, even when her husband went away on business in South America, but she was incensed by the debacle which followed when the French armies collapsed in the summer of 1940 and the Germans entered Paris as conquerors and occupiers.

However, aged 45, as a heroine in one world war and the mother of three teenage children, it might be thought that Mary had done enough and certainly as much as many another in one lifetime.

2

THE AMBULANCE CONVOY

On 10 May 1940, after eight months of phoney war, the German Army and Air Force began its blitzkrieg on Belgium, the Netherlands and Luxembourg and soon crossed the border into France. On the morning of 15 May, Winston Churchill, the newly appointed British Prime Minister, received a telephone call from his French counterpart saying, 'We have been defeated. We are beaten; we have lost the battle.'[1] Churchill flew to Paris the next day where he saw that the French government was already burning its papers and preparing to evacuate the capital. When he asked, '*Où est la masse de manoeuvre?* [the strategic reserve which had saved Paris in the First World War]', he was told, '*Aucune*' – there was none. For Churchill, this was the most shocking moment of his life.[2]

Pessimism in French government and army circles mirrored folk memories of the siege of Paris in 1870–71 and the German attack on Paris in 1914. As refugees and defeated soldiery from the north and east flooded into Paris, defeatism soon turned into panic, and organisation broke down. Over the next three weeks the exodus from Paris itself swelled into a flood.

Mary had offered to help in the evacuation of the wounded and when asked to stand by at an hour's notice to take charge of an ambulance convoy, she promised to be ready. Meanwhile she saw to the safety of her own. She asked the Red Cross if they would escort Barbé to Bordeaux, but when she was refused because it would be too much responsibility, Mary sent all three of her teenagers by bicycle to Vannes, some 500km away in Brittany, to a Jesuit college where their father had been educated, trusting that a priest there would look after them.

Then she set about cleaning and tidying her apartment in the rue Erlanger and packing her possessions away. Mary, though anxious for her children, felt bound by her promise to remain available to lead an ambulance convoy out of

Paris. Below her the streets grew silent. As others recalled, the social services, the Red Cross and the French government were fleeing south, having burned any papers that they could not carry.[3]

Mary was tuning to the BBC from London when, at 11 one morning, the telephone rang at the rue Erlanger and a male voice asked, 'Comtesse de Milleville?'

'*Oui.*'

'Ah, thank God! We didn't really expect to find you in.'

'What on earth are you talking about? I've been waiting here for days.'

'Yes, I'm sorry, but things are very difficult at this end. Did you know that the whole of the Red Cross have disappeared?'

'That doesn't surprise me. What do you want me to do?'

'A convoy of ambulances is waiting at Porte St Cloud. We want them taken to Bordeaux.'[4]

'Very well, are they ready now?'

'Yes.' Her caller continued, 'May I thank you, Comtesse? It is good to know that the English keep their word. *Bon voyage.*'

Mary dressed for the journey in her blue field uniform with its white apron and white wimple and, of course, the ribbons of the medals that she had been awarded in the First World War. As she locked the door of her apartment and went out into the street she met an old friend, André Huget, a tax official, who cried out, 'Ah! Madame, I was coming to see you where you were. There is no time to be lost. The Boches are already in the outskirts of the city. Where are you going?'

'What the hell do you think I am doing?'

'Would you like me to tag along and help?'

'In other words you want to get out of Paris. Have you got a permit to get gas?'

'Yes, I have.'

'Then follow me.'

At Porte St Cloud, Mary found eleven ambulances filled with men; some of them had been operated upon that same morning. There were some fifty or sixty men in stretchers and on the floor of the ambulances, and walking wounded sitting beside the drivers. There were no requisition papers, no petrol coupons, no instruments, no bandages – in fact, in Mary's words, 'no nothing'.[5]

Mary's travels over the next two or three weeks, her journey westwards out of Paris towards the Brittany coast, south across the front of the advancing German Army, on to the foothills of the Pyrenees, and her return to Paris, are at once confused and incredible. According to one version, she drove via

Rambouillet to Rennes, Nantes, Vannes, Bordeaux, south to Pau and back again, via le Pyla and Poitiers to Paris. Whatever her actual trajectory, the experience would influence events later in her career when running an escape line.

Undismayed by the lack of resources, Mary set out with her own car at the head of the convoy, flying the Red Cross flag on a pole. Huget brought up the rear of the column. The first 14km, along roads thronged with refugees, took seven hours. The only relief came when German aeroplanes flew over and the refugees dived for cover. Mary used the sudden opening in the line of traffic to speed ahead until, exhausted and exasperated, she decided to draw into a farmyard. There she requisitioned the entire farm, 'Everything you've got here. All your milk and all your eggs and your wife – she's got to make omelettes,' and she wrote out her own requisition papers.[6]

The next morning she gave her promise to the wounded soldiers, 'You will not be prisoners, that I swear by everything that is holy.' On returning to the road, she peremptorily stopped the traffic by walking into the carriageway waving her Red Cross flag. For the next 16km she walked down the road waving the traffic aside, shouting, 'Red Cross! Right of passage!'[7] For three days and nights Mary's convoy took its westerly route through Rambouillet and towards Rennes, before turning south for Bordeaux. When she was tired of walking, Mary shared the driving with Huget, whose own car had broken down and been abandoned.

Her first brush with the invading Germans was at a crossroads where a German motorcycle patrol was holding up the traffic for a column of troops on their gleaming bikes who sped across her path. She immediately engaged in verbal battle, 'I'm the Red Cross. Kindly grant me the right of way. International law – right of way must be given to the Red Cross.'

A German officer nodded, but did not smile, 'Yes, that is the law. Bring your vehicles up and we shall allow them through.'

Only a few minutes before, the ambulance drivers and some of the fitter patients had been berating Mary and blaming her that they might not reach the coast in time to be evacuated before the Germans arrived. Now she ordered them, 'Into the ambulances! Follow me!'

Twenty kilometres further on, a tank blocked the road. It made no difference to Mary, who once more dismounted and advanced on the tank, waving her flag, 'Red Cross. We have the right of way. Will you kindly remove your tank?'[8]

The response from a wild-looking officer in field-grey uniform was surly, but as Mary continued to argue with him another officer, 'tall and smart, though not particularly good-looking', slowly walked over.[9] Not for the first time, Mary's heavily accented French gave her away. 'Madame, may I ask what nationality you are?'

And, despite her score of years married to a Frenchman, she replied proudly, 'I'm British.'

'I knew you couldn't be French,' he answered in perfect English. 'Now what can we do? You are right. Of course we will give you right of way. Where are you going?'

'In a few more miles I intend to turn south for Bordeaux.'

He may have been surprised at Mary's roundabout route, 'What maps do you use for selecting your route?'

'The *Michelin Guide*.'

'That's no good. I will give you a good map. Now, if you follow my directions implicitly, you should have no further trouble. Drive your ambulances at about 25 miles an hour, or even up to 30, and you will move ahead of our tanks. Then you'll come to the armoured cars. When you reach them, raise the Red Cross flag and carry on, keeping to the left-hand side of the road. Directly you get past, increase your speed and there should be no more difficulty. What do you intend to do when you have got to Bordeaux?'

'To deliver my wounded.'

'May I give you a little advice? If you can, move down to Pau. Bordeaux will be in the occupied zone, but Pau will not be occupied.'

Mary could hardly believe her ears. Pursuing her circuitous route she went to La Chapelle, outside Vannes, where she was surprised that her children had not arrived. Only a little nonplussed, she continued southwards via Pontchâteau and Angers until she reached Pau, 200km south of Bordeaux.[10] It was typical that here Mary should have what she called a 'blazing row' with the doctor in charge of the military hospital. The doctor claimed, 'I can't take any more people.'

Mary replied, 'You can't take any more? Well, you're ruddy well going to. I am a British subject and a British officer and you're ruddy well going to.'

'Well, your ambulances may be useful.'

'Yes, except one, I'm keeping one.'

'No, you're not; you haven't got orders to keep one.'

'Nevertheless, I'm keeping it. And you can pick it up somewhere on the street as I certainly shan't bring it back to you, but I happen to need it.'

Mary needed the ambulance because she had met some French officers outside Bordeaux and had promised she would return to pick them up if she could. It was another round trip of several hundred kilometres and she packed them in like sardines. Afterwards, she liked to think of them as the 'first of the Free French'. Her second arrival in Pau was greeted by one of the young men's parents who feted her. Mary recalled that she also got a bath.[11]

Only when she had rested did her thoughts revert to her children and she set out in search of them. Unknown to her they too had cycled south, and by chance at le Pyla, south of Bordeaux, she met her son Maurice. The next moment, in a most un-Mary-like manner, she was clutching Maurice to her; even she could not trust herself to speak. Maurice and his siblings had met a school friend and his parents who had brought the children south, and now they could be reunited with their mother.

While sipping coffee, Mary had to decide what to do. She would go to Confolens, where a French official had promised her a set of new tyres if she could give him a lift to his home. Maurice, she decided, would cycle to Bordeaux and stay there to sit his baccalaureate, but he would tell Oky and Barbé to cycle to Poitiers where Mary would rendezvous with them. Huget, who was still with Mary, could scarcely believe his ears and at once protested that the children should not be expected to cycle such a long way. He received a lashing of Mary's tongue, 'Shut up, André. You know the trains aren't running. Anyway, do you want them to be picked up? Of course they'll be perfectly alright, they've plenty of money and they can take their time. Nobody will stop a couple of kids who are pedalling along the country roads.'

Huget raised his eyes in despair, but Maurice knew better than to disagree with his mother. At dawn, mother and child separated. There is no report of Mary crying at this new parting from her teenage boy in wartime. Instead, she drove away with her French official and his promise of a set of tyres, and a young Belgian hitchhiker who had told her, 'I'm making for Paris, Madame.'

'Jump in. We are not going there directly, but you should get there in a couple of days.'

The Belgian boy immediately offered to pay his fare. 'I wouldn't dream of taking your money, but you can pay for your ride by looking after my tyres.' The tyres were worn to the canvas and he did indeed earn his ride during repeated stops to mend punctures.

When they reached Poitiers, Mary settled to await the arrival of her children. She waited for six days until, dirty and dishevelled but brown under the summer sun and full of high spirits, they were reunited. Strapping their bicycles on the roof of the car, Mary and her children set out for Paris.

3

PARIS, JULY 1940 – WE'VE ALREADY BEGUN!

When Mary returned to Paris after her epic journey, she found that the flight of French government on 10 June 1940 had been followed by some 2 million Parisians. It was a strangely empty city that the main German forces entered four days later. William Bullitt, the American ambassador in France, who had stayed in the capital to help supervise the orderly transfer of the government of Paris, reported to Washington that the German Army was inside the gates of Paris and that all was quiet. Only a few French gendarmes were on the streets as German tanks, armoured reconnaissance cars, anti-tank guns and motorised infantry paraded down the Champs Elysées while a handful of sightseers watched in silence.

On 14 June the French government had moved again, from Tours to Bordeaux, where it had gone after the German invasions of 1870 and 1914, and on 22 June it signed an armistice with Hitler's Germany. The armistice gave Germany control over the north and west of France, and introduced an internal boundary, called the demarcation line, between the occupied zone and so-called free zone. This line ran for some 1,200km, from the Spanish border to Switzerland, and soon it would only be permitted for Frenchmen to travel between the two parts of their own country if they possessed a pass, or *ausweis*, issued under German authority.

Meanwhile Charles de Gaulle made his famous *Appel du 18 Juin* for Frenchmen to rally round him, 'I, General de Gaulle, currently in London, invite officers and French soldiers … to put themselves in contact with me. Whatever happens, the flame of the French Resistance must not be extinguished and will not be extinguished.'

By the end of the month, however, the French government had moved for a third time, to Vichy, a spa town in central France, and there on 11 July Marshal Philippe Pétain, a hero of the First World War but a reactionary in his old age, was sworn in as head of a collaborationist French state. Henceforth, that part of France and its overseas territories that he governed would be known by the pejorative 'Vichy'.

Meanwhile, Mary returned to Paris on 3 July where she was appalled at the breakdown of French morale. As she told Peter Morley many years later:

> We were not very proud of the French. We were sick to death of them, and we knew that some of us had to stay here who could stand up to the Jerries, and could help the people through. And the French wouldn't have done it until you could collect them together, this sacred few, but at that time there were very, very few of them. What gave me the idea that something was to be done was what Edith Cavell had done in the last war, was necessary and had to be done in this war. Who? There was nobody in Paris, or nobody who could do it, so I said there you are, darling, you are to do it.[1]

Mary's reference to Edith Cavell, not the only time she summoned up this image of the martyred nurse, is telling. Edith had been arrested and executed in 1915, when Mary too was a nurse. The memory of the death of one of the leaders of her profession, which was seared into her mind, would have been reinforced by Herbert Wilcox's 1939 Oscar-nominated film, *Nurse Edith Cavell*, which starred one of the most glamorous actresses of the age, Anna Neagle. Edith's hospital in Brussels had been overrun by the Germans: Mary's Paris had fallen under German occupation. Now, in 1940, Mary was nearly the same age as Edith had been when she was martyred, and a desire to emulate Edith Cavell would account for some of the reckless things she was about to do.

Mary was amazed at the number of German troops who thronged the city. These were combat troops, who had not yet been replaced by second-line, inferior, occupation troops. They were smartly dressed, of excellent physique and, at this stage of the war, on their best behaviour. Mary, who also liked to look smart by wearing her Red Cross uniform, was amused by how much she attracted the eyes of the occupiers. She noticed, too, that mixed among the population of Paris were men who, to her eyes, must be stragglers from the British Army who had failed to make their escape from the beaches of Dunkirk or from any of the other evacuation ports in northern and western France.

Mary looked with some scorn on German soldiers who were sightseeing and enjoying themselves, including large numbers of them at the Tomb of the Unknown Warrior, 'standing reverently beside the flame and giving the Hitler salute'.[2] She resolved to do whatever she could to resist the occupation, and her first thought was to help the stragglers to escape capture by the Germans. Her son Maurice recalled:

> She considered that her job was to not think about herself. She didn't even think about us [her children]. She was so busy and her heart was really in getting these people out. There was no other thing. It primed everything. She wasn't a mother anymore; she was an officer doing a job which she considered was to be done.[3]

When Mary had returned to her apartment in the rue Erlanger she had discovered that Michèle Cambards, the daughter of a French friend and a girlfriend of Oky, was living there.[4] Soon, others turned to her for leadership and two young men, also friends of Oky who had presumably heard of Mary's adventures in June, soon sought her advice on how to leave Paris. They had heard de Gaulle's appeal to join him in England to continue the fight and wanted to join him. In addition to these loyal Frenchmen who wanted to leave Paris and to join the Free French, there were still many hundreds of British soldiers hiding north of the Seine.

Mary invoked the image of Edith Cavell, telling her children:

> If we start to help [these] people to get out of the country, we shall be running a grave risk. You may think it's a great adventure, but remember what happened to Edith Cavell in the last war. We don't know if there are any British troops in Paris yet, but I am sure there must be a few stragglers not so far caught. So from the beginning we must train ourselves to carry out our job with secrecy and efficiency. It's no good helping anyone if we have the slightest doubt about them. This is what I propose to do. I'm going to put some soil in that large bulb bowl, and I shall make anyone we help swear on the soil of France to fight for his country before we raise a finger to help him.[5]

The practical difficulty was to know where to cross the demarcation line between the occupied and unoccupied zones of France. When Michèle Cambards told Mary that her former governess was living on a farm that she had inherited from her parents at Sauveterre-de-Béarn, in the Pays-Basque and near the border with neutral Spain, she was despatched to the south to find out more. Two days later, she was back with the remarkable news that the governess' farm actually straddled the demarcation line between the two zones of France. The farmhouse was on one side and the cowsheds on the other and the fields stretched well into unoccupied France. The governess would be delighted to help, and the farmer had suggested that the easiest way to cross would be for escapers to cross with the cows early in the day for the morning milking.

So, on her 18th birthday, a hot July day in 1940, Michèle initiated the escape line by leading her two young compatriots, Oky's friends, on the first stage of their journey to join de Gaulle in England. Soon Oky had piloted his own first French escapers to the farm and a brisk traffic that was to last for several months had begun.[6] Michèle recalled that in the first six months of the German occupation she and Maurice helped about fifty men to cross into the unoccupied zone of France, and that about a half of these were British. Before the line of demarcation was closed, the majority of the journeys were by train and Michèle and Maurice sometimes made the round trip two or even three times a week. It was exciting and they made a little pocket money by smuggling goods in the burgeoning black market.[7]

Mary financed operations with her own money, but she had a jolt when on 4 July she went to her branch of Lloyds Bank in the Boulevard des Capucines where, seeing German guards at the door, she walked by without faltering in her step. It was the same at the Paris branch of Westminster Bank. She returned to her flat frustrated, but grateful that she had kept her jewellery with her and not put that into any bank vault.

Mary turned to the American consulate for help, but there she was brushed off with the response that every Briton left in Paris was short of cash and she was not a special case. Being Mary, she decided to apply directly to the ambassador, but in the lobby of the embassy she met an old friend, 69-year-old Cecil Shaw. In 1939 the *New York Times* described Shaw as 'Colonel Shaw of Paris'.[8] To Mary, Shaw was a blimpish figure and, ever anxious to improve her social acquaintances, a '12th lancer', but he was much more interesting than that.

Cecil Arthur Shaw lived at the Ritz Hotel, he was 6ft tall, balding with white hair at the sides, and a red nose which indicated his penchant for a lifestyle that was paid for by his American wife. Shaw's many decorations included the Distinguished Service Order (DSO), won heroically in 1901 during the Boer War.[9] He became an amateur film-maker in the First World War and transferred to the newly formed Royal Air Force, from which he retired on health grounds as a flight lieutenant in the stores department in 1922.

Shaw's curious career is explained by the knowledge that before the First World War he had worked in military intelligence in India, South Africa and Rhodesia, where he had met 'Uncle' Claude Dansey. Dansey was a career intelligence officer who, in 1936, set up a shadow secret intelligence agency that ran in parallel with the Secret Intelligence Service (SIS), and to which he recruited expatriate Britons who had settled into foreign communities and businessmen working for British companies abroad. Shaw was almost certainly one of Dansey's agents recruited into the Z Organisation.[10]

Without telling Shaw why, Mary explained to him that she had run out of money, and when he learned of Mary's distress, he told her, 'Don't worry, m'dear.' Turning to an American clerk, Elizabeth Deegan, who Mary already knew, Shaw asked if Mr Sutton of the British Interests Section was in.

'Always, to you, Colonel Shaw.'

'Good, I want to introduce him to the countess.'

Inadvertently Mary had stumbled upon a nexus of people who were working overtly in the British Interests Section of the US embassy and covertly helping British servicemen to escape from occupied France: Shaw; the American Elizabeth Deegan, one of whose tasks was to visit the hospitals and prisons and check on whether there were any British there;[11] and a British consular official, Edward Sutton. Sutton was described as hardworking and mild-mannered, from Guildford in Surrey, in his forties, with his thinning hair carefully drawn across his scalp, who seemed to have a perpetual look of worry.[12] In fact, Edward John Sutton was a locally employed English clerk at the British consulate general in Paris who had volunteered to work for the British interests section in the US embassy.

Reports of escape and evasion in the National Archives at Kew reveal Elizabeth's closeness to Sutton. When a British soldier, Private A.A.L. Lang, evading capture by the Germans, reached the American embassy, 'Sutton, an English clerk in charge of British interests at the American embassy', gave him 50 francs and when he returned to the embassy, 'Mrs Deegan gave me another 250 francs, a map, food and clothing.'[13]

Sutton, in his overt official capacity, had funds which he used to put distressed British citizens on an allowance, and when Shaw vouched for Mary, he put her on the highest rate available – 1,682 francs and 20 centimes a month. All that Shaw asked of Mary was whether she still had her car, and they parted with the colonel saying, 'Goodbye, Countess. Glad to have been of service. Perhaps we'll meet again soon.'

If Shaw and perhaps Sutton were working for the Z Organisation and the SIS, it is likely that one of them cued Oky, possibly through Mary, because he returned

from an early trip to Sauveterre-de-Béarn, having met Major William Higgins
at Mauléon, some 15km to the south of Sauveterre, in the Vichy zone of France,
and about 30km through near empty countryside from the Spanish border.
Higgins was another likely candidate for Dansey's Z Organisation, a director of
Duco, the French chemicals and vehicle paint company, and married to the sister
of a famous Basque tennis player, the so-called Bounding Basque, Jean Borotra.
Higgins was well integrated into a Basque society which was antipathetic towards
central government – whether it was in Paris ruled by the Germans or in Vichy.
The route over the Pyrenees from Mauléon was relatively easy and the major
knew several guides living in the foothills who were prepared to guide men over.
Higgins had already helped several English soldiers to cross the Spanish frontier,
as well as many young Frenchmen who wanted to join the Free French.

Back in Paris, Mary was shocked when she returned from a meeting with
Shaw and Sutton to find Oky in her flat with two English soldiers, dressed
in civilian overcoats but with obvious dirty khaki uniforms underneath, very
dishevelled and downhearted. They had taken refuge in a Salvation Army
hostel, but the hostel still worked its peacetime routine and turned the homeless
onto the streets after breakfast. 'They've got nowhere to go, Mother. They've
spent two nights at the Salvation Army hostel, but they're not allowed to stay
there during the day. All they've been doing is walking about and sooner or later
someone's bound to pick them up,' explained Oky.

'Then we'll go into the bag, mum,' added one of the soldiers. 'We can't spend
the war in a cage, can we? After all, it's only just begun.'

'No, of course not,' was Mary's terse reply.

The solution was clear, and that same night Oky took the two soldiers, now
dressed in old and inconspicuous clothes, by train to Bordeaux and Dax and
on to meet Major Higgins. While Oky was away, Mary met Shaw again, who
expressed some concern about her car, 'Sooner or later it's going to be requisitioned or stolen, Why not arrange to have the German Red Cross markings
painted on it? It might give you some protection.'

Mary agreed.

'Bring the car round and I'll arrange for it to be done. By the way you might
be able to do something for me in return. Quite a few British men are interned
in Fresnes and I like to go there when I can, taking some food, and a football to
kick about. Are you game to come?'

Mary knew that Fresnes, a large nineteenth-century prison 19km south of
Paris, had been taken over by the Germans. 'Of course, so long as you can get
me some petrol.'

The next day Shaw asked to meet Mary at the Place de la Concorde, where he showed her the car, now embellished with the emblem of the German Red Cross – an eagle clutching a red cross in its talons. Mary grimaced as the pair set out for Fresnes, 'There's no knowing what I shall be able to do now.'

On the journey Shaw took Mary into his confidence, 'We've got to start trying to get our men out of the country.'

'We've already begun,' Mary replied tersely.

'I guessed as much. I've had my eyes on you from the beginning. How do you do it?'

'That's my affair,' answered Mary, still tight-lipped.

'All right. I'm afraid you must take charge, though. We've got to concentrate on getting officers only back to England. The army needs them desperately. I know another woman, Madame Bonnefous, to whom we can leave the smaller fry.'

These are the words Mary put into the mouth of Cecil Shaw when she was secluded post-war in a hotel in southern England with Barry Wynne, who was taking notes for the book which eventually became *No Drums … No Trumpets*. That there were others involved in the escape business would have been obvious, but it seems unlikely that Shaw would unnecessarily disclose to Mary the name or identity of the others and thereby put them at risk. This disparaging remark about Catherine Bonnefous and 'the smaller fry' may have been inspired by Mary's post-war jealousy or spite.[14]

In fact two 60-something-year-olds – Catherine or 'Kitty' Bonnefous, an English woman married to but separated from a French wine merchant, and Etta Shiber, an American widow – had independently established their own escape line for British soldiers who had missed the evacuation at Dunkirk. Etta had met Kitty in a dress shop when she was visiting Paris in 1925, and when her husband died in 1936 she moved to Paris to live with Kitty. In June 1940 they stayed in Paris until the last minute, when their eventual flight was slowed by the throng of refugees on the road.

Later, Etta would recall the fright and the fear on roads crammed by Parisians on foot, on bicycles, in horse-drawn, and even dog-drawn, vehicles and some, like them, in cars, and the terror of being machine-gunned by the Luftwaffe. When they stopped to search for food, they found instead a British airman and, on the spur of the moment, decided to hide him in their car. When they were turned back at a German checkpoint, they were obliged to return to Paris where he became the first of some 150 evaders, many brought to Paris by a fearless, patriotic priest, Abbé Christian Ravier, who they helped to escape from occupied France.[15]

Both women would be arrested and Catherine sentenced to death, but after Etta's plight had been reported in the American press, Etta was eventually exchanged for an infamous German woman spy held in the USA. Their story (although names were changed and events reordered to prevent them being of use to the Germans) was told in a wartime best-seller, *Paris Underground*, published in the USA in 1943.[16] The book compares well with Wynne's *No Drums … No Trumpets*, and in some aspects Wynne may have plagiarised Etta Shiber, either deliberately or subconsciously.

Etta's account is substantiated by the reports of escapes and evasions received by the War Office in London, which included multiple references to the work in 1940 of Shiber and Bonnefous. There are several references to Shaw when, for instance, the adventurous multiple escaper Lance Corporal J. Lee Warner of the Queen's West Surreys applied to him at the American embassy for help in his final and successful escape. Shaw gave him 500 francs (less than £5) and told him to go to the Salvation Army.[17] However, the reports only contain one reference to Mary Lindell, and that is the escape of Major Jimmy Windsor Lewis.

Meanwhile, Mary still had to work out how exactly she was going to get Shaw's officers across the demarcation line and into unoccupied France.

FRANCE, AUTUMN 1940 – COME WITH ME!

The French Red Cross now appealed again to Mary. She was approached by the fair-haired, plump and giggly Mademoiselle Pau, 'The fact is, Countess, I've remembered that you've got a car and that somehow you've managed to keep it on the road. What naughty things are you doing?'

Mary glared icily at Pau.

'We have a difficult problem with which I am sure you will sympathise. Every day people are bringing us children, even babies who, in the melee of the last few months, have been separated from their parents. Most of the parents are on the other side of the demarcation line and the children are stranded here in Paris. Would you consider taking them over the border into unoccupied France?'

Mary, whose regard for the French was somewhat diminished, pursed her lips and had almost formed a 'no' when she thought, 'My God, I've struck oil!' Cautiously she asked, 'What would this entail?'

'We have the children, of course. We might even be able to get hold of a little petrol. All you have to do is get permission from the Germans.'

'Surely, you don't seriously suggest that I should do that?'

'We thought you might somehow be able to wangle it.'

'How many of these kids have you got?'

'Two are waiting already.'

Mary promised to see what she could do, 'Make out the papers as soon as you can.'

'I have them here already, Countess. We knew you wouldn't refuse.' Pau rummaged in her handbag for the documents. 'When will you go?'

Mary remonstrated, 'Give me a chance! I haven't even seen the Germans yet. Things are getting more and more difficult, as you know.'

'You'll manage, my dear.'

Once the door had shut on her startling guest, Mary could barely contain her excitement, and went at once to the American embassy to find Shaw. 'I've hit on a wonderful plan. The French Red Cross want me to take some children into unoccupied France. I haven't worked out all the details yet, but if I arrange to make the first journey in two or three days, will you have an officer ready for me to take?'

'I've got two English officers who are watching a football match this very afternoon.'

'All right. Bring one of them to the embassy and I'll come down and collect him.'

At the rue Erlanger she talked to Michèle Cambards about her plan, 'I can't drive the car and look after a squealing infant, so you'll have put on an apron and come as a nurse. It's bound to look plausible to the Jerries.'

Mary had another idea: amongst the Paris population of Russian émigrés, she knew a prince who was friendly with the Germans and she went to him to explain the task which the French Red Cross wanted her to do. 'We've got all the necessary French Red Cross documents, but I need an *Ausweis* from the Germans to cross the frontier. Do you know anyone who could help?'

'I know them all,' the prince smiled. 'Let's start at the top. How would you like to see the military governor?'

'Why not?' she said, thinking he was joking.

To Mary's astonishment he immediately rang the Hôtel Crillon and spoke to the general's aide. After a brief conversation he asked Mary, 'Will it be convenient tomorrow morning at eleven?'

Mary nodded, and thanked him profusely. It appealed to her sense of humour to think that she, born in England, was about to ask for a pass from the German governor of Paris to help a British officer to escape.

Next morning she was escorted into the governor's office, where a general kissed her hand before listening carefully to her story. Afterwards Mary claimed that this general was Otto von Stülpnagel, but he was not appointed *Militärbefehlshaber in Frankreich* (military commander in France) until October that year. Whoever the general was, he agreed without hesitation to send Mary and her Russian prince to the office of a subordinate who would issue the precious *ausweis*.

The subordinate was Hauptmann Klaus von Bismarck, who was charm personified. The prince explained that the general had told them to come to Bismarck's office where the necessary forms would be made available for an 'angel of mercy' – with a sweep of his hand he indicated Mary – to cross the demarcation line with a child who had been separated from its parents. The request was plausible: the war had separated some 90,000 children from their parents and the French Red Cross had assumed responsibility for reuniting them.[1]

Bismarck studied the French Red Cross papers. 'I see, one nurse, one child. Who drives the car?'

'I do,' said Mary.

'It is a long way for you to drive.'

Mary seized her chance, 'Of course, I shall take a mechanic with me.'

'Ah, I see, the Countess de Milleville plus one mechanic, one nurse and one child,' he spoke as he wrote, he signed the *ausweis* and stamped it twice.[2]

Mary, secretly hugging herself, put the papers in her bag and with her prince took leave of Bismarck. Later, at the American embassy, she left a message with George, the porter, for Shaw, 'Tell him I'll soon be ready.'

Next day she returned in her car and parked it outside the embassy, only to be told that Robert Murphy, the charge d'affaires, had given permission for her to bring it into the embassy grounds and park it next to his. Inside the embassy Mary spoke to Elizabeth Deegan, who told Mary in a hushed whisper, 'Countess, I've got a boyfriend for you.'

'Where will I find him?'

'He should be already sitting in your car, my dear.'

Mary drove home with a young captain. He was a gunner in his early twenties, fair haired, blue eyed and, in Mary's opinion, very English-looking. He had no papers. In the rue Erlanger she told him to exchange his uniform trousers for a pair of slacks and then walked him to a photographer friend. The next stop was at the *Préfecture de Police* where Mary knew a police inspector, Noël Riou, and in his private office she persuaded him to make out the necessary French identity papers.

Mary had one last conversation with Shaw in the hallway of the American embassy. Shaw smiled when he heard the arrangements she had made, but what, asked Mary, was she to do with her mechanic, assuming that she succeeded in crossing the demarcation line? Evidently Shaw was already aware of the covert activities of the Reverend Donald Caskie, who was at the British Seamen's Mission in Marseilles. 'You must tell him to make for Marseilles and when he gets there to go down to the docks. Without having to speak anyone, he will be able to find the Seamen's Home. At the home he will find the Reverend Donald Caskie. He is a Scottish priest and will do all he can to help him. Fortunately we have sent substantial funds to Caskie, direct from the War Office by way of an American in Cannes. Caskie is using the home as a front. This is the best we can do, I'm afraid.'[3]

This sounded good to Mary, but Shaw added, 'Not as good as all that. In Fort St Jean in Marseilles there are over 400 members of the British forces, and we have been unable to get them out. Tell this young captain that whatever happens, he must consider it a point of honour not to disclose Caskie's name. Right, Countess, all I can do is to wish you *bon voyage*. And, by the way, Murphy is a bit concerned at the number of visits you are making, he has made it look as official as he can by allowing you to park your car beside his, but as a neutral he naturally has to be careful.'

'Well, damn it, I am officially in the French Red Cross and I've reason to be coming here.'

'Yes, I know, but just be careful, that's all. Off you go, and good luck.'

Mary slept well and at five o'clock the next morning she set out with Michèle and the baby on the back seat of the car and the English officer, now known as 'Marcel Trideau', beside her in the front whilst she drove.[4]

'Trideau' felt ill at ease: if arrested, the worst he could expect was a prisoner-of-war camp, but the two women faced arrest and summary execution. Mary only laughed at his worries for her and Michèle. They met a few German convoys but otherwise the journey south-west towards Champagne-Mouton was uneventful, until suddenly, rounding a bend they came upon a German roadblock manned by guards pointing sub-machine guns at the car, and Mary braked to a stop.

'Why the hell are their Schmeissers at the firing position?' whispered 'Trideau'.

'Don't talk, you fool, it's perfectly in order.'

A German sergeant walked to the driver's window. Michèle pinched the child, who began to squawk. Mary spoke in French. Giving the sergeant just sufficient time to glance at them she produced the *ausweis*, and then one by one, but rapidly, the sheaf of documentation which she had acquired in Paris.

The sergeant glanced into the car and shouted at one of his men, who lifted the barrier, and with a cheery wave they were through. A hundred yards further on was a French post, but here there was only a cursory check and then they were in unoccupied France. They drove on chattering and laughing like children let out of school.

Mary turned left, taking care to stay south of the demarcation line and outside of German-controlled France, and drove toward Confolens. There, she remembered, lived the French official who, on her return from Pau after her ambulance convoy only a few weeks before, had promised her a set of tyres if she would drive him home. It was dark when she found the old man's house, and he became nervous when he realised that Mary had others with her in the car, but she bolstered his confidence with a pretty speech about the gratitude of France and Great Britain.

Next, skirting the internal border between occupied and unoccupied France, Mary drove to Limoges, where she bought 'Trideau' a ticket for the train to Marseilles and gave him some pocket money. Her next stop was Châteauroux, where the child's parents lived, and there she and Michèle spent the night. They had a new problem – how to replace her mechanic for the return journey to Paris? It was Michèle who, while Mary slept upstairs, solved this problem by recruiting a young man in the bar of the hotel.

Two days later they were all safely and without incident back in Paris by mid July. Mary's first thought was to report to Shaw and she drove to find him at the American embassy, but she was shocked to be told, 'I'm terribly sorry, Countess, but there's another passenger already waiting in your car. This fellow is highly important and I've given him a lot of information. See what you can do, will you, m'dear.'

'You don't waste much time, do you? We haven't even got another child yet, let alone the petrol.'

Shaw sympathised over the petrol shortage, 'Even the head porter at the Ritz can't help me. The embassy's dry, I don't know what we're going to do.'

The highly important fellow was Major Jimmy Windsor Lewis, who had been wounded on 25 May 1940 and had walked out of a prison hospital on 13 July in Liege, Belgium, in workman's clothes supplied by the hospital sisters. Some of the people he had approached for help were too scared so soon after the shock of defeat, but others willingly gave him money or advice, food and a bed. Loyal Belgian policemen had escorted him to a civilian hospital and from there, on 18 July, Windsor Lewis reached Paris, which he knew well from before the war and where he thought he had friends. However, the hotels he had stayed at pre-war – the Crillon, the Bristol and the St James – had all been taken over by the Germans, and when he found his friends they gave him money but would not let him in.

Windsor Lewis reached the American embassy on 19 July 1940 where he posed as an American who had lost all his documentation in an air raid over Ostend. He was introduced to Sutton, who handed him over to Shaw – who put him in Mary's car. The poor response of Windsor Lewis' pre-war Parisian friends to his requests for help was in sharp contrast to the reception he now received at Mary Lindell's home. In his debrief to MI9 at the end of the year, Windsor Lewis wrote, 'Mme de M., who was a Red Cross worker, took me in and told me I could stay there as guest of the family for as long as you wish, and in our hands nobody will find you.'[5]

Windsor Lewis remained hidden in Mary's flat in the rue Erlanger for two weeks, except for jaunts to the photographer and Mary's visit to Inspector Noël Riou in his office, who thumb-printed him and issued him with the identity card of James O'Brien, a journalist from neutral Ireland.[6] Windsor Lewis also visited Colonel Horace Fuller, military attaché at the American embassy.[7] Fuller had watched the fall of France from the safety of the US embassy, had met senior German military leaders over dinner at Maxim's, and had much useful information to pass on. On one of his visits to Fuller, Windsor Lewis asked if the Germans really meant it when they put up posters announcing the death sentence for anyone helping or harbouring Allied soldiers and airmen.[8]

'Of course they do.'

'Then I can't possibly stay at the countess' flat; by my presence I am risking not only her life but also the lives of her children. I simply cannot do it.'

'There's only one thing for you to do then. You'd better go to the American express and buy a ticket home.'

Once more, a transatlantic joke failed and Windsor Lewis did indeed buy a railway ticket to Spain, but it was for a train leaving the next day and, as he had nowhere else to go, he returned to Mary's flat. Mary went white with rage when she found out what he had done. 'You bloody, bloody fool …' she began, and continued for ten minutes. 'What the devil do you think you are doing? It's true that there's some risk, but if you mess about like this you really will put my life in danger. Now just listen to me …'

No death threat was going to deter Mary, but the urgency of the occasion was impressed upon all. When, after two weeks the French Red Cross still had not produced a child to be carried across the frontier, Mary decided to change the process. Presenting herself at Bismarck's offices she was horrified to walk in on Bismarck berating a group of Frenchmen who were asking for passes to cross the newly established demarcation line. 'I'm so sorry. These people infuriate me,' he said shooing them from his presence. 'But what can I do for you, Countess?'

'I don't think it's much use asking from what I've just heard. You see I'd come for another *ausweis*. I have to fetch a poor little child from the other side of the border and bring it to Paris this time.'

Charmed, Bismarck replied gravely, 'Oh, but I think it is in order for the Red Cross to go,' and ordered a subordinate to 'kindly make out the papers for the countess'. Turning to Mary, he asked, 'Do I understand you mean that you will be going alone with your mechanic this time?'

Mary nodded.

'Very well, we'll soon have that done. By the way do you have plenty of petrol?'

Mary looked glum, 'One never has enough petrol, Herr Hauptmann.'

'Of course not.' He told his underling, 'Make out a permit for eighty litres of petrol. This is a mission of mercy.'

Once back at the rue Erlanger, Mary announced her departure would be the next day, as soon as the curfew was lifted. The mechanic was, of course, Windsor Lewis, and at 5 in the morning on 8 August she drove him out of Paris in her car. He and Mary kept their aplomb when, outside Étampes, a Luftwaffe sergeant stepped into the road waving his helmet and stopped the car, and enquired in poor French to know where they were going.

'Orléans.'

'Just my luck, an angel comes along but she's going the wrong way.' For a moment Mary thought of driving on, but the idea struck her that a German passenger like this might just make things easier for her, and she asked where he wanted to go – 'Chartres'.

'Well, it doesn't really matter to us whether we go through Chartres or Orléans. We'll give you a lift.' As the young flyer walked round the front of the car, Mary told Windsor Lewis to get in the back and not to speak. The German was pleasant enough, but after few minutes' silence he asked if she spoke any German.

'*Non.*'

'Do you speak English?'

When Mary cautiously answered, 'Yes', the German roared with laughter.

'Good, because I haven't had an opportunity to learn French yet, we have been too busy bombing England. This morning I nearly did not come back.'

'What happened?'

The pilot explained that he had become lost in fog over the Bristol Channel, chased by Spitfires, run out of fuel and been forced to bail out over France. He spoke such good English because he had lived there before the war for two years. Suddenly, he turned to the mute mechanic in back and asked, 'Who's this?'

'My mechanic.'

'He doesn't look very intelligent.'

'No, you're right, he isn't. He's a little simple-minded.'

After a few kilometres the sergeant remarked, 'You speak very good English, Madame.'

'So do you, but I had an English nanny and we were always made to speak English at meals.'

'Strange. I learned my English in Hanover, but I visited England before the war. It is a nice country.'

Mary drove on until they reached Châteaudun, about 65km south-west of Chartres. Her ordeal was not over because her passenger insisted that she should stop at the German headquarters, which was in the town hall. Mary hoped to be on her way, and smilingly said, 'Well, goodbye.'

The German turned to her and said, 'No, no, not yet. You must come with me!' The German flier wasn't finished in his torment of Mary, and insisted that she accompany him past the German sentries and inside the headquarters. She locked Jimmy Windsor Lewis in the car, while the German beckoned her to follow him. Guards clicked to attention and someone shouted, '*Gott in Himmel!*' and noisy conversation broke out in German.

The German led Mary upstairs and stood listening before large double doors, put his finger to his lips and suddenly threw the doors open. Luftwaffe officers, who had been drinking and chatting, gathered round Mary's guardian who, once he could free himself from the crowd, told her, 'I have told him that you were the only person kind enough to stop on the road to give me a lift.'

Once again Mary made her excuses – she had an aunt who would be waiting with supper for her further along the road. Her hosts, who had thrust a glass of wine into her hand, were sympathetic and one of them asked what they could do for her. 'Madame, you have been most kind. Is there anything I can do in return?'

'I … I really don't think so.'

'Let me see, perhaps some chocolate or sugar?'

An older officer asked, 'What about some petrol?'

'Gentlemen, we never have much petrol, you know. Your bombers and tanks use up so much of it.'

'Leave it to me,' said the older officer, and returned in two or three minutes. Then, thanking her again for her kindness, he proffered a wedge of petrol coupons, 'With my compliments, they are valid for use at French and German pumps.'

Mary had hoped that this would be the happy end of her ordeal, but the young flier asked another favour, 'Do you think you could possibly go out of your way another two or three kilometres and drop me at my airfield?'

'Certainly, I will do that with pleasure.'

And there he insisted on a ride along the perimeter track of the airfield so that he could show off. 'Look at these wonderful aircraft!' he cried, as Windsor Lewis, from the back seat, silently counted the number and different types of fighters and black-painted bombers.

Fifteen minutes later, back at the main entrance, the German finally said goodbye. As he leaned over to shake hands, Mary realised that Windsor Lewis' shirt sleeve had worked up his arm to reveal his tattoos. They included '*Floreat Etona*' ('Let Eton Flourish') on his left forearm and on his right arm she could clearly see the leek of the Welsh Guards. Somehow, the German did not recognise these. As they finally drove on their way, Mary broke the tension by shouting at him, as she might at a naughty child, 'For God's sake, sew your buttons on properly!'

The stop at Châteaudun had delayed Mary and Windsor Lewis; it was evening and Mary was exhausted and enervated. They had only gone 10km when they entered the little town of Cloyes-sur-le-Loir and arrived at the Hôtel St Jacques. She drove through the arch which led into the courtyard before she realised that the hotel was now a German officers' mess, where the landlord was allowed to keep only a handful of rooms and a table or two for the occasional French traveller. Mary and her mechanic ate dinner in a dining room crowded with German officers who, fortunately, were engrossed in their own conversation.

As the landlord showed them to their rooms at the end of a corridor he made a curious remark. 'I'd like to point out, Madame, that your rooms are at the end of the wing and should you get nervous during the night, you can always drop out of your window into the river.'

Mary started at this, 'Are you mad or something? We've come here to sleep, not to swim,' and she stumped into her room.

Early next morning they had tiptoed down the corridor and out of the hotel, when suddenly and quietly a door opened and the landlord beckoned them silently, whispering that though the hotel could not provide breakfast because of the food shortages – which were already affecting even rural France – his wife had a cooked breakfast waiting for them. Afterwards he refused payment, telling Mary that she should never pass the hotel without calling on her new friends.

They drove on early next morning past Tours and Poitiers to Ruffec, on the road to Bordeaux, where Mary wanted to call on an old friend, Marthe Rullier. Marthe, who had been a nurse with Mary in the First World War, lived in a house on a small estate with a long drive outside Ruffec. German officers were billeted at the Rulliers', but Marthe and her husband Paul were much more worried, when they heard of Mary's plans, at the rumours that the demarcation line had been shut. To make sure, Mary drove on alone into the centre of Ruffec and to the local German headquarters, where she interviewed the newly appointed town mayor. He was surprised to examine her *ausweis* and its signature, as it was Bismarck's superior who had issued the order to close the border. Mary argued that she therefore could have no better authority than Bismarck's and the hapless German acquiesced. Would the countess want to cross now, in which case he would send someone with her, or would she prefer to do so in the morning which would give him time to warn the guards?

'We'll cross tomorrow morning, first thing, if we may.'

'Very well, I will inform the guard to expect you.'

And so it was: the soldiers at the border post at Champagne-Mouton were expecting her, she brandished Bismarck's pass, and they did not even ask Windsor Lewis for his identity card. Once through the barrier and on the unoccupied French side, they turned east and stopped at Confolens for lunch, before going on to Limoges, where Mary brought Windsor Lewis a train ticket for Marseilles, gave him enough food for a couple of days, and they said their goodbyes.

Once, when Mary told this story to a spellbound audience, one of her listeners asked, 'Did he get back to England?'

Mary hooted with laugher, 'Yes, we met in London eighteen months later.'

Indeed, after several more adventures lasting three months, Windsor Lewis reached London in December 1940. In France, Mary continued to lead a charmed life, although one which would become much more dangerous for her.

5

A FAMILY AFFAIR

Mary had decided that while Sauveterre-de-Béarn was a good place for her French evaders to cross the border, it was too far away for the British to use and the round trip too long if they were to be escorted by members of her family. Also, too many applications for an *Ausweis* to Bismarck would begin to look suspicious.

Mary needed another route for her escape line and she decided to take Marthe Rullier into her confidence. She was looking for a farm which, like Michèle's governess' farm, straddled the border. Marthe's husband, Paul Rullier, an insurance salesman who had been used to travelling on business, knew just the place that, within a short while of the border being formally closed, had sprung into use by the French as a crossing between the two zones. The route crossed two adjacent farms; one, owned by a farmer called Maxim,[1] lay in occupied France west of Ruffec, and the other, Marvaud near the village of St Coutant, was owned by Armand and Amélie Debreuille and lay in unoccupied France.

If not on her earlier visit with Windsor Lewis, then on this visit, Mary made acquaintance with Roger and Germaine Rouillon, proprietors of the Hôtel de France in the centre of Ruffec.[2] Satisfied that hers was a workable system, Mary returned to Paris. It was not long before the new escape route was operating, with her two sons, daughter Barbé, and Michèle acting as couriers and, claimed Mary, taking two or three men each week.

At this stage of the war Mary's resistance work in helping Frenchmen to leave France to join de Gaulle's Free French and helping escaping British soldiers to return to Britain was entirely freelance. Apart from the funds that she received through Cecil Shaw, she had no sponsorship and no training in clandestine techniques. Indeed, she used very little artifice at all and relied very much on the force of her own personality. And as far as possible she made it a strictly family business, with only a few friends she could trust allowed into her circle of deception and disguise, and she took terrible risks.

Shaw continued to bring her escapers who he thought she could help. Also, Riou, Mary's policeman friend, had realised her connection to Shaw and the American embassy, and he called on her at home. Riou, who was one of the first among the Parisian police force to take up the struggle against the occupying Germans, knew of plenty of stragglers and would-be evaders, but he had no means of passing them across the border and knew of no escape line to the south. His proposal to Mary was that they should co-operate: he would round up the stragglers and Mary would smuggle them out of Paris.

However, security was not all it should have been within Mary's small group, and a rare instance of her taking any precaution was when she adopted the code name 'Marie', and made her family and all her contacts swear to deny any knowledge of her if they were caught. However, if a lone French policeman, Noël Riou, knew of Mary's activities, then it was only a question of time before the Germans too began to suspect her.

Nevertheless, it was a surprise one day when Barbé answered the door to a well-dressed German officer and a civilian.

'Mamma, there are two gentlemen to see you.'

Mary met them in the hall. 'Do come through to the lounge.'

They were a uniformed German officer, who was tight-lipped, and an Austrian in plain clothes who led the conversation, 'Countess, I see you are a member of the French Red Cross.'

'That's correct.'

'We understand that you do a lot of travelling.'

'That's also correct.'

'To where, in fact, do you make your journeys?'

'Oh, that depends, across the demarcation line, of course, and to various towns in the Free French zone.'

'What exactly is your reason for going there?'

'I take children who have been separated from their parents and reunite them.'

'I see. On what authority do you make these journeys?'

'On the authority of the French Red Cross and, of course, I have an *ausweis*. Surely you don't see anything wrong in this, do you? I am in the French Red Cross and this is part of my job.'

'Not at all, but I would like to see any documents you might have, supporting your claim.'

'Certainly, I have all the documents,' Mary indicated the papers which were stacked on the mantelpiece, and the civilian looked through them.

'Yes, Countess, they seem perfectly in order to me.'

Earlier that day Mary had taken delivery of a parcel of clothing, which she had been asked to take with her on one of her journeys across the demarcation line. The uniformed officer, who seemed less at ease than his colleague, lighted on the parcel, 'What is in that?'

'Some underclothes, which I have accepted from a lady for delivery into unoccupied France, where her son happens to be. Is there anything wrong with that?'

'Not at all, but you'll appreciate that we have to be very careful. Do you know exactly the contents of the package?'

'No, I'm afraid I don't. As far as I know, it's all underclothes. If you've got the slightest doubt about it why don't you open it?'

Slowly the Austrian civilian undid the string and folded open the brown paper to reveal neatly folded vests, underpants and bars of soap. The two men began a bickering argument in German which was too fast for Mary to understand, and the Austrian seemed to win. 'Thank you for your co-operation, countess. We shan't trouble you any more today. We bid you good afternoon.'

The relief in Mary's flat was palpable. Her children, who had made themselves scarce, found their mother by the window looking out onto the street and trying to marshal her thoughts and her emotions. 'Is it bad, mamma?' asked Oky.

'I don't know, I just don't know.'

Mary's first thought was that to run now would be a giveaway to the Germans, and to carry on as if nothing had happened would be best. Then there was another knock on the door. The civilian had returned. In a loud voice he said, 'I'm terribly sorry, countess, I'm afraid I forgot my gloves.' She could see that he was smiling and, uncertain what was happening, she beckoned him to step into the hall. She felt uncomfortable and, for the first time, not a little afraid. At that moment Barbé entered carrying a tray of tea. Seeing the silver and the china, the Austrian exclaimed, 'That looks inviting and brings back many happy memories. You English love your tea!'

Mary was stunned and before she could recover he showed her a document from his briefcase. It was a warrant for her arrest. 'Don't worry, I am not going to arrest you. This scene brings back so many happy memories. You see I am an Austrian and we too enjoy our tea. I shall come back the day after tomorrow, countess.'

Mary's quick wits had returned, 'Why not come at teatime?'

'Thank you, I shall be delighted. At four o'clock?'

'That will be most convenient.'

Mary took great care over tea on the next Friday: there was a silver teapot, Wedgwood cups and even scones. The Austrian was appreciative, 'This brings back memories of England when I was a boy. My cousin was military attaché in London, and I spent the happiest times of my boyhood when I visited him.'

She was suspicious of his emphasis on her Englishness. She knew that in mid July the Germans had rounded up some 670 British subjects and imprisoned them in Fresnes.[3] She must also have been worried that her English contact at the American embassy, Edward Sutton, had disappeared.

The Austrian continued, 'I am not certain yet what you are doing, but I must admit that your papers are absolutely in order. I have checked them. But tell me, who gives them to you?'

Mary did not want to compromise Bismarck by naming him, 'They are signed. You can see perfectly well for yourself.'

'But how much do you have to pay the officer?'

Mary glared, 'Absolutely nothing, he merely performs his duty.'

'I'll tell you what I want to know. A number of our officers have been corrupted lately and many of them have sold papers like these for money.'

'You could never buy the officer who signed these papers!'

'Would you mind if I took one of your *ausweis* with me?'

'Not at all, please do.'

Over tea they began to discuss England, and the Austrian disclosed why he had not arrested her, 'Countess, I have a pretty good idea of what you are doing and I know you do it because you consider it your duty. But I warn you, if we uncover your game, nothing I can do will save you.'

'But I'm doing absolutely nothing.'

'For the time being I'm going to invite myself round every Friday because I've been instructed to watch you. So, if you persist in travelling abroad, please make certain that you do it on any day except Friday. That is the day reserved for me.' With this warning the Austrian thanked her for his tea, playfully ruffled the teenaged Barbé's hair, slowly walked to the hall and left.

Just two days later, on the Sunday, Mary heard that there was another Englishman waiting to go down her escape line. She knew she was now a marked woman, probably being watched by the German Army's security police, the *Sicherheitsdienst* (SD). Despite misgivings, she decided that she must behave as though nothing had happened, and that she must continue her activities, which included her cover of ferrying children north and south across the demarcation line. She therefore applied for another *ausweis* – which was promptly granted.

She was able to complete a round trip and be back in the rue Erlanger before it was time for Friday's tea ceremony with her Austrian tormentor. It was with some surprise when she answered the door that he stood there with an orderly who carried an enormous bouquet of flowers. 'Countess, Count von Bismarck has sent you these flowers and hopes you will accept them with his profound gratitude.'

'But why?'

'You see, I checked on the papers you gave me. When I saw Count von Bismarck and told him that you said that he couldn't be bought, he wished to thank you for speaking for his honour.'

'Perhaps you will kindly tell the count that his flowers are beautiful and that if, after the war, we are both still alive, I hope he will offer me flowers again. But now, I am afraid, he is my enemy and I cannot accept them. If he will permit it, I suggest that they are sent to the American hospital at Neuilly, where there are British soldiers and officers lying wounded, I can only accept them on these terms.'

The Austrian laughed, 'I told von Bismarck that you wouldn't take them and, to be frank, I'm glad you haven't, because you are staying true to yourself and true to the judgement I have made of you.'

* * *

Not even neutral US citizens were safe in 1940 Paris, and on 17 September 40-year-old Kathryn Lewis disappeared from Hôtel Le Bristol, which had been taken over as a home for the American embassy staff and American nationals. Kathryn, accused of taking photographs of military subjects on the Paris streets, was held incommunicado for a week by the Germans in Fresnes Prison while embassy staff searched police stations, hospitals and even morgues for her. She was held for several more weeks until December when, without charges or trial, she was allowed to leave France.[4]

In the heady days after the fall of Paris, there had been something of a free-for-all in helping British stragglers to reach unoccupied France. However, by October 1940, when two of the stragglers, Captain D.B. Lang and Second Lieutenant John Buckingham, reached the American embassy they were told that they 'could no longer help us, financially or otherwise. The Germans were tightening things up and they [the Americans] dare not run any risks.' Lang reported that he went away 'almost in despair … but returned the next day in the hopes of something'. Lang was lucky: he met Kitty Bonnefous, who he reported 'was very willing to help us … another Edith Cavell [who] would stop at nothing to help British … reach unoccupied France'.[5]

Sutton had been arrested and would spend the next five years in solitary confinement in Germany.[6] Now Mary learned that Elizabeth Deegan, who had been her point of contact at the American embassy, had also disappeared. It was several days before her arrest was announced in a German communiqué and reported in the Paris newspapers.[7] On 1 December Elisabeth Deegan had left her apartment on what she thought was a routine visit to Cherche-Midi, a nineteenth-century French prison which had been taken over by the Germans:

> Two German civilians, presumably members of the German Secret Police, who called at her apartment and invited her to go to the Cherche-Midi prison to visit one or more British prisoners. This was the second time within a week that she had been invited by the German authorities to visit acquaintances at the Cherche-Midi prison … later in the day she returned under escort to obtain warm clothing. In the evening a friend of hers received a message from an unspecified source that she was comfortably lodged and that while it would be impossible for her to be at the embassy for work on 2 December, she would doubtless report for duty on 3 December. Mrs Deegan did not report for work on 3 December.

In fact, she was being held by the Germans and charged with 'conniving in the escape of British officers'.[8] A week after her arrest, and following a frantic search, Elizabeth Deegan was located. She was being held under arrest in a small hotel. Once found, the Americans protested against her detention and she was released on 14 December, but the Germans promptly asked for her to be recalled, along with two other US embassy officials, Cecil M.P. Cross and Leigh W. Hunt, who were alleged to have helped in the escape of a British officer and to have hidden Sutton in the embassy grounds. By Christmas Eve, Elizabeth was in Lisbon.[9]

Over tea on 20 December, Mary's Austrian visitor gave her more bad news. 'Look,' he explained, 'I'm going on leave. I must ask you not to leave your flat for any reason whatsoever when I have gone, except to shop. You are now to come under strict surveillance and everything you do will be known at SD headquarters. When I come back,' he turned to Barbé, 'I shall bring you some magnificent Austrian chocolates. You'd like that wouldn't you?'

Mary cut in, 'She's a pig and she'll eat any pig's food.'

Generously the Austrian laughed, 'But promise me, Countess, that you will not move.'

'I won't move. I can't move, as a matter of fact, because after the last child I took over the demarcation line my car isn't here anymore.'

'I'm not asking you where your car is. I have never asked you where your car is. All I am asking you is not to make any journeys while I'm away.' And with that he wished Mary and her family a happy Christmas.

Meanwhile Etta Shiber, who had been held for questioning by the Germans between 26 November and 14 December, was rearrested on 22 December, though the charges against her were not known.[10] Eventually, according to a German communiqué of mid February, she was accused of being 'an accessory to others under arrest and charged with aiding in the escape into the free zone of military fugitives'. Cecil Shaw, too, had been arrested.

Mary Lindell must have realised that with her friends detained or fled, a net was closing around her. She did warn Michèle Cambards that something was wrong and that she should disappear for a while, and this was the last time that they saw each other for the rest of the war,[11] but she appears to have given no thought to escape for herself or her family.

PARIS, 1941 –
THE COURT MARTIAL

T here are several hundred reports of escapers (from prisoner-of-war columns being marched towards Germany and from prisons there) and evaders (those who had not been captured) from occupied Europe, held in the National Archives at Kew. They are known as E&E.

Once an escaper or evader had reached British territory, typically Gibraltar or England, he was interrogated about his experience and for the lessons that could be learned from what he had done to succeed in his flight. In 1940 and early 1941 most of the evaders were soldiers who had missed the British evacuation from the north and west of France. After 1941, most of the evaders were Allied airmen who had crashed or been shot down over Europe. The reports, which are not complete or comprehensive, generally consisted of a main report outlining the escape and, filed separately, an appendix with details such as the names and locations of those who had helped in the escape or evasion.[1]

The question must be, how many of these E&E in 1940 did Mary Lindell help? Estimates of those left behind from the British Expeditionary Force vary between 2,500 and 10,000. According to the one-armed Jimmy Langley, who had himself escaped from a prison hospital in Belgium and who, as a staff officer, would in 1941 join MI9 (the British escape agency in London), there were maybe 2,500, and perhaps as many as 3,000, British servicemen left in France after the evacuations from northern and western France.[2] Other reports put the number much higher, maybe as many as 4,000 or even 7,000,[3] while Etta Shiber in her wartime account put the number as high as 10,000.[4]

Reports from individual places varied wildly: Lance Bombardier J.G. Enoch, who escaped from St Valery, gave the lowest estimate, reckoning that there were 300 escaped British prisoners of war in northern France, while Gunner

C. Hillier, who escaped from France and reached Spain via the Pyrenees in December 1940, informed that in one town alone there were, 'to my certain knowledge 48 other ranks hiding in Calais and at least 250 in the vicinity'.[5]

Not all of these would escape France. Some settled down with French girls for the duration of the war, or went into hiding with Belgian and French people and waited to make their escape from the north.[6] Donald Darling, when he was sent to Spain to organise that end of the escape lines, thought initially that there might be as many as sixty to 100 men who would need to be evacuated. In practice, in the twelve-month period from June 1940 there were 1,000 reports by E&E from all around Europe.[7]

These numbers are difficult to reconcile with historical and anecdotal evidence or to attribute to particular helpers. While a few individual helpers in Paris, like Kitty Bonnefous, Elizabeth Deegan, Mary Lindell and Cecil Shaw, are mentioned by name a few times in the early reports of E&E, the many Belgian and French men and women who helped the E&E appear anonymously or are simply referred to as 'friends'. The majority of E&E travelled to Marseilles, where they were helped by Donald Caskie, Ian Garrow and later 'Pat'. Very many more made their way across the eastern Pyrenees to Spain. Popular crossing points of the German-imposed demarcation line were Vierzon and Loches, and Perpignan was a crossroads for E&E travelling north to south towards Marseilles or east to west towards Spain. Routes across the Pyrenees followed several ancient Jacobean pilgrim routes.

Notably too, after the fall of France, American consular officers throughout occupied and non-occupied France helped British sailors, soldiers and airmen to escape. The assistance of staff at the American embassy in Paris and the American consulates in Lyon and Marseilles seems to have been particularly well co-ordinated.

As for Mary Lindell, the bare facts about the ambulance convoy of wounded French soldiers and Mary guiding the convoy from German-occupied France to Pau in the non-occupied zone of France in June 1940 are not disputed.

Then there are many more Frenchmen – youths who Mary helped to escape between July and October 1940 from Paris in order to join the Free French. Maurice, Oky and Michèle Cambards made the round trip between Paris and Sauveterre-de-Béarn two or three times a week. Michèle put the number of people they escorted at about fifty, but she also suggested that about half this number were British evaders.[8]

Mary only acknowledged a handful of evaders: two unnamed English soldiers who she sent to Higgins in Mauléon;[9] 'Marcel Trideau', an unidentified captain of artillery;[10] and Jimmy Windsor Lewis, whose escape is well corroborated;[11] as well as at least one 'Englishman'.[12] Up to December 1940, 'Mary did not give up her work … but continued to make occasional "visits" out of town.'[13]

So, in the period from June to December 1940 Mary, her family and Michèle may have helped two dozen Englishmen to avoid capture by the Germans and perhaps twice as many Frenchmen to leave France. By contrast, Kitty Bonnefous and Etta Shiber had taken far more risks and they had helped more than 150 men to evade capture.

Most of these efforts had ended by the Christmas of 1940, and for several days over Christmas and the New Year of 1941 Mary and her family lived in limbo. She must have known that the Germans would be watching her, but she could not have known that the French police also had her under surveillance.

On 9 December the collaborationist French government in Vichy had forwarded a report from Châteauroux to the police in German-occupied Paris that Mary was helping loyal Frenchmen to leave France to join de Gaulle in England. On 27 December 1940 and 2 January 1941 the police in Pau also reported their general suspicion that Mary was carrying out unspecified activities in support of '*l'ex Général de Gaulle*', and on 11 January there was a report that she had given a Breton, Edgard Tupët-Thomé, advice to go to the British or American consulates in Marseilles with 'a view to joining the army of former General de Gaulle in England'. Mary had been heard speaking out in favour of de Gaulle and advising other youngsters to join the Free French abroad. On 25 January 1941 the Vichy government demanded to know more.

A subsequent police report revealed that Barbé de Milleville was also under investigation for assisting '*un depart en Angleterre*' and she was under strict surveillance. To the investigating policeman the teenaged Barbé (she was barely 15) appeared unusually grown up and he reported her age as 'about 20'.[14]

Then, shortly after the Christmas holiday, at half past seven one morning, the German military police came with a warrant to search her flat. As far as Mary was concerned the only incriminating object in the flat was her British passport, which during the search Barbé snatched from a drawer and hid under her clothes. The German search was thorough, but they found nothing and their questions were perfunctory, but included the seemingly odd question, 'What important people do you know in Paris?'

Mary gave the name of a young actress and the mistress of Otto Absetz, the German ambassador in Paris, Corinne Luchaire. However, she could not give an address, other than that it was a pink house in a particular street. The Germans seemed satisfied and left. Nevertheless, Mary was shaken and after they had gone it was a further shock to realise that they had missed a pistol which was lying on top of a wardrobe. Maurice was told to get rid of the gun, and the children were drilled in an emergency procedure.

First, no one would enter the flat without a special ring at the door. Then, since the Germans seemed to prefer early morning calls, the family would rise early too, let the beds become cold and remake them. Mary would go to the back door and, after a pause, the front and back doors would be opened simultaneously to disguise any noise, and Mary would slip out into the street. Maurice would leave via a balcony, shin down a lamp post and disappear through the cellar of an adjacent block. Oky and Barbé would be left to deal with any visitors. Mary hoped that the Germans would not arrest her estranged husband, who had returned to Paris and lived and slept in his study, or Oky or Barbé because they were so young.

Mary's rudimentary security routine failed on its first test, when the Germans returned three days later. Mary got to the street, but had a premonition that Maurice had not got away and that she could not leave Barbé to face the wrath of the Germans. She calmly returned to the flat through the back door. 'And where have you been?' demanded one of the Germans.

'That's none of your business.'

'Where have you been?'

'I've told you already, I don't care to say. It's none of your business.'

'It is my business, very much my business. Tell me where you were last night!'

For once Mary was nonplussed, but looking sideways at Barbé and then at the German, she said, 'You are not very tactful in front of my children. You know perfectly well that I didn't sleep here. Do you want me to tell you with whom I slept?'

'No, I'm not concerned; I didn't know that you were that kind of woman.'

'After all, Paris is Paris.'

'I have many questions which I wish you to answer.'

'Very well, but let's sit down in front of the fire.'

'We wish to have the names of all the people with whom you are in contact. Of course you know Colonel Shaw.'

'I'm afraid I don't know any Colonel Shaw.'[15]

'If you start trying to be clever, I shall be forced to take you away.'

'Very well, gentlemen, perhaps it's warmer with you.'

'In more ways than one. Come with us!'

On 8 January 1941 Mary was taken away for questioning by the SD. She knew that they had already arrested Elizabeth Deegan and Etta Shiber, but she was appalled when they began to ask her about Noël Riou and Catherine Bonnefous. At the mention of their names, she hoped that her interrogators did not notice her slight shiver of fear. Worse was yet to come.

'What about Captain Windsor Lewis?'

'I'm terribly sorry, but I don't know any of these people you mention.'

'But you had that gentleman in your flat!'

'It's the first time I have heard of it. Was he handsome?'

'Yes, very handsome.'

'What a pity I missed him, he sounds just my sort.' The questioning dragged on into the afternoon until her interrogators asked again about Shaw. 'I've already told you, I don't know that gentleman.'

'But he knows you.'

'Does he? How nice for him.'

'Yes, Colonel Shaw does know you.' At last Mary felt she was on safer ground. She and Shaw had agreed, if ever they were questioned, to deny any knowledge of each other: now she realised that her interrogators were fishing in the dark.

There was one other fateful exchange. Invited to write to Barbé and ask for her toiletries to be sent to her, Mary snapped, 'What shall I write, that these swine are arresting me?'

After a day of stonewalling her interrogators, Mary was taken to Cherche-Midi, where she was at once at odds with the prison staff. On the first morning:

> They came in the morning and threw in a broom and said, 'Sweep this out,' and I said, 'No, British officers don't sweep out.' And I said, 'I'm your visitor and you do the sweeping.'
>
> 'We'll fetch the commander.'
>
> 'You can fetch God Almighty, it doesn't worry me.'
>
> 'You must sweep out your cell.'
>
> 'Then why the heck aren't they written up and put for all to see.' I said, 'You've made a mistake. You pay for it. As to sweeping out your cell, absolutely nothing doing – N O – no. That's the end of the story.' And I never swept it. And I never swept it in any prison.

After several days in solitary confinement at Cherche-Midi Mary was put into a cell with Etta Shiber and another woman. Quickly Mary and Etta guessed that the stranger was a stool pigeon and were cautious in what they said. Later, both would recall their time together in a cell: Etta's wartime account was fictionalised for its propaganda value and to protect individuals who were still in German hands, while Mary's post-war account was fantasised to cast the best light on her.[16]

Then, on 6 February 1941, Mary was tried by a German military court. The actual charges against Mary are unknown but there were several possible counts against her. She had helped British soldiers to evade capture, but her blanket denial of any knowledge of evaders seems to have protected her, and if the Vichy French had any proof against Mary, not even they made such evidence available to the German court. There was a possible offence that Mary had failed to turn herself in when British nationals were interned in August of the previous year, but the Germans at least seemed to accept that her marriage had given her French nationality. The wider German investigation seemed to be concentrated against Etta Shiber and Kitty Bonnefous (who, by Etta's estimation, had helped more than 150 British soldiers to cross the demarcation line).

But Mary had insulted the German Army, and she was found guilty and sentenced to the seemingly light sentence of two and half years' imprisonment. The accusation was that she had said, 'These swine are going to arrest me.' Mary's defence was convoluted:

Just supposing that I had said 'These swine are going to arrest me', are you not aware of the meaning of the word 'swine' in England? In German you say '*schwein*' and it means 'pig', but in England 'swine' means a wild boar, an animal of courage and ferocity. Therefore in my context I was praising the German army, not deriding it.

It is not clear whether Mary tried to explain this in French or German, or even English, but when pigs or *porc* became boar or *sanglier* and were translated, the German officer who was president of the court was nonplussed. If this was explained in English, Mary had come dangerously close to admitting her real nationality.

Typically Mary had faced the court dressed in the blue of the French Red Cross uniform with her medal ribbons. Now Mary's counsel pushed what advantage she had gained by asking for her 1918 citation for the award of the Croix de Guerre to be read out. The president read this through in silence and then, to Mary's amazement, he stood up and saluted her before the court withdrew.

Ten minutes later they returned to announce that her sentence had been reduced to nine months' solitary confinement, which Mary served in cell number 119 at Fresnes, where she was taken on 25 February.

The American Etta Shiber and her friend Kitty Bonnefous were not so fortunate. A few days later, on 7 March, Etta was sentenced to death for helping British soldiers to cross the demarcation, though after strenuous appeals for clemency by the American embassy her sentence was commuted to life imprisonment, and later she would be exchanged for a German internee in the USA.[17] The same court also condemned Kitty to death, a sentence which was also commuted to life imprisonment.[18] Kitty survived a dreadful three years in German prison camps and an equally dreadful several weeks at the hands of her Russian liberators.[19]

In one aspect, all the women were fortunate: in 1940 the German Army governed Paris and there were forms of trials – albeit the rough justice of a *Wehrmacht* court martial. The occupation began with a velvet glove, but the iron fist soon emerged.[20] The *Wehrmacht* had been ordered to exercise restraint in their dealings with the population of the occupied enemy territory 'as befits a German soldier', which they at first succeeded in, while maintaining a strong physical and visual presence,[21] but by early 1941 the Gestapo was to begin interrogations under torture, summary executions and deportations without trial.

LYON, SPRING 1942 – DOWN THE RABBIT HOLE

Fresnes Prison, some 8km south of central Paris, had been built in the late 1890s as a model prison, but little had been done to modernise it in the intervening half-century. There were three main blocks: the largest one for men, another for women, and the third was the prison hospital. Inmates recall the endless corridors, the cells measuring about 7ft by 10ft, the furniture being fixed or chained to the walls, and having to wash themselves and their clothes in the single toilet bowl. It stank, and the paint was peeling off the walls, which were covered in graffiti.

The Germans took control of Fresnes, though many of the French staff remained in place and used the prison as a punishment centre, a holding camp for prisoners whose cases were still under investigation and as a transit camp for those awaiting deportation to Germany. There was no heating and the cells were frequently crowded, and even in modern times Fresnes Prison has been labelled as one of the worst prisons in Europe, the cells filthy, cold and damp and the meals mostly inedible.

Nine months in Fresnes broke Mary's health and left her with a persistent chest complaint. Mary left only a brief memoir of her imprisonment at Fresnes, where she was held in solitary confinement, and no one else has left a memory of meeting Mary there in 1941.[1] Her claim that she was at Fresnes while Henri Honoré d'Estienne d'Orves was a prisoner and heard the Frenchman singing to cheer up his fellow prisoners,[2] and that she heard others communicating between themselves by using the water pipes, are probably false memories. She also claimed to have counted every brick in her cell, recited every poem and play in her head, and looked forward to Sundays when she could receive visitors.

Maurice came to see her on her first Sunday in prison, but the following Sunday, 9 March, there was no sign of him. It was the following Sunday before Barbé came to see her. 'Maurice has been taken,' she whispered. 'It was the gun.'

On Monday, 3 November 1941 Mary was released from Fresnes. She had already been warned through Barbé's new, German friends that fresh papers were being prepared for her internment as a foreign national at Vittel. As she stepped into the corridor, the wardress whispered, 'If your family are not out-side the gates, don't wait, it may be very dangerous. They are expecting papers to order your further detention.' Maurice, her husband, was coming by car to collect her, and Mary walked along the road in the direction of Paris until, suddenly, she saw his car. Quickly she climbed in alongside Oky and Barbé. Maurice turned the car and they drove off towards the city.

Her son Maurice, who had been arrested by the Vichy Police on 9 March 1941 for illegal possession of a pistol and sentenced to eleven months' imprison-ment, was being held in the prison at Troyes. Despite the danger to herself, the following Sunday, 8 November, Mary went to visit him. Young Maurice was cold and ill, and Mary at once took off her only sweater and gave it to her boy, whispering that she was going to make a long journey. Mary had determined to go down her own rabbit hole.

Although ill health detained Mary for some months in Paris, Oky helped her to escape from her own flat, and he and Barbé saw her off on the train from Paris to Ruffec. Poor Mary was not to know that the tearful, ashen face of her second son running down the platform and waving to her would be the last time that she saw him.[3] Though her marriage to Maurice was ended, he was at hand in Ruffec to escort her to Marthe Rullier's house where she slept, despite there being Germans billeted there, while Maurice stayed in town at the Hôtel de France.

The next day Mary also visited Ruffec, where she met Gaston Denivelle, retired Colonel Ernst-Henri Gua, the chief of the local resistance movement, and a new recruit to the Resistance, police Lieutenant Henri Péyraud. Many years later, Péyraud recalled his meeting with Mary, commenting on her dress and English accent, 'She spoke our language with a pronunciation which was unquestionably English and also wore the uniform of the French Red Cross. But the accent!'[4]

Mary had made useful contacts, but there was little she could do until her own health was better and Maurice junior was out of prison. That evening Maxim escorted her across the demarcation line. Large doses of Doctor Collis Browne's Chlorodyne – a mixture of laudanum, cannabis and chloroform –

were necessary to still her cough, and at the next farm (Armand's) Mary collapsed and for several days she would lie in bed sweating and sleeping.

At last she was well enough to move on by bus and train to Limoges and then Lyon. There she found refuge in a flat in Lyon belonging to a Jewish lawyer, M. Bloc, until one day she had a visit from an American, George Whittinghill, who told her:

> I'm afraid that I learned about your presence in town only because there has been a certain amount of gossip. In the circumstances I do not advise you to remain here any longer. The Vichy police are extremely active and I don't think it will be more than a few hours before they learn about you. I have taken it upon myself to come up and warn and offer you an apartment in another part of the town where you should be safer for the moment.

Whittinghill was another American link in the escape lines which were spreading throughout occupied and Vichy France. He was in charge of the British interests section, working from the former British consular offices and was in 'very active', close touch with the French Resistance. In the US consulate proper in the Place Beauvau his fellow vice consul, Constance Ray Harvey, was in touch with the Resistance further north, and especially in Belgium.[5]

Harvey, though she had never lived or been stationed in Britain, was very pro-British. In Bern she had rented her flat to the British military attaché Cartwright, and she was a friend and admirer of the British air attaché 'Freddie' West.[6] Harvey and Whittinghill provided passports for Belgian, British, French and other citizens who wanted to leave France, and they smuggled diamonds and sent intelligence reports from all over Europe to the American military attaché in Switzerland, Barnwell R. Legge.[7] Later, Harvey and Whittinghill also worked closely with Virginia 'Ginny' Hall, who had joined the ambulance service at the beginning of the war, escaped from Vichy France to London, where she was recruited into the Special Operations Executive (SOE), and returned in August 1941 to Vichy France where she worked, under the cover of a correspondent for the *New York Post*, with the French Resistance.[8]

Whittinghill may not have been wholly convinced of all of Mary's claims when she related these to him, but he was authorised to put distressed British citizens on an allowance and he agreed to pay Mary, starting on 28 February 1942. Once she was safely relocated in a Lyon suburb, Whittinghill explained his idea that Mary should leave France under the cover of one of the many elderly English governesses who were stranded on the continent and needed help to leave for Britain.

Nevertheless it took several months before she could obtain an exit visa, and then only through the alertness of one French policeman, Jo Peronne. Peronne spotted Mary in the street, recognised her Englishness and, instead of betraying her, arranged a pretend robbery. He then issued Mary a certificate which stated that all her documents had been stolen.

While Mary was waiting for her documentation, she befriended 'Jacques', a young Belgian who was introduced to her by Whittinghill and, presumably, Constance Ray Harvey and her Belgian contacts. One day, as Mary sat in his office, Whittinghill speculated, 'If my memory serves me correctly you were anxious to obtain a British passport for your son. Naturally, I am sure you realize that we Americans cannot issue such documents.' As he said this he dropped his eyes to a small, slim, dark-blue book lying on his desk, and almost immediately he added, 'Excuse me, countess, I must go and have a word with my secretary, I'll be back shortly.' A highly delighted Mary returned to her flat with the passport of a young Australian, Tom Groome, who Whittinghill had already helped to escape to Spain.

Less happy news came from Paris: Mary learned that there had been fresh proceedings against her and that *in absentia* she had been condemned to death by a court in Paris. Nevertheless, Mary insisted on staying in Lyon until the summer of 1942 when she could be sure that Maurice had been released from prison, and then, with more foolhardiness, she took Maurice for a short holiday to Monaco. There she explained to Maurice that he must lie low for the next while until she returned.

Mary was plotting to resume her escape lines activity, and on 14 June Pat reported that she was offering to help prisoners of war to escape, but that she needed funds.[9] She was determined to go to England, to gain official recognition for her escape work and, just as important, to obtain funds. Only once she was assured that Maurice could stay in the relative safety of Monaco with a loyal French family did Mary, armed with no more than her new certificate and her charm, take the train via Perpignan to Portbou on the border with Catalonia.

At Portbou the railway gauge changed, and while Mary waited for the Spanish gauge train to arrive she was asked to surrender all her papers, but she had only Peronne's certificate. A French inspector of police insisted, 'I must have your official papers.'

'I'm sorry, I haven't got them. You see all my papers were stolen, the Lyon police gave me this receipt.'

The policeman smiled, 'This is a new idea but it's very good. It's the first time I've come across it. Where did you get this idea?'

Mary was nervous and did not know whether this was a loyal Frenchman or not. 'I don't know what you mean, I tell you I lost all my papers and the police gave me this document to cover them.'

To her surprise the policeman offered her lunch – still Mary did not trust him, but the policeman was giving her cover, 'No one will speak to you now that I am with you. Otherwise you might receive the attention of certain gentlemen.'

Mary dare not put her thoughts into words but hoped that her eyes expressed her gratitude. Only when she settled in the train did she realise that she had left her Red Cross coat behind in the restaurant, and standing at the window she asked her new friend to fetch it. 'Don't worry, I'll take it back to Lyon for you. Tell me the name of the man who gave you those papers and I'll give it to him.'

Mary had recovered her wits, 'Inspector, I will make you a present of the coat. The commissary of police at Bellacour in Lyon will confirm that my papers were stolen. What more do you want?'

The inspector stood grinning in the hot sun to wave Mary off while she collapsed into her seat. Spain could not come too soon. But she had forged another link in what would become her new escape line.

At the British consulate in Barcelona, she was greeted by a delighted Harold Farquhar, Consul General, otherwise known as 'Agent Horse'. Having first heard of Mary from Jimmy Windsor Lewis, he had been expecting her for over a year.

LONDON, SUMMER 1942 – MARY GOES TO TOWN

N ews of Mary's arrival in Barcelona caused something of a sensation in London. The British Consul General in Barcelona, Harold Farquhar, had already proved rather more effective than the British ambassador in Madrid, Sir Samuel Hoare, at helping refugees, amongst whom there were many escapers and stragglers, to reach Gibraltar and Lisbon. Hoare had banned any activity such as aiding British servicemen to reach home, as he thought this might be prejudicial to Anglo-Spanish relations. Farquhar turned a deaf ear to these instructions and, under the code name of 'Horse', had spent a good deal of his own money in helping servicemen who reached the Catalonian capital.

Farquhar had already heard of Mary from Jimmy Windsor Lewis, who had passed through his hands two years before, and presumably he had noted others who had tales of having been helped while in France by a somewhat larger than life character – an Englishwoman who was reported, somewhat incredibly, to be dressed in a French Red Cross uniform which belonged to the previous world war.

Farquhar's equanimity was not, therefore, disturbed when the lady herself appeared at his door in late July 1942, 'I'm delighted to meet you, I heard all about you from Major Windsor Lewis, and I've been expecting you for over a year.' Soberly he reported the facts to London: sitting in his office was a woman, dressed in a French uniform and wearing numerous First World War decorations, with a British passport and claiming to be a distressed governess who had crossed the border by train, having obtained a visa from the American consul in Lyon for travel to Spain and Portugal.[1]

In London, the 26-year-old, one-armed Jimmy Langley, who had been wounded and captured at Dunkirk and escaped through Marseilles, was now known as 'P15' and was responsible for liaison between the Secret Intelligence

Service and MI9. MI9 was a little-known branch of Military Intelligence responsible for assisting servicemen like himself, who found themselves behind enemy lines. In practice, most of Langley's work involved giving support to the French Resistance in their work on escape and evasion lines in north-west Europe. Langley's section in London consisted of just two officers, himself and Airey Neave, Neave being one of the first and few Allied servicemen to escape from the high-security German prison at Colditz Castle.

Langley and Neave were the same age. Jimmy was plain 'Jimmy', but other MI9 agents were Michael Creswell in Madrid, who was 'Monday', and Donald Darling, who was 'Sunday', and so Neave took the code name 'Saturday'.[2] When 'Jimmy' in London read the telegram from Farquhar he turned to Airey Neave, 'Crikey! This is fantastic, read on!'

Langley and Neave sent for Windsor Lewis' escape report and sure enough there, in the middle of a five-page report, was a discreet reference to 'Mme de M.', who was a Red Cross worker and who had obtained papers including an *ausweis* from the German authorities and calmly driven Windsor Lewis through the German lines and across the border into non-occupied France. She had since been arrested and imprisoned for nine months and now she was in Spain, offering to return to France and start a new organisation, but she needed funds and a wireless operator. She would shortly arrive in London from Lisbon, where she had also been interviewed by Darling.

Darling recalled, 'It did not occur to me that she might try to seek employment with my service.' He identified some of her weaknesses, 'Her challenging attitude towards anybody who denied her what she asked for could land her in trouble in France, where she was already, probably, known to the French police and to the Gestapo.'[3] To Langley and Neave these seemed like the adventures of a noblewoman in the pages of an eighteenth-century novel, not France in the 1940s.

Mary had already made her way to Lisbon and by flying boat to Shannon in Northern Ireland and on to Poole in southern England, where she arrived on 28 July 1942. Two days later there was an insistent ring at Jimmy Langley's flat above Overton's Restaurant at the bottom of St James's Street, which served as an office. When Neave went down the dark stairs to answer the bell, there, in the bright sunshine of St James's Street, dressed in a royal-blue uniform with the fabled row of British and French decorations, stood the slight figure of Mary Lindell. Neave knew she was in her mid 40s, but she looked much younger. Neave noted her chestnut hair and her finely proportioned face. She was very feminine, 'but in her expression there was intensity, a stubbornness which somehow did not fit her smart appearance'.

As soon as she spoke, Neave understood that she was very English and used to getting her own way. 'I have received several messages at my hotel asking me to meet Captain Langley. Does he happen to be in?' The tone was peremptory, and she looked Neave up and down as though he were the butler answering the door. Then she laughed.

Neave was shaken. 'Let me introduce myself, I am Airey Neave of MI9. We are expecting you.' The handshake was predictably vigorous and together they climbed the stairs to Langley's flat. Neave noted that, despite her gruff manner, she was still beautiful and he saw how easily she was able to charm the Germans – if she wanted to.

The meeting with Langley started badly: there was a rule that people like Mary arriving from the Continent should not discuss their affairs with others. 'I have already seen Jimmy Windsor Lewis, of course.' She had also already met many of the Frenchmen whom she had helped in her ambulance convoy all those many months ago in June 1940. Langley and Neave were wary of Mary and asked for her story of the war to date, which she told with some verve.[4]

'And you still want to go back to France after all this?' asked Langley.

'That is what I am here for.'

'Have you contacts in France that are still safe?'

'Yes, a large number.'

Their meeting ended after some small talk in which Mary told Langley and Neave that Kipling was her favourite author and that Edith Cavell was her personal heroine. When she had gone, Neave asked Langley, 'Well, what do you think of that?'

'I've got nothing to say at the moment, except that I want a very large whisky and soda.'

Looking back, Jimmy Langley reflected:

Mary was a very brave, courageous woman who wanted to have everything her own way. When she first got in contact with us in London – or rather we got in contact with her – from the moment she arrived in England, from the word 'go' she was, to put it mildly, difficult. She wanted to have her own way, she wouldn't obey any instructions given by us and they had been given really for security reasons. She had made it clear she wished to go back and she was obviously fit to so do, but she did get across people. There's no doubt about that. And a lot of the high-ups in MI9, those who did meet her, came away with the impression that she was alright in very small doses.[5]

Mary's version was slightly different:

> I'd been freelance, there was nobody in occupied France to give you direc-
> tions, and I was doing this entirely on my own, and when Neave, Langley and
> company said, 'Oh, you no longer are', I took rather a dim view. I said, 'I'm
> not going to be pushed around by you people.'

But Mary also realised that the only possibility of getting back to France was
by plane, and the only way to get a plane was by playing along with officialdom
– and officialdom took some time to decide what to do with Mary. It was a
principle that anyone who had been in the hands of the Germans was suspect
and should not go back into the field, and on these grounds, and because he
was a misogynist who did not like sending women into the field, Langley and
Neave's boss, Colonel Claude Dansey, had to be convinced to let Mary go back.
To Dansey, letting women run anything was against his principles, even if MI9
was in dire need of agents.[6] Not only was it unusual for any prisoner to be given
up by the Germans, but Dansey was also worried that by using threats to her
children, Mary might have been turned and become a double agent who would
inform on others. In Dansey's opinion, even the redoubtable Mary Lindell was
liable to blackmail of this kind.[7]

When another line, Comet, was penetrated and many of its agents and *passeurs* lay in Gestapo hands in fear of torture and death, Langley in MI9 pleaded
for MI6 to do something to save them, but Dansey told him, 'Your trouble,
Jimmy, is that you love your agents.'[8]

Dansey may also have known that, as a result of other arrests in Paris, the
Germans wanted to interrogate Mary again and that the Vichy Police had
orders to help find and arrest her. On the other hand, Mary was well aware of
the risks of going back. Other escape lines across France had suffered a series
of setbacks and there was a desperate need for a new line from the occupied
into the non-occupied zone of France.

At the merest suggestion of doubt in her, Mary took strong personal affront
and she insisted to Langley and Neave that she would return to France with or
without their consent. Langley later described her as 'a woman who brooks no
opposition but prefers to use a battleaxe rather than the more usual feminine
charm when dealing with difficult males'. Langley accompanied her to a meeting in which Claude Dansey intended to tell her that he would not let her go
back to France. He wrote afterwards:

Dansey never got round to that as Mary took control of the interview and informed him of all his shortcomings as far as helping evaders was concerned. When he pointed out that he was only trying to save her life she replied that it was not her life he was interested in but his reputation.

Beaten, Dansey relented, and Mary was prepared for her return.[9]

The task of training and controlling MI9's difficult new recruit was given to Airey Neave. One challenge was to try to team her with a wireless operator who, at this stage of war, was provided by the SIS, and there was a very small field of candidates. When he had chosen, Neave told Mary, 'He speaks perfect French and has lived in France, but is actually an Australian.'

Mary said quietly, 'And his name is Tom Groome.'

Neave was astounded, 'How on earth do you know that?'

Mary took from her bag the photograph which she had taken out of the passport that George Whittinghill in Lyon had given her for Maurice to use.

'Incredible, incredible, I would never have believed it. Anyway, he's your man.'

But when they met, Mary took a personal dislike to Tom Groome. Her dislike was instinctive – an instinct which was reinforced when they were taken up in the back of a Lysander and Groome was airsick – and it was mutual.[10]

When by chance, one afternoon in London, Mary met 'Jacques', the young Belgian she had befriended in Lyon, she made up her mind that she wanted 'Jacques' as her wireless operator. However, there was a pressing need for her to return to France and 'Jacques' could not be trained in time. If 'Jacques' could be released from the Belgian Army to be trained as a wireless operator, he would be sent out later.

The only possible alternative was for Mary to communicate with London by courier. Since Mary already knew George Whittinghill in the American consulate in Lyon, and he could communicate by diplomatic bag with the US embassy in Switzerland, it was agreed that she would send her messages to London via Whittinghill to Colonel Henry Cartwright, British military attaché in Bern, Switzerland.

Also in Switzerland was Victor Farrell, the former professor of English at the St Cyr Military Academy in France. Farrell had been British consul in Geneva since the beginning of 1941, in succession to Frederick van den Heuvel (who remained in Switzerland as head of the British SIS). Both Heuvel and Farrell were members, of course, of Dansey's pre-war Z Organisation. Cartwright, who in the previous war had made repeated attempts at escape from German prison camps until he eventually broke out of a camp and walked nine days to Holland, was an expert at interrogating escaped prisoners of war and Allied airmen who crossed into Switzerland, and he too was connected to the SIS.[11] Together these men helped to make Switzerland, the only neutral country bordering on Germany and with land frontiers to France, Austria and Italy, a nexus of intelligence for Dansey in London. Furthermore, Farrell had his own wireless transmitter/receiver in order to keep in touch with London.[12]

Meanwhile, Mary received training in coding and decoding, and also in Lysander operations, including the laying of flare paths and the signals to aircraft. Her cover, she insisted, would remain her Red Cross uniform, but she agreed to adopt a field name. She would become 'Marie-Claire'.

Neave had no doubt about her capacity to bluff her way past mere mortal men such as railway guards or sentries, but he was more worried about the dangers to Mary herself. Her French papers remained in the name Ghita de Milleville. Part of Mary's argument for retaining her own surname was a paradox: she was so well known in France that if she was recognised at a hotel using another name, it would arouse suspicion. However, in her absence, the Germans in Paris had condemned her to death in the name of de Milleville.

Langley recalled:

> Perhaps one broke a security rule by sending someone back who had already been in Gestapo hands and was known to the Germans, but it was simply a case that we had to have more people, and as she volunteered to go back, we then trained her to send her in again, knowing the risks we were taking, or rather – let's be fair – the risks she was taking.

It was never easy to resist Mary's enthusiasm and fearlessness, but the risks were even greater than Dansey, Langley or Neave imagined and, perhaps, had these been fully assessed her mission might have been cancelled.

RUFFEC, WINTER 1942 – TWO IMPORTANT PARCELS

S o, after just three months in England and a holiday in the West Country, Mary was escorted by Neave to Tangmere, near Chichester, an airfield used as a base by 161 RAF Squadron to fly agents in and out of wartime France using its black-painted Lysander aircraft.

Mary returned to France on the night of 26–27 October 1942, flown by Pilot Officer John Bridger in Lysander V9353 on Operation Achilles. The aim was to land 'Marie-Claire', as she was now to be known, at Thalamy Airfield, 12km east of Ussel, which had been used before by the Lysanders.

The journey was not accomplished without amusement. Before she dressed in flying clothing and donned a parachute, Mary went to the loo, but was disturbed by a knock on the door. 'What the hell! I haven't finished, I want to do a wee-wee.'

'Well, the pilot wants to speak to you.'

Mary was furious: she thought the pilot wanted to give her a message of reassurance about the flight. He was a Canadian, 'I'm sorry to have pulled you from where you were, but I want to thank you for what you're doing for all of us.'

'Don't be silly, you're the heroes.'

'No, when I put you down, I know where I'm to sleep, but you don't.'[1]

For Bridger, older than most of his colleagues in RAF 161 Squadron and more experienced – with over 4,000 hours flying in his logbook – and less articulate than the others, even dour, this seems a rather unusual and long exchange.[2] To Mary, Bridger was (with her usual tendency to exaggerate), 'One of the really big pilots during the war.' The exchange, she thought, was, 'Priceless. It was the most thrilling thing that ever happened to me in the whole war. He was sweet.'

The weather in the first October moon period was very bad and the cloud so thick over the landing areas in France that most missions were cancelled, and the second moon period was therefore busy.[3] Mary's fellow passenger in the back of the Lysander was an RF Section agent, Ferdinand Rodriguez.[4] Having taken off at 20.58hrs on a Monday evening, Mary recalled seeming to skim the Channel at wave height until Bridger climbed over the coast of France 'like a hunter at full gallop'.[5] She saw two or three lights winking at her from the ground and only when the aircraft bucked and reared did she realised that these were anti-aircraft guns firing at her.

The rest of the flight was in cloud and Mary marvelled that the pilot could find his way, but through breaks in the cloud she saw the occasional town or a river shining in the moonlight. At altitude it was bitterly cold in the back of the aircraft and, despite their brief acquaintance, Mary and her fellow passenger huddled together for warmth. When Mary heard Bridger throttle back and felt the Lysander begin to sink she realised that they must be near the landing ground. At 1,000ft Bridger began to circle, and then she heard his voice over the intercom, 'Look, down there on the port side. I'll have to circle. I can see only one light.'

The aircraft banked steeply and Mary peered into the night: she too could only see one light. Were there other pinpricks of light down there? Bridger called over the intercom, 'Shall we have a try?' For most pilots on these special flights the minutes on the ground seemed like an eternity. The lights were supposed to be arranged in an 'L' shape. They would land into the wind, taxi in a tight circle and come back to the start ready for a quick take-off. The time on the ground was usually no more than two minutes, enough for one set of passengers to disembark and another set to climb aboard. If anything untoward happened, the pilot would open the throttle and race off into the dark.

Mary felt uneasy. What if the Germans were down there? She looked at Rodriguez, who nodded, and she called, 'OK'.

Bridger called back, 'Don't open the canopy until I give you the word. If I'm the slightest bit suspicious, I shall take off immediately.'

They landed at 00.32hrs on 27 October, but all was not well. The agent who was supposed to be in charge of the landing reception committee had fallen asleep on the train and missed his stop at Ussel. Another resistant had extemporised a flare path using solid meta-fuel, and Bridger, who wanted to spend as little time on the ground as possible, was held up. First, Mary and Rodriguez began to hand out the stores that covered the floor of the aircraft, then, as Rodriguez reached down for the last of the bicycle tyres, he pulled the release handle of one of the parachutes. The draught from the engine caught the canopy and the cabin filled with its voluminous silk enveloping them both.

That was grimly amusing. 'What the hell's going on in there?' called Bridger, 'For Christ's sake, don't waste so much time.'

'Don't panic, one of the bloody parachutes has come undone.'

'Well for God's sake, stow it away.'

For a few moments they fought to push the fabric into the cockpit and then clambered out into the night, stepping off the aircraft's ladder onto the soil of France. Bridger was expecting return passengers for England, but no one appeared. 'Well, have I got two passengers, or not? I don't intend to wait very much longer.' Bridger looked round, saw no one, raised his hand in salute and with a roar took off into the night. A few minutes later the rest of the reception party arrived, inebriated and without any return passengers. Mary and Rodriguez made off into the night on their own, away from the irresponsible and drunken reception party.

Mary's first, self-appointed task was to collect Maurice from Monaco. Travelling by train via Limoges to Toulouse, her sense of danger was so dull that she sent a telegram announcing her arrival, and once there, she went to find her son at the Imperial Hotel. Next morning, mother and son took the train to Lyon. She needed to re-establish contact with George Whittinghill and with Police Inspector Jo Deronne. She had told Langley and Neave before leaving London that her escape line would be based on the small town of Ruffec and her headquarters at the Hôtel de France. So, while she made her way there, she sent Maurice to Perpignan to explore ways of crossing the Pyrenees into Spain. Whether Mary had made a prior arrangement with Roger and Germaine Rouillon, owners of the Hôtel de France, is not clear, but it was convenient, not least because other members of the Rouillon family also ran the buffet at the Gare d'Austerlitz in Paris, which was the terminus for trains to Bordeaux, via Ruffec, and all the Rouillons were active in the Resistance.[6]

Mary had barely taken her coat off when Gaston Denivelle, a true patriot, arrived to tell her that there were at least six airmen being hidden in the area between Angoulême and Poitiers. Mary arranged for them to be moved at once, using her well-established route across farmland east of Ruffec.

She also heard of Henri Péan, a priest in the small town of Draché. Péan had been serving in the French Army in 1940 when he was taken prisoner. Released in 1941, he immediately took up the work of the Resistance, in all its forms: the escape of refugees, illegal passages across the line of demarcation, intelligence gathering, the distribution of BBC news, hiding secret agents, repatriation of

Allied airmen, production of false identity cards, the reception of parachutages and, later, helping to hide French boys from the forced labour organisation.

Péan, it was rumoured, said Mass with trousers and boots under his cassock so that he could return to his resistance work without delay, but he belonged to no organisation and preferred to deal with whichever resistance group best suited his purpose. Mary had to travel up to Châtellerault, between Poitiers and Tours, to meet Péan where, at the house of the Goupille family in La Haye-Descartes, she gave the priest 50,000 francs, but she advised him to keep a low profile. Péan ignored her advice and handed over another half-dozen downed airmen who he had been hiding in the district.[7]

Meanwhile, on 1 December 1942 Mary returned to Lyon to meet her son Maurice, make contact with Inspector Deronne and replenish her funds from George Whittinghill at the US consulate. Even though the German Army had crossed the demarcation line after the Allied landings in North Africa in November, the line was not annulled until 1 March, and Mary was in Lyon only a couple of days before she attempted to cross northwards from what had been the so-called free zone – not by the familiar farms east of Ruffec, but by another way, across a mill near Blois on the River Loire and well north of her usual route. It was to prove disastrous.[8]

Mary was escorted by a resistant called 'Pierre', and she was riding on the back of a tandem bicycle steered by another resistant, 'François', when they were run down by a car, said to be driven by two collaborators – probably they were smugglers. Her companion was hurled into the air and fell screaming into the verge. Mary hit the bonnet of the car, rolled over its top and fell bleeding and still into the road. She was so deeply unconscious that the villagers who heard the commotion and came scurrying along thought she was dead. Their bodies were carried for 5km on a farm gate to a farmhouse where the farmer dug a grave for Mary but refused to bury her until a doctor had certified she was dead.

The local doctor was on his rounds, but when a chemist, who arrived with plaster of Paris and bandages to treat 'François', was asked to sign the certificate, he insisted on seeing her body first.

'It's alright. She's dead. Just sign a certificate.'

The chemist insisted and after being allowed to examine the body announced, 'Quick, fetch some hot bricks.' He treated her with an injection of camphor oil, a cure more normally used on horses with breathing difficulties, but also on humans in a state of catatonia. Mary woke with a start: she felt cold, but no pain. The chemist now insisted that she should go to hospital. 'The only hospital

I know where there is a patriotic surgeon is in Loches. His name is Martinez, but it's over 20km away.'

So severe was the pain when they tried to move her to an ambulance that Mary fainted again. The stretcher would not fit down the stairs and she had to be carried down in an eiderdown. 'It can't be helped. If she's to be saved, we must get her there.'

X-rays in the hospital at Loches showed that Mary had multiple fractures. 'Why on earth didn't you tell us?'

'Tell you what? That I am in agony?'

'You shouldn't be alive. You've got five ribs broken and all of them compound fractures. Your lungs, liver and intestines should all have been pierced, especially after being carried for five kilometres across fields. It's a miracle that you are still alive.'

For two or three days she lay strapped, but without anaesthetic because the doctor thought she might not be able to withstand the shock. Maurice, summoned from Lyon to his mother's bedside, was shaken to see her so pale. The doctor advised that, given her age, her bones would take longer to mend and that she should stay in hospital for seven weeks.

Mary, however, was conscious, very much aware and indomitable. She was still in charge, and she gave orders to Maurice to tell Gaston Denivelle to keep the escape line going while she was immobilised. When she heard that two airmen had arrived on 19 December at Ruffec, claiming to have been shot down on the night of 6–7 December in eastern France, she was certainly not too ill to demand their names and numbers for an identity check. They were Sergeants H.O. Robertson and H.J.B. Canter. Unfortunately they had arrived when Mary was on the other side of the demarcation line and too ill to travel to meet them.[9]

Still in hospital on Christmas Eve 1941, Mary and Maurice shared a dinner while he reported on his progress in establishing a new route over the mountains into Spain. However, when he returned to Lyon after the holiday he found a message from Armand Debreuille saying that he had 'two important parcels of food for him'. 'Parcels' was a code word for an evader – someone who needed to be hidden from the Germans and wanted to escape from France.

Whether Mary had any inkling exactly who her 'important parcels' were, or whether she had received any briefing, even verbal, in London to expect any unusual evaders, or whether she made any connection with the news of an attack on shipping at Bordeaux is not known. Certainly she was bored by the inactivity of being in hospital and when Maurice made a third visit to Loches to bring his mother the message, she swung into action.

She issued her detailed orders. Maurice was to go to Ruffec for the 'parcels'. She told Maurice:

> I'm not supposed to be out of here for another three or four weeks, but obviously I can't stay here. I shall also go to Lyon and make sure everything is in order. Go to Armand and tell him you will pick up the men on 6 January. You take the men from the farm on bicycles to Roumazières and pick up the night train to Lyon. The stationmaster will help you, but don't take any risks.

Two days later, though feeling weak, Mary discharged herself from hospital and travelled by train via Limoges to Lyon. She also made the decision that she could not cope with Robertson and Canter and, disappointed, they returned on 17 January 1943 to Paris to restart their attempt to escape. The one thing Mary could not do was tell London by wireless what had happened to her or give any news about her 'important parcels' – whoever they were …

THE PRIDE OF POMPEY

While Mary was hospitalised, Gaston Denivelle had been contacted by Lise de Baissac. Two months earlier, de Baissac and Andrée Borrel had been among the first female agents of SOE to be parachuted into France. Andrée Borrel went to Paris to work as a courier for the Prosper network run by Francis Suttill. Lise de Baissac established a safe house in Poitiers for her work as a courier and liaison officer between the Prosper network in Paris and the Scientist network, run by her brother Claude de Baissac, and operating in Landes and the Vendée.[1]

Lise was in touch with London through her brother, though whether Denivelle knew this, or was trusted enough to be told, is unknown.[2] Nor is it known whether Denivelle told Lise that, while Mary was *hors d'combat* (literally, unable to participate) he was running the Marie-Claire escape line. Even if Denivelle and Lise de Baissac had realised the full extent of each other's involvement in covert operations, it is doubtful whether this or knowledge in London of Mary's hospitalisation would have altered any of the events in the winter of 1942–43.

Bordeaux, in the Second World War, was a major port where ocean-going ships berthed in the broad Garonne River above its juncture with the Dordogne before running out to sea as the Gironde. It was also a haven for blockade runners who brought valuable cargo from around the world to feed the German war machine. The Scientist network sent intelligence to London about the movements of blockade runners and their cargoes, and was planning an attack by smuggling explosives on board the ships.

Meanwhile, earlier in 1942 Major H.G. 'Blondie' Hasler, Royal Marines,[3] had submitted a plan of attack to the chief of combined operations (CCO) which called for teams of canoeists to paddle up the Garonne and place limpet mines on ships alongside the quays in the centre of town.[4] Thus, there were two plans of attack: one sponsored by SOE and the other by CCO. The submarine HMS *Tuna* duly delivered Hasler and his Royal Marines to the mouth of the Gironde on the night of 7 December 1942 for a raid that was called Operation Frankton. The marines paddled by night and hid by day until they reached the port, some 96km from the sea, and where six ships were mined. Mountbatten called Operation Frankton 'the most courageous and imaginative of all the raids ever carried out by the men of Combined Operations', but only two of the twelve canoeists survived. These two were Blondie Hasler and his crewman, Marine Bill Sparks.[5]

The full details of Operation Frankton have been vividly and definitively told by Paddy Ashdown in *A Brilliant Little Operation*. Hasler and Sparks scuttled their canoe and trekked to Ruffec, north-east of Bordeaux, which they reached on 18 December 1942. Though unknown to Mary when she left England only a few weeks earlier, her return to France had been part of a wider plan to increase the marines' chances of escape, though the briefing given to Hasler regarding their proposed escape after the raid was vague.[6] The addresses of safe houses and names of willing helpers would not, of course, be given. Like aircrew, Hasler and his men had to be content with only general directions.[7]

Hasler was told only to expect to find someone from the French Resistance at Ruffec, a briefing which, in the words of Paddy Ashdown, was 'more to do with hope than deliberative planning'.[8] The operation order that Hasler gave verbally to his marines (as it was too precious even to write down) called only for them, after scuttling their canoes, 'to proceed independently in pairs in accordance with the escape instructions', and 'on reaching a British consul in Spain he is to be informed that the party consists of Combined Operations personnel escaped from a raid but no further details'.[9]

In practice it was not possible to say more. Normally no one going to wartime France, whether aircrew or commandos or agents, were given the details of any escape line,[10] though in planning Operation Frankton the staff of Combined Operations had indeed discussed with Langley and Neave at MI9 the possibility of putting the canoeists in touch with an underground organisation which would help them find their way to neutral territory. Otherwise, the commandos had no choice but to accept that they would be taken prisoners and, after Hitler signed the infamous Commando Order, capture now meant death.[11]

Towards noon on 18 December Hasler and Sparks walked into Ruffec. They looked and smelled like a pair of vagabonds, and though they walked past a gendarme and stood bewildered on a street corner, they knew not what to do next. According to Sparks, they were looking for the Café de Paris but, as he grumbled to Hasler, 'There is no Café de bloody Paris.'[12] The two men had clearly forgotten the name of the rendezvous in that part of their briefing.

Tired and hungry, they decided to spend their last remaining francs on a meal. Because it looked too smart, they rejected the Hôtel de France, where the Rouillons might have swept them up, and instead they opted for a workingmen's café-cum-hotel called the Toque Blanche. In a small town where defiance of the Germans and smuggling people and goods across the line of demarcation was an industry, Hasler and Sparks had stumbled across friends who would help them in their escape. Yvonne Mandidaud, who served the two marines with potato soup, was unfazed when Hasler paid their bill with a 500 franc note wrapped around a handwritten note asking for her help. Yvonne and her brother, René, sent for the local schoolmaster who addressed them in English, 'Who were you told to contact?'[13]

Whatever Hasler had been told in England, and whatever he had passed on to his marines, Sparks heard him say, 'We were told only that friends of England would be here to help us.'

'Why did you come here?'

'We had nowhere else to go and we were hungry.'

After a second interview, this time with Germaine Rouillon who Sparks described as 'a little old lady', Hasler and Sparks were accepted for what they were, and not German deserters or, worse, German agents provocateurs. The next evening they were smuggled across the demarcation line and hidden on Armand and Amélie Marvaud's farm. Significantly, besides the Rouillons at the Hôtel de France and Gaston Denivelle, several others in Ruffec who were part of Mary Lindell's escape team sponsored by MI9 had already been recruited by Lise de Baissac to work with the SOE in the Scientist network, and part of Lise's business for the SOE was to smuggle agents. When Hasler and Sparks turned up unexpectedly in Ruffec, all turned now not to Lise but to Mary for her help and expertise in spiriting them out of France. A message was sent via Maurice in Lyon, a message which eventually reached Mary in her hospital bed.[14]

When Sparks learned that the escape line was run by an Englishwoman called Marie-Claire, he gave in to his male chauvinism. He was unhappy that his fate should be in the hands of a woman, but when he met her he was one of the first to appreciate Mary Lindell's raw bravery, telling his biographer, 'She was one of the most extraordinary and courageous people I could ever hope to meet.'[15]

When, soon after Christmas 1942, Hasler and Sparks, in their hiding place on the Marvaud farm, heard about Mary's road accident, they were temporarily downhearted, but soon cheered up when they were told that her son would be coming to collect them. When Maurice arrived, Sparks' sense of humour failed him again, 'Nobody ever looked less like an agent. Nineteen years old, good-looking and speaking perfect English, he was more like an Oxford University student.'

At first, Maurice's manner was a little too cavalier for Sparks' liking, as though their escape was all some sort of schoolboy adventure. However, he seemed to know exactly what he was about; he smiled and did his best to reassure the marines, even though they had to accomplish the first part of their journey without identity cards. Maurice explained that the Marie-Claire escape line southwards across the nearest part of the Pyrenees had been blocked by the Germans, and that he was going to take the two Royal Marines by bike and train to where his mother was convalescing in Lyon, some 320km eastwards and away from Spain. Soon Sparks appreciated that Maurice was as smart and shrewd as anyone he had ever met, and despite the lad's manner Sparks placed his confidence in him.

'If anyone says anything,' Maurice told them, 'just pretend you don't under-stand and sort of grunt "Breton". You'll pass easily enough for one of those peasants from Brittany who doesn't speak French!'

The journey to Lyon passed without incident and the two marines were taken by Maurice to a luxurious flat, presumably belonging to an M Bloc (a Jew), where they met a small, middle-aged woman in a Red Cross uniform, who had a heavy strapping around her collar bone. This was Sparks' first impression of Mary, who was then aged 47:

> We knocked on the door and this is where we got our first look at Mary. Lovely little lady, small. It was very surprising that she was so small – and very heavily bandaged from her accident. Her arm was in a sling – but she was the master power, and seeing my commanding officer taking orders from a little lady was very humorous for me. But she left us in no doubt that she was the governor.[16]

Maurice introduced them, 'This is my mother.'

'I'm so sorry that you had to hide out for so long at the farm,' Mary told them at once. 'I'm afraid my route across the Pyrenees has closed and I've got to open a new way through. Now, come and have some lunch.'

Sparks, despite his male chauvinism, was impressed:

> There was something of the English matron about her. She was fearless, a touch arrogant, but very jovial, and although she was a woman, she was very

much the governor. I had arrived feeling unsure about putting my life in the hands of a woman, but within ten minutes I had every confidence in her.[17]

Over a convivial lunch Mary carefully checked Hasler and Sparks' stories. She also showed she was used to command, and turned to Hasler, 'That moustache is going to come off. You can't go around Lyon sporting a moustache like that. You look too English.' When Hasler returned from the bathroom having trimmed a little off his moustache, Mary pounced. 'It's still too much. Back to the bathroom!'

When he returned a second time he announced, 'There I've taken the bloody thing right off.'

Sparks could hardly suppress his mirth, 'Well, ma'am, do you realise that that was the pride of Pompey, that was!'

Mary laid down her rules for escapees, which including no dalliance with the local girls. She also arranged for their photographs to be attached to genuine identity documents issued by a contact in the town hall, and she took them to a safe house. After a while, however, even Mary had to admit defeat and hand Hasler and Sparks over to another escape line – Albert Guérisse's 'Pat' line.

Mary went in person to their safe house to break the news. With one sleeve tucked into her coat pocket and her coat draped over the shoulder, her arm still in a sling, she announced, 'Come on, lads, we've got a journey to make on a tram,' and she led them to the suburbs of Lyon, calling out in English when they reached their destination, 'I say, Bill, we're getting off here.' Sparks shrank inside his shirt collar and felt that everyone was looking at him as he slid out of the tram, sweating with fear. Mary was doubled with laughter at having given him a scare.

As they parted on the pavement in the growing darkness of the city, Sparks thanked Mary and she wished him good luck, 'Cheer up, Bill, you'll soon be on your way home.' Sparks reflected that she was not only a courageous woman and a highly organised resistance fighter, but had become a good friend too. He wondered, however, how long Mary would be able to evade the Germans with her incredible devil-may-care bravado:

The impression she gave me was one of safety. I felt safe when Mary was about. Even though she spoke English, and she had very funny ways – I don't think any other organisation thought a lot of her ways – this girl really gave me confidence. She was afraid of no one and she passed this on to everyone. Anybody who had dealings with her felt the same way.[18]

NEWS FROM FRANCE

With a route for her escape line over the Pyrenees not yet re-established, Mary Lindell was obliged to hand her two important 'parcels' over to 'Mr Carter', who represented another escape organisation, the Pat, or PAO, line. The Pat line, which ran through Marseilles, was organised by the Belgian doctor, Albert-Marie Guérisse, masquerading as a French Canadian under the name of Lieutenant Commander Pat O'Leary. The line helped scores of downed American and British pilots and other escapers to reach Spain, some by sea and others over the Pyrenees.[1]

The arrangement between Mary and Guérisse was necessary, but was not one which was wholly amicable. Guérisse had reported Mary's activities to London as long ago as June 1942, stating that she was English and able to assist prisoners of war to escape but needed finance. Then, soon after Mary had returned from England at the end of October 1942, Guérisse had complained that Mary was using his contacts, presumably in Lyon or Toulouse, and threatened to stop work unless she was forbidden to do so.[2] Mary reciprocated, accusing Guérisse of claiming successes for his line which were really hers.[3]

Hasler and Sparks were not to know how lucky they were. In January and February 1943, as they were conducted through Vichy France, south to Marseilles and, after a pause, westwards to the Spanish border, the Pat line was being rolled up behind them. After the Allied landings in North Africa the previous November, the Germans had crossed the demarcation line and occupied the remainder of France, and the activities of the various German agencies, including the Gestapo and the Feldpolizei, had increased significantly. Guérisse's organisation was penetrated by traitors, and as Hasler and Sparks journeyed into safety the members of the Pat line were being arrested.

Ironically, the Australian Tom Groome, who MI9 had wanted to send with Mary as her wireless operator, was one of the first to be caught, although it was by carelessness rather than through treachery. Groome had landed in France by the felucca *Seadog*, landing on the night of 3–4 November 1942 on the south coast of France, near Port Miou, between Marseilles and Toulon, in the company of Mary Herbert, Marie-Therese le Chêne and Odette Sansom.[4]

Inexplicably, MI9 had given Groome the field name of Georges de Milleville – he thought the name might already be suspect, and Darling, who he stayed with in Gibraltar before boarding the boat, advised him to change it as soon as he could.[5] However, Groome was arrested in early January 1943 after he had been detected by German direction finders. He had set up his wireless at a house at Montauban, north of Toulouse, the home of Pat Cheramy, who was married to a French doctor and whose English name was Eleanor Maud Hawkins.

As if to confirm the distrust that Mary Lindell had had of him, Groome had failed to observe one of the rules that all wireless operators were taught in the SOE's schools – to move his transmitter often to reduce the chance of being located by direction finders. He was transmitting without a lookout, and he and his courier, Edithe Reddé, an employee of the French Post Office and well placed to bring him encoded messages for transmission, were located. His host and hostess were also arrested.[6]

Groome and Reddé were in an upstairs room and so absorbed in their work, Groome in his earphones transmitting his messages in groups of five and with his revolver by the set and Reddé sitting beside him, that they did not hear someone silently enter the room until Groome felt a gun at his back. 'Finish that message. If you stop you will be shot.'

However, Groome had the presence of mind to leave out the security check from the message he was sending and when Langley and Neave received the message marked 'Security check not given' they were warned that Groome was probably in German hands. Taken to Gestapo headquarters in Toulouse, the first words of his interrogator were, 'Our detector vans have been listening to you for two months.'

As a Gestapo officer began his questions to Groome and Reddé, suddenly Groome leapt up onto a desk and jumped through a window, breaking the glass. He dropped 30ft to the pavement below and sprained his ankle, but managed to limp down the street through groups of pedestrians to hide in the doorway of a house. However, when the Germans raced down the stairs and out into the street, Groome was betrayed by 'a craven bystander' and he was dragged back to the German headquarters.

In the confusion Reddé, who did not know whether Groome had survived his jump or not, was left unguarded. She peeped out of the room where they had been questioned, saw a number of girl office workers walking down the stairs, and simply followed them out into the street without being challenged. Once outside she hurried to a hotel, rushed upstairs to the first bedroom she could find and hid herself in a wardrobe. When nothing happened after half an hour, she crept out again and went to find Guérisse. Astonished by the girl's story, Guérisse wondered if she had been planted by the Germans, but once he had confirmation of her story he put her on the escape line from France.[7]

Pat Cheramy was not so lucky and after several months imprisonment at Aix-La-Chapelle she was deported in October 1943 to Germany where she would meet Mary Lindell in Ravensbrück.

Reddé met Bill Sparks in Marseilles, where he was being hidden on the top floor of a block of flats with Hasler and a group of RAF evaders in crowded quarters overlooking the Observatory Gardens. The flat was rented by a member of the Pat organisation and run by a French family called Martin.

Sparks described Reddé as extremely jolly and companionable but at least 16 stone, and when he thought she showed an inclination to want to get even closer to him he remembered Mary's orders, 'No women!' Sparks comforted himself with the thought that their quarters were too crowded to allow any intimacy, but that even if he rejected her and Reddé threw him off the balcony, at least she was not going to turn him over to the gendarmes. He might not have liked to know that later, when Edithe was training as an agent to return to France, she was assessed as 'a very good shot with the pistol: better than most of the men'.[8]

During the next month the population of the flat grew to include a Belgian prince, Werner de Mérode, and others, until on 28 February 1943 Guérisse told them that next morning they would be leaving for Spain.[9] Hasler, Sparks, de Mérode and Sergeant J.G. Dawson travelled by rail to Perpignan and by road to the foothills, and then they walked for four days without incident to arrive at Bañolas in Spain towards the end of the first week of March.[10]

Guérisse had said goodbye to this party at Perpignan, noting in his dairy that they were 'a Belgian [Mérode], an aviator in the RAF [Dawson], a British Lieutenant belonging to a commando [Hasler], a British aviator [no – this was Marine Bill Sparks] and an American aviator [unidentified]'. He was thus unaware of the identity of Hasler and Sparks, who been in the custody of the Pat line since January.

Even if he had known, he had already lost his wireless operator, Groome, and even as he was writing in his diary the Gestapo were closing in on Guérisse.

In the round-ups which accompanied the collapse of the Pat line, another of those arrested was the female journalist Ragna Fischer, a Danish national working for a Swedish newspaper in France, who was also a *passeur*. Ragna would meet Mary Lindell in Ravensbrück in the following year: her account in the Swedish newspaper *Göteborgs-Posten* of her arrest and life in Ravensbrück would be one of the first to reach the free press.

Meanwhile, in London there was no news of Hasler and his Royal Marines, but relying on a German news broadcast that indicated none of the commandos had survived, Hasler and his men were officially listed as 'missing' on 24 January.

* * *

Mary, however, needed further medical treatment for the injuries received when she was run over, and she needed cash to support her own escape line. So, after she had inserted Hasler and Sparks into the Pat line on 2 February, Mary crossed into Switzerland where, in Geneva, she gave Victor Farrell a detailed account of the Marie-Claire line and passed on a coded message which Hasler had entrusted to her. When this message reached MI9's offices in London in the early hours of 23 February, the code could not be deciphered: evidently Hasler had not only forgotten the name of the rendezvous in Ruffec but he had forgotten how to encrypt his report. It took the patience, imagination and skill of a WRNS officer, Mary Hamilton, working through the night to break Hasler's impromptu code, but when at last it could be read it was the first news that Hasler and Sparks were alive.[11]

Mary's part in the escape of Hasler and Sparks, and in bringing Hasler's coded message to Switzerland despite her serious injuries, marked another highpoint of achievement in her life and this alone was sufficient to merit some award. Mary might have chosen to take refuge in Switzerland, yet she was an extraordinary woman and had more to contribute to the Allied victory in the war.

Mary had come to the notice of the Swiss Army and of the police, who noted that she stayed at the Hotel Gotthard in Bern before moving to the Hotel Terminus and then to a private house to stay with Mme Morin at the Villa Vaudijon in Colombier. The Swiss investigation confirmed that in June 1943 she was still suffering a from a fractured collar bone. She also made contact with Paul de Saugie, and it was de Saugie who twice helped her to cross the border from Switzerland into France by the simple expedient of climbing a wall in the garden of a villa outside the village of Ville-le-Grand, between Annemasse and Geneva.

De Saugie was another who fell under Mary's spell. During the war he met many agents but Mary stood out. She was, he recalled, always dressed in her uniform with a row of ribbons on her chest, 'She did everything with a smile and she was so plucky, and she always spoke about the "dirty Germans" and she was really quite different from the others.'[12]

THE MARIE-CLAIRE LINE

Nominally at least, according to Swiss archives, Mary spent the next seven months in Switzerland where she was supposed to attend regularly at the British consular offices in order to collect a small allowance which was due to her. However, ignoring advice to rest in Switzerland, Mary insisted upon returning to Ruffec and de Saugie helped her to make clandestine entries into France, so she missed several attendances. And once more Mary clashed with the Establishment: her absences were noted by Henry Cartwright, whose office paid Mary her allowance as a refugee, and he refused to pay her for those weeks when she had not been in Geneva. Like Dansey in London, he had met his match in Mary, who took her womanly revenge by ordering several outfits of clothes in the shops and asking for the bills to be sent to Cartwright.[1]

In France, she had decided to abandon the route through Sauveterre-de-Béarn in favour of a route more to the south-west, and crossing not directly into Spain but into Andorra; in the following weeks of the spring of 1943 she worked diligently on setting up her escape line. This ran to the foothills of the Pyrenees by road or by railway, as far as possible through Toulouse and then through the small towns and hamlets of Le Vernet, Pamiers, Varilhes, the railway junction at Foix, Luzenac and Ax-les-Thermes, towards the terminus of the mountain railway at Latour-de-Carol, and then the safety of Andorra. If there were German or Vichy French checkpoints anywhere along the route it was easy enough, she thought, to jump off the slow-moving mountain train and walk across country, and there were also numerous safe houses along the route.

The escape line depended upon the trust and loyalty of scores of French men and women, and Mary was generous in her praise:

Most of them knew me vaguely because I'd always been down in that part of the country, and they knew that I'd been through the 1914 war, got the Croix de Guerre and, of course, that made a terrific difference to them. They were all peasants, I mean really, really peasants, some of them couldn't even write, but absolutely brave, they would have done anything on earth when they'd got their Englishman, their English pilots, their English pilots were just gods for them, they would have given their lives.

Back in Ruffec she found that Gaston Denivelle and Geneviève or Ginette Favre[2] and others on the Marie-Claire escape line were overwhelmed by the increasing numbers of evading airmen.

She soon heard that the priest at Foix, Abbé Armand Blanchebarbe, was already actively resisting the German occupation. Blanchebarbe, born at Lorry-lès-Metz in eastern France, had objected to the new Germanification of Lorraine and been expelled from his parish in November 1940, settling during the war at Foix with his sister, Marie-Louise, as his housekeeper and taking charge of the ancient pilgrim church of St James.

Like Father André Péan to the north of the Marie-Claire escape line, Blanchebarbe worked with several groups of resistance. In Foix, these included the local branch of the nationwide group known as Combat, and with Irénée Cros, the head of the local *Mouvement Unis de la Résistance de l'Ariège* (MUR), which organised escape lines into Spain and Andorra.[3] Blanchebarbe's church gave cover for meetings with members of the Resistance who met discreetly in the sacristy.

Other refugees from Lorraine were involved in a *réseau* (network) who provided safe houses. Among these refugees were Madame Ména, who sheltered men at her house in Bouychères, outside Foix, and Gisquet, a customs officer who had notice of the times and routes of German patrols and was able to tip off the French and Spanish guides so that very few were intercepted in this part of the Pyrenees.

When Mary and Blanchebarbe met, she found him only too keen to help escapers and evaders on the Marie-Claire line to flee into Spain. After the American and British landings in North Africa in November 1942, the Germans had occupied Vichy France and frontier guards, mainly Austrians, had been posted in the Pyrenees. There, a 20km-deep forbidden zone had been declared where special passes were needed. Nevertheless, a steady trickle of refugees continued to cross the mountains and after February 1943, when the *Service du Travail Obligatoire* (STO) threatened to deport all young men to forced labour in

Germany, the trickle turned into a torrent. Blanchebarbe was deeply involved in this traffic.

Blanchebarbe became another one of Mary's fans, describing after the war an incident when, confronted in the abbé's sacristy by a suspected traitor, she showed her determination:

> I had no idea that she was armed. She stood in front of him and put a gun to his face. She had not one revolver but two, and held one in each hand and put one in his face and then she said if you betray us I'll blow your face off and if this pistol doesn't work then I blow your guts out with this one. I admired her a lot. She was a little woman but I had such admiration for her, she had so much sang froid. For a woman, that Mary was a great man.[4]

The respect was mutual, Mary's view of Blanchebarbe being that 'he was rather special, he was really a great man, he was brave, but unconsciously brave, it was just in him'.

Mary accompanied her 'parcels' as far as possible, and at least once a month she was in Foix. Somewhere beyond Foix, as the railway wound through the deep valley and up towards its terminus at Latour-de-Carol, at the engine driver's signal of two hoots on the whistle, escapers would jump off the slow-moving train and be met by guides who would show them on foot over the mountains into Andorra.

There were numerous tracks which led off to the south. The passes were generally some 1,500–2,000m high, and the distance from the road or the railway was less than 30km – a day's walk for a fit man, properly dressed and equipped. Unfortunately, many men and women when they reached this stage of the journey were not fit and rarely were they properly equipped. In Mary's estimate, it was a long, stiff day's walk, but in practice the journey often took several days.[5]

All went well until in July 1943 when, on a second visit to Switzerland to replenish her funds, Mary received a card postmarked in Monte Carlo on 24 June and addressed to 'Mme Charles Morin in Colombier, Switzerland'. The postcard told her that her son, Maurice, was in hospital. This was veiled language to tell her that Maurice had been captured by the Germans and was being held in the prison at Fort Montluc in Lyon.

Mary tuned to Victor Farrell for help and the reply from MI9 in London read, 'Secure release without delay – stop – finance as required.' Armed with funds by Farrell she crossed into France, and from the station at Annemasse was in Lyon within four hours.[6]

Maurice's capture, Mary thought, was his own fault because he had broken her 'no girls' rule. 'You see, when you do a job like that [in the Resistance], you do not run after the girls, and he had a girl friend who happened to be a Jewess.'[7]

In fact, Maurice had been betrayed by a love rival, and it was obvious to Maurice that the young man who had turned him in had told the Germans a fair amount about the de Millevilles:

> He knew my mother, he knew she was my mother, he knew she had been in England, and the Germans said so to me, and it was obvious that when they put the question they wanted answers which they already had. Well there you are! Beat the shit out of him and he'll tell you! As it happens I didn't, or anyway I'm not conscious of having done it, because I can tell you that at certain times I was feeling fairly bad. But I think that at that time they had already beaten so much out of you that it was not possible to tell them anything.

Mary agreed, 'He didn't say anything, they didn't get anything out of him.'

The head of the Gestapo in Lyon was Klaus Barbie. Barbie, who had been head of the Gestapo in Lyon since November 1942, had not yet entered into the full ferocity of his outrages against the civilian population and, in particular, against French Jews. He was also susceptible to a pretty face and to bribery,[8] and so Mary summoned Barbé from Paris. In the months since Mary had last seen her, Barbé had grown into a young woman. Mary might have been shocked if she had also known the extent of Barbé's friendship with the German occupiers of Paris.

When she arrived, Mary demanded, 'How much do you think you can buy Maurice for?'[9]

'It's difficult to say, mamma. Fifty or sixty thousand francs plus expenses, perhaps.'

'Very well, when can you meet this man, Barbie?'

'I could try to fix it for this afternoon. He has already asked me to tea, but I'd prefer to meet him in a café and have a drink.'

'Very well, Barbé, fix it as you think best.'

Barbé returned from her meeting with Klaus Barbie with the news that he wanted to meet Mary. Alerted by this, Mary, leaving 60,000 francs with her daughter, went into hiding and left instructions for a rendezvous at a hairdressing salon the next day. Mary could not sleep, but the next morning Barbé reported that the bait had been taken. It seems that Maurice was a prisoner of the SD and not of the Gestapo, but Barbie promised that he would be released by 11 a.m. Mary was slowly learning some field craft and asked for a watch on the prison to see that he was not being followed after his release.

But at 11 a.m. there was no Maurice. 'If that brute double-crosses me!' exclaimed Barbé.

'Let's give him until 12.30, and then you must telephone again.'

At 12.30 p.m. there was still no Maurice and when Barbé rang the Gestapo chief he seemed genuinely enraged and promised that Barbé would see her brother by 3 p.m. that afternoon. At a 2.45 p.m. on 13 August, after three months in jail, Maurice staggered out of the jail and Mary's surveillance was able to reassure her that he was not being followed. Mary met him in a safe house:

> He looked just like God's wrath. He was so thin the poor little devil, and as he came forward to kiss me, his glasses dropped off and to my horror he went down on his knees and was feeling about, feeling for these things. 'I said, what's the matter?' And then he told me that to try and make him talk, they had beaten him with these chains across his eyes.[10]

In Mary's understated words, Maurice 'had had a very, very cheap time'. She thought he had been blinded and arranged for Maurice to receive the best treatment, before leaving that same night for Switzerland. Lyon was far too dangerous for her.

While the Germans were intensifying their search for Mary and gathering a case against her, they seemed to have looked everywhere apart from Ruffec. Meanwhile, Paul de Saugie, Mary's contact inside the Swiss Secret Service, had provided her with a new identity as he just happened have a set of documents, including the birth certificate and the marriage certificate, of a Comtesse de Moncy. Since Mary's lingerie was embroidered with the same initials, this was the identity she now adopted.

Undaunted, Mary returned to her work. Maurice recalled:

> My mother had a very narrow channel of interest. Her channel of interest was getting Allied airmen out of the country, and the fact that she was out-spoken, outspokenly patriotic and didn't know what fear was – anyway she didn't express it at any time – made a lot of people follow her blindfoldedly.

Mary's image of herself was simple:

I represented in my little tu'penny ha'penny mind, I represented Great Britain who was standing up against the world and fighting for it, and I wasn't going to let Great Britain down. It just didn't enter my head. And I wasn't frightened. If you're shot, well you're shot and that's the end of the story, isn't it.

Maurice recovered quickly from his maltreatment at the hands of the Germans and was able to run the line between Ruffec, Lyon and Toulouse. What Mary needed was for someone to feed the line from eastern France, and by chance Maurice had met the Comtesse Pauline Barré de Saint-Venant, who was using the name Alice Laroche.

Surviving descriptions of her are unkind: a wartime depiction of her is 'a large woman, well built. Fat, about forty-five years of age, pointed nose, dyed Titian hair.'[11] A contrasting picture is of a woman 'aged about fifty, 5 ft. 8 ins. or 5 ft. 9 ins. tall and of masculine appearance and looked pregnant. She has dark hair going a little grey.'[12] For once, Mary's was the kindliest, telling Rossiter in the 1970s that Pauline was a 'tall, vivacious woman in her forties with a confident rather domineering air'.[13]

Pre-war, Pauline had been a member of a Fascist group[14] but, in 1940 and like Mary, she had been affronted by the German invasion and had aided the escape of French prisoners of war and civilians from Alsace-Lorraine out of occupied France into the unoccupied zone. However, her associates had been arrested and in July 1943 she was faced with having to recreate her escape line, which she based at Hôtel Richelieu, and she began to run E&E from the Gare d'Austerlitz to the Spanish border.[15] Two months later in Lyon she met Maurice de Milleville, who, on his own initiative, agreed to pay Pauline for every airman brought to the Marie-Claire escape line.

However, when Mary first met Pauline she had only one word for her: she was a 'harridan'. And for spite, she added, 'she was about 48, older than me, round a nasty age, her hair was dyed'.[16] It was a case of the pot calling the kettle black, for both pot and kettle were of the same age, had had similar wartime experiences and were of similar temperament. It was a tragedy that they could not co-operate – a tragedy which would lead to the death of one of them. Their dislike for each other was exacerbated by the shortage of funds needed to service the escape line and to cover even the minimum costs of the scores of men being kept in hiding and smuggled across France.

The operation of an escape line was an extremely expensive business and its finance had to be kept covert. The funds needed to pay off potential enemies and to compensate genuine expenditure incurred in its purposes were frequently underestimated and Mary was no exception to this rule.[17] In October 1942, when Mary returned to France by Lysander, she had brought with her 250,000 francs (at the exchange rate of 300 francs to the pound). MI9 had offered her more, but Mary had seriously underestimated the costs of running an escape line and she had refused.

Without a wireless operator she could not arrange for a parachutage of more money and so she was obliged to make repeated crossings into Switzerland to obtain funds. Thirty years later, when interviewed by Margaret Rossiter, Mary would reflect ruefully on rumours that Guérisse and his Pat line were funded in instalments of 5–10 million francs each. Perhaps this was an exaggeration, but she also knew of wartime rumours that some agents of MI9 and SOE had set up their girlfriends in well-furnished, luxury Paris apartments using funds received from London, and she had heard post-war stories that many funds had not been returned and had been used to buy property on the Mediterranean coast.

Mary's Marie-Claire line seems to have been well-run financially. Mary insisted that anyone lodging an escaper or evader should be paid 100 francs per person per day in the country and 150 francs per day in the town, and that expenses like the cost of new shoes and clothing should be covered. When one of her agents had to travel she allowed 50,000 francs as 'security' or 'safety' money to be used for bribes, but this was returnable if it had not been used, and she allowed a further 10,000 francs for the agent's expenses, of which he or she was allowed to keep any balance. In addition, Maurice had agreed to pay 10,000 francs (some sources say less) to Pauline de Saint-Venant for each airman that she fed into the Marie-Claire line,[18] assuming that each 'parcel' was hidden for a month and new clothes and documents had to be paid for. There were officials to be paid off for favours or for just looking the other way, and there were guides to be paid for escorting 'parcels' through the mountains. The finances required to run an escape line ran into millions of francs.

When Mary returned from one of her visits to Switzerland in September 1943, Farrell in Geneva had advanced her 50,000 francs, still far too little to match the needs of the trickle of E&E, a trickle which was beginning to grow into a flood.[19]

It is not possible to say accurately how many escapers and evaders passed down the Marie-Claire line, or indeed the other escape lines, or made their way independently across France and through the Pyrenees. An accepted French number for those who left France across the Pyrenees during the Second World War is 33,000. The Pyrenees form a barrier 24–32km wide of crests and valleys that were then, and still are, sparsely populated, and in the 1940s they were mostly known to herders, hunters and smugglers. The early routes across or around the mountains were at the western end of the mountain chain via Biarritz across the Bidasoa River to Bilbao, and at the Mediterranean end of the mountains into Andorra and Cataluña. It would take about ten hours for a fit man in fair weather to cross these extremities of the Pyrenees.

As the war drew on and German control tightened on the crossings, the routes shifted to the higher, more difficult areas of the mountain chain. Even in July or August the passes at the highest parts of the mountains could be blocked by ice and snow, which would begin to form again in October. In the harsh winter of 1943–44 many crossed via the lower mountains west of Perpignan, and when that became too dangerous the line from Pau via Oloron-Sainte-Marie was reopened. Mary Lindell, for example, used the 'Higgins' route via Mauléon in the autumn of 1940, used other routes in 1941 and 1942, and reverted to the route through Mauléon at the end of 1943.[20] Often the routes followed medieval pilgrim routes to Santiago de Compostela.

The rugged foothills were tough going for the average hiker,[21] but the real problem for those forced to take a circuitous route on minor tracks in order to avoid patrols was that they were poorly equipped and had already endured months of malnutrition. Those who had been in hiding for several weeks, or even months, were especially unfit. Nevertheless, most crossings (more than 25,000) were successful – the majority by men who left France to join the Free French forces. Some 1,500 men, women and children were defeated by the mountains and turned back; some 3,800 were caught by the Germans and deported to Germany; and about 1,100 died on the crossing or in Spanish internment camps.

The French number includes 900 civilians who were 'Poles, Belgians, English, Canadians, and Americans'. To these numbers must be added the uniformed escapers and evaders. There is no reliable audit of these. Neave wrote that there was:

> … no separate total for those who reached safety from occupied France, Belgium and Holland … the fairest estimate which can be made is that over 4,000, including Americans, returned to England from these occupied countries, before the Allied landing in Normandy in June 1944.[22]

Clutton-Brock gives a higher number of 1,000 Royal Navy and British Army personnel, 2,100 RAF airmen, including men from the British Empire, and 1,500 United States Army Air Forces (USAAF) personnel (the USAAF numbers appear low and should perhaps be raised by another 1,200 or so to match official American statistics). The bulk of the sailors and soldiery escaped in late 1940 and early 1941, having missed the evacuations from Dunkirk and the ports of western France. In subsequent years it was downed airmen who made up the bulk of the numbers of evaders.[23]

So, the estimate of E&E, mostly Allied airmen, ranges widely from 4,600–5,800, and attributing these to specific escape lines is problematic. According to Clutton-Brock, 288 Allied military personnel passed along the Comet line from Belgium to Spain in the years 1941–44,[24] though other sources put this much higher – at more than 500, including 116 men who were personally escorted by Dédée de Jongh.[25] Several hundred men left France via Marseilles in 1940 and 1941, organised by Ian Garrow, and when Albert Guérisse took over from Garrow with the Pat line in June 1941 another 300 men left France by this line, up until Guérisse's arrest in early 1943. These included some sixty-seven E&E who were evacuated by the Royal Navy using HMS *Tarana* or the felucca *Seawolf* from southern France in 1942.

As many again were taken off the French north coast via the Shelburne line, another of the escape lines, the Bourgogne line, which operated successfully from early 1943 onwards and with remarkably few losses of either helpers or evaders, is credited with helping 315 evaders, though there may be some double-counting of E&E, who were also handled by more than one organisation, including Comet.[26] This still leaves several hundred E&E who presumably made individual escapes through France and were helped by uncounted and anonymous, brave, patriotic French men and women.

Mary Lindell's contribution to these escapes must be measured against these imperfect numbers. She had been one of the first, a self-starter who had sprung into action in 1940 when the rest of France lay supine and shocked under the German heel, when she had helped several British servicemen and French evaders to reach Spain. After nine months' imprisonment, she had made her own escape. Then, despite the great risks to her personal safety, she had volunteered to return to occupied France to set up an escape line for the Cockleshell raiders and she stayed on to run the Marie-Claire escape line based in Ruffec. By her own estimate, in 1942 and 1943 she made only a modest additional contribution to these numbers. 'Well under a hundred,' she told Margaret Rossiter, 'Because I wasn't at it for very long.'[27]

Unusually modest, she omitted to tell Rossiter that for most of 1941 she had been in prison and in the first half of 1942 she needed to convalesce after a road accident in which she had been left for dead. Then she was preoccupied with getting her son out of the hands of the Gestapo; she made several crossings into Switzerland to obtain funds from Victory Farrell, the SIS/MI9 agent in Geneva, and despite all this, her escape line was still active enough for Pat to complain in October 1942, within a few days of her landing in France, that Mary was using his contacts and he threatened to stop work unless she was forbidden to do this.[28]

Darling, the man who was 'Sunday', put the number credited to the Marie-Claire line in 1943 as low as eleven, 'in spite of the very worst luck',[29] while after Mary Lindell's arrest in November 1943 Michael Creswell, the man who was 'Monday', reported from Spain that there were ninety-seven men hidden in Paris and in need of money.[30] These were the men who Pauline would take over, on what was now *her* escape line and known as Marie-Odile.

Notwithstanding the difficulty of marrying individual escapers and evaders to specific escape lines, some of the escapes that Mary organised are well documented.

PYRENEES, AUTUMN 1943 – SNOW UNDERFOOT

O n the night of 13–14 June 1943, Quebecois Sergeant Joseph Sansoucy RCAF was flight engineer in a Stirling bomber of 75 (New Zealand) Squadron when it was shot down over Normandy. He found many people willing to help him, including a gendarme who gave him food and a map, a fisherman who rowed him across the Loire and a farmer who took him into hiding. In July 1943 Sansoucy reported, 'I cycled over to Draché to find the local priest who was connected with an organisation.'[1] The priest was, of course, André Péan.

Péan hid Sansoucy for several weeks in Sepmes, between Châtellerault and Tours, in the care the Comtesse Marie-Thérèse de Poix at the Château de la Roche Ploquin. Marie-Thérèse was one of the many brave Frenchwomen who kept the flame of the Resistance alive, but in the dark days that followed she would be arrested and thrown into Ravensbrück.[2]

By the end of August, Péan had contacted Mary who sent a young girl from Ruffec, probably Ginette, to collect Sansoucy. He was taken to a safe house where he met an American known only as 'Haviland'. 'Haviland' has not been identified: he is described as a naturalised Frenchman, a member of the American Ambulance Service, who lived on a farm about 25km south-east of Ruffec.

One of the escapes organised by Mary involved Gaby Tritz, who would in turn be rescued by having her named placed on Mary Lindell's list in April 1945. Gaby Tritz had sheltered several evaders including, for several weeks in the summer of 1943, Sergeant James Sparkes. Sparkes had special reason to avoid capture by the Germans. He flew in the Lancaster bombers of 101 Squadron RAF, which suffered the highest casualty rate of any RAF squadron: their aircraft carried two large, vertical antennae rising from the middle of the fuselage and were fitted with secret radio intercept and jamming equipment operated by a crew member, usually someone with a German or Jewish background. Sparkes was the only survivor of his aircraft when it was shot down on the night of 27–28 June 1943.[3] Moving from safe house to safe house via Candé to Champtocé-sur-Loire to Nantes he briefly met Sergeants Alan Sheppard and Charles Trott. Sheppard was a wireless operator and Trott was flight engineer of a Lancaster of 115 Squadron which had been shot down in the early hours of 20 June.[4]

Sparkes was taken to Poitiers where he stayed from 13–25 July in the rue Riffault with Gaby Tritz. While there, he learned that Gaby was from Alsace. In 1914 she had been an au pair in England when, fearing internment as an enemy alien (Alsace was then part of the Kaiser's Germany), she had fled to Kansas where her brother was a doctor. Gaby had spent her twenties in the USA where she had married and divorced, and then had married again (this time to a Frenchman) and returned to France where the Second World War had overtaken her. Gaby was able to move Sparkes onto Châtellerault, the rendezvous where Péan often handed evaders over to the Marie-Claire line.

Next, on 13 August Gaby took an American sergeant, Albert Carroll, into hiding in her home and two days later she took in two more, Edward Chonski and John Zioance: all had been shot down in their B17 bomber, 'The Mugger', of 303rd Bombardment Squadron – somewhat inappropriately known as the Hell's Angels – on 4 July 1943. According to Carroll, who stayed some weeks with Gaby, she had already sheltered another English sergeant besides Sparkes. Carroll and his fellow crewmen reached the Pyrenees via Foix in late September, and were back in England on 19 October.[5]

Meanwhile at Ruffec, Sparkes, Sheppard and Trott were reunited and joined by a fourth airman, the Canadian Sergeant Phillip Whitnall.[6] Whitnall was the wireless operator of a Whitley, from 296 Army Co-operation Squadron, that had been shot down on 18 April. Whitnall was wounded and had been convalescing and in hiding with the same French farming family ever since. Several promises of help had failed to materialise, but Whitnall's fate changed when 'a man who travelled regularly to Switzerland' met Marie-Claire on one of his trips: this may have been Michel Hollard.[7]

When Mary Lindell learned of Whitnall's plight, she promptly offered to help. First she sent him an identity card, a ration card and a medical certificate saying that following a throat operation he could not speak for two weeks. Then 'a girl from Lyon', almost certainly Ginette, escorted Whitnall by train to Ruffec where Mary met him at the station, and from there he was taken by bicycle to a farm where 'Haviland' lived. Whitnall had lost track of the date, but when all was ready he and 'Haviland' walked to the main road, where they were met by Mary, and they returned together to Ruffec where he met the three other sergeants at the Hôtel de France.

Early the next morning they set out in a large party comprising Mary Lindell, a policeman in plain clothes (probably Péyraud), four sergeants (Sheppard, Sparkes, Trott and Whitnall), and the driver of the truck (one of the Regeon sisters). They travelled via Toulouse towards Foix in the foothills of the Pyrenees. Meanwhile Sansoucy, who spoke good French but with a Canadian accent, and 'Haviland' (whom Sansoucy called 'de Havilland' and described as 'a naturalised French American') went by train to Limoges and Toulouse. They had been warned by Mary to avoid German patrols by leaving the train at Le Vernet and walking to a rendezvous south of Foix. They were indeed stopped as they left the station by German soldiers, who fortunately did no more than take a note of their names and addresses, which were, of course, false.[8]

The rendezvous was at Varilhes, still some kilometres short of Foix, where Mary left the four sergeants in the hands of her *passeurs*, and after a week of short marches with Spanish and French guides they were joined by a party of about twenty French civilians and walked into Andorra on the morning of 17 September. By 6 October they were back in England.

In late September two Polish airmen arrived in Ruffec: Sergeant Piotr Bakalarski and Sergeant Witold Raginis, who had been prisoners of war and had escaped from a working party in a mine near Cracow. It had taken them a month to cross Europe to Montlucon where Raginis' parents lived. From the *Maison de Prisonnières* at Lunéville they were taken under mock-arrest by a gendarme to Lyon where, on 23 September, they were taken to the grand-sounding but rather lowly Hôtel Claridge where they met 'Mme Laroche … She handed us over to Maurice, the son of Marie-Claire'.

Bakalarski noted that on 23 September Mary Lindell 'was then in Switzerland, and her organisation was short of money'.[9] Maurice presumably paid or promised to pay Pauline, checked the Poles' identities and took them to a series of safe houses until Ginette Favre came to escort them to Ruffec, where they arrived on 4 October. Mary was now keeping seven rooms at the Hôtel de France, but Bakalarski and Raginis were only allowed one night there before being taken to a safe house outside Ruffec where they stayed until 23 October.

Meanwhile an Australian pilot, Allan 'Mac' McSweyn, and an older New Zealand soldier, Jeff Williamson, had also escaped from a prisoner-of-war camp in Germany. McSweyn had chosen Williamson as his partner because Williamson spoke fluent German and knew the railway network. They also reached Lunéville, from where they were escorted in handcuffs (probably by the same gendarmes who had 'arrested' Bakalarski and Raginis) to Nancy and from there to Lyon. There, while McSweyn and Williamson were waiting to meet Pauline, they were found in the Turkish baths by Maurice de Milleville who, on his own initiative, took them to Ruffec where they arrived on 8 October and were met by Mary Lindell.[10]

They were joined by 20-year-old Sergeant Stanley Philo, who had been shot down on the night of 15–16 August west of Paris while returning in his Lancaster bomber after a long-range raid on Milan. Philo, who spoke no French, walked westward as far and as quickly as he could. He was helped by several families en route, including the Helleux family in the village of Senonches, the postmaster at Azay-le-Ferron and a Mme Shields, the widow of an American. He was glad when he was taken in by the Resistance at the Château de la Boussée on the Loire. His feet were badly swollen and blistered and he was sheltered there until 18 October when he started his journey to Ruffec, which he reached after two days.

Philo's trudge across France had brought him into the welcoming arms of Mary Lindell. The French border zone with Spain and Andorra had been turned into a forbidden zone for which a new pass was required, but Mary had her own printer, photographer and forger working for her, and new passes were ready by 20 October. Philo was quickly equipped: 'Marie-Claire got me new clothes and shoes and an identity card for the frontier zone as well as a work certificate.'[11]

Mary ordered McSweyn to stay in Ruffec, while Raginis and Williamson, and Bakalarski and Philo made their way in pairs – one French speaker and one German speaker in each pair – via Bordeaux and Toulouse, where on 23 October Mary said goodbye to them and they travelled on south-west towards the border with Spain. The four met again in Urs, close to the border with Andorra, where they spent the night of 24 October in a cave.

Next morning they were soaked by a heavy downpour which turned into an unseasonably early snowstorm, their sodden clothes becoming stiff and frozen. When the party separated, the 38-year-old New Zealander, Williamson, would die of hypothermia, but the three others reached Andorra after trudging through thigh-deep snow and taking twelve hours to climb one col – a climb which might normally have taken half an hour. Bakalarski, Philo and Raginis would eventually reach Britain via Spain and Gibraltar, but Williamson's tragic death marked the beginning of the end of the Marie-Claire line.

Back in Ruffec, McSweyn was joined by three more evaders: Flying Officers Mike Cooper and Harry Smith, and Sergeant Len Martin. Cooper's Spitfire of 616 Squadron had suffered an engine failure on 16 August over Calvadoa and he had bailed out and landed in a tree which, until that moment, had been pregnant with fruit.[12] Martin and Smith were Canadians whose Halifax bomber of 419 Squadron had been shot down on the night of 16–17 September 1943 over Calvados in northern France. All three were sheltered by peasants until, on 20 September, they were collected by pony and trap from their separate hiding places and escorted by circuitous routes which took them to the outskirts Paris.[13]

On the last leg of their journeys Ginette Favre brought them by train to Ruffec, where they arrived at the end of October. Martin described Ginette as a girl of 'about 20, but looking about 12'.[14] By contrast, Cooper remembered being greeted at the Hôtel de France by 'a middle-aged, wrinkle-faced woman wearing a Red Cross uniform who asked if they had had a good journey'. Cooper later recalled Mary's speech:

> I am an Englishwoman married to a Frenchman after the last war. You will know me as Marie. I have been parachuted into France with the object of setting boys like yourselves safely into Spain. I spare neither money nor effort to carry this out. You boys must trust me and obey me completely, or go away now.[15]

Cooper's account (*One of the Many*, published in 1997) of his journey along the Marie-Claire escape line, during which one of the guides died, is one of the most complete available. The details of other escapes come from the reports that the men filed once they had reached safety and now held at the National Archives at Kew. They are, in general, reports of unalloyed bravery and resource by the individuals concerned and by the numerous ordinary French people who, at great risk to themselves, helped them. Mary made no such reports, and she told a rather different tale:

> When you suddenly get unfortunate lost men, do you know when a man, whether he's one of those wonderful pilots, so brave that he can't see straight – when he's shot down and when he's on the run, he becomes like a little boy, about that big, a little scared boy. Honestly they are, they're all scared.[16]

Mary told Rossiter:

I can still see in Ruffec two Canadians, I called them Big and Little Canada.
Well, Little Canada was so terrified that he burst into tears and when we went
down to meals I had to have Little Canada sitting at my table and say, 'Look
here, Little Canada, eat or I don't.'

'Mary, I can't.'

'Don't be a fool.'

Then when they came down, he simply sat in the train and held my hand.
Not love, it was just that he thought it was safe. A little boy.

Mary was resolute: when handing her charges over to the guides she told them,
'Look, if you have any trouble with this little bastard, shoot him and forget it.'
But she was also sympathetic:

I don't know if you realise the situation in a foreign country, occupied by the
enemy, and not knowing anything, suddenly being handed over to something
and then saying 'Oh, God, it's a woman, this is dreadful isn't it.' And yet
suddenly they feel safe. It's a peculiar situation. I loved the whole lot of them.
They were too sweet, too ridiculous, most of them, and I never even knew
their names.

To most escapers and evaders, however, Mary looked, and was, very businesslike;
she impressed them, they trusted her and were prepared to wait on her word.[17]

THE LOVERS

There was one man who baulked at Mary's commanding presence: Captain George Tsoucas, a Greek officer in the British Intelligence Corps who had been captured in September 1942 during a raid by the Special Boat Service on a Luftwaffe airfield on Rhodes. Tsoucas, who was a generation older than the 20-year-olds who comprised the bulk of the escapers, had already made three escape attempts: from a ship in Parts Harbour, from an Italian prison camp and from a German camp.[1]

This time, his escape companion was Captain 'Buck' Palm of the South African Air Force (whose Hurricane fighter of 94 Squadron had been shot down over the Western Desert on 29 November 1941, and who had since also become a veteran escaper). They had made their way on foot from Germany, crossed the border near Marainville and, following local advice, had made their way to the *Maison des Prisonnières* at Lunéville. There, a friendly captain of gendarmes gave them clothes and fake identities and escorted them 'under arrest' to Nancy,[2] where he handed them over to Pauline, who was introduced to Tsoucas and Palm as Mme Alice Laroche. Two days later Pauline took them via Paris to Ruffec, where they arrived on 3 November.

Pauline was keen to know what had happened to McSweyn and Williamson (who she had last heard of in the Turkish baths in Lyon), and by asking for the young Comte de Milleville, Pauline soon found Marie-Claire at the Hôtel de France. Mary went white with fury when she heard of Pauline's arrival, but decided to see the woman. They had the first of several blazing rows in the Hôtel de France.

In the report of his escape Tsoucas wrote that he was not impressed by what he saw of Mary Lindell, 'The whole village knew about her and her private car and the trucks which she hired, and she was very indiscreet in talking English to escapers and evaders in the hotel.'

Tsoucas' version of events was, 'Marie-Claire and Mme Laroche had a terrific row. Mme Laroche resented the insulting way in which Marie-Claire spoke to the French people. They quarrelled so violently that I had to separate them in the hotel.' Tsoucas' escape and evasion report is querulous in tone but this may be accounted for by Mary's reaction when she discovered that Tsoucas and Pauline – both in their mid 40s – were canoodling in a bedroom in the hotel and thus breaking her rule of 'No women!' And in a room for which she was paying.

Tsoucas' views may also have been influenced when Mary told him that her priority was to get airmen out of France and that others did not seem to have the same urgent need. Tsoucas could not, and did not, tell Mary all of his exploits, but based his claim to priority passage on being an intelligence officer, telling Mary, 'I think you had better send me home immediately'.

Mary, who did not know Tsoucas' full background but who had taken a dislike to him, replied, 'That's quite out of the question. This is an escape route for airmen. Naturally, we'll do what we can, but there is no possibility of your getting preferential treatment. If you have vital information to disclose, I could, if necessary, make arrangements to have it sent to London. But as you've only just come out of a prisoner-of-war camp, where you've been an interpreter, I can't see what vital information you could possibly have.'

'When I get to England I shall report you,' was Tsoucas' response.

'You can do what you like.'

And then Tsoucas blundered. 'I am superior in rank to you,' he shouted.

'That's just where you make a mistake, young man [in fact Mary was only four years older than Tsoucas]. If there were a general here, he would come under my command, and, I've no doubt, would be happy to do so.'

A less biased, but nevertheless alarming, view of Mary and her use of the Hôtel de France in Ruffec emerges from a report by Germaine Rouillon's brother, M. Lemétayer in 1945:

> We were beginning to be disturbed that Mme de Milleville was taking absolutely no precautions to hide her presence at the hotel; she was attracting the attention of the guests with her foreign accent, her lively arguments in the corridors of the hotel with Mme Laroche, and also by her prolonged stay in Ruffec. We persuaded M. Rouillon to ask Mme de Milleville to leave the hotel.[3]

Rouillon's request was unfortunately the start of another row which burst out in the Regeons' house. Gaston Denivelle and Pauline wanted reimbursement for their services, and Mary had difficulty paying: eventually she left Ruffec without settling her bill – some 23,000 francs – at the Hôtel de France.[4] Nevertheless Tsoucas and Pauline were included in the party which, on 7 November, set off from Ruffec in a truck. The others were McSweyn, Cooper, Martin, Palm, Smith and Tsoucas, escorted by Mary, Jean Péyraud from the gendarmerie, and the sisters Henriette and Therese Regeon who owned the truck.[5] Mary was, of course, in her uniform and her cover was that the Red Cross were taking a party of bombed-out refugees – deaf, dumb and shell-shocked – to a resort in the south. When the truck's rear axle broke, Mary had to persuade a farmer to lend them his truck in return for several litres of fuel and, no doubt, some of her precious hoard of francs.

Travelling eastward, they reached Saint-Yrieix-la-Perche, a small market town south of Limoges, half an hour after the train for Toulouse had left and they were obliged to spend the night in the station hotel. As they trooped into the dining room 'all the other customers stopped eating and sat back to watch us'. Then, to their horror, they saw a German officer also in the dining room. Fortunately he did not pay much attention to Mary and her large party, even though Mary was in her Red Cross uniform and typically she announced in her loudest voice and in English that all Germans were idiots.

Next morning they were alarmed to find the same German officer pacing the platform, but fortunately he took no action before they boarded the train for Toulouse, where they changed for Foix. At Pamiers, a couple of stops before Foix, on the evening of 8 November, Abbé Blanchebarbe rushed onto the platform to announce that a large party of French refugees and their guides had been captured by the Germans and that it was too risky to go on. Blanchebarbe arranged for them to spend the night in Pamiers and, crestfallen but undeterred, Mary returned with all her party to Ruffec on 13 November.

There, Mary and Pauline quarrelled for one last time. By now Rouillon was fed up with the women and he had heard from Péyraud that the gendarmerie had been ordered by the Germans to keep an eye on the hotel. Mary decided to close her Ruffec headquarters and to move further south to Pau. Maurice had already reconnoitred a new route which took a clockwise sweep through south-west France along the railways via Limoges, Toulouse, Tarbes and Pau and up the Pyrenees via Oloron-Sainte-Marie and Tardets-Sorholus.

Once more Mary was adamant that airmen of all ranks had priority over army officers, and rather surprisingly after he had criss-crossed half of Europe and had reached so close to the Spanish border, a disgruntled Tsoucas went off with Pauline to Paris. There he spent much of the next three months in Pauline's company before she escorted him to the Spanish border in March 1944.[6]

On 22 November Mary escorted McSweyn and his four companions, Cooper, Martin, Palm and Smith, by train from Limoges to Oloron-Sainte-Marie and from there by bus to Tardets-Sorholus. There is no hint in any report by the Canadians, Martin or Smith, that either of them even held hands with Mary. Rather, McSweyn reported:

> The group reached Tardets-Sorholus about 18.00. From there we walked … to Montory where we arrived about 22.00 hours. After we had had a meal Marie-Claire left us with our two guides … At midnight we set off in the pouring rain. We walked all through the night and about 04.00 hours it began to freeze hard.[7]

McSweyn had been told that the journey was only about 20km and that the way was easy, which in fair weather would have been so, and they carried no food or drink with them. Dragging and half-carrying each other, the party stumbled into Spain leaving one of the guides wrapped in a groundsheet and buried in the snow. This was the second death on the way over the mountains. If McSweyn and his party's experience was bad enough, they were at least men in their twenties. Mary was a generation older: she had suffered years of food shortages in France, her health had been broken during a cold, damp winter of malnutrition in prison at Fresnes, and she had been run down and left for dead, yet still she could lead men along the roads between the mountain villages and her spirit was undaunted.

Perhaps, she was not strong enough to make the crossing of the Pyrenees in that foul weather. But, knowing that the Germans were closing in on her, now she had her opportunity to make good her own escape by crossing the mountains. However, there was duty to be done and she knew that there were others on the Marie-Claire escape. So, letting the five men to make their way to freedom, Mary chose to walk at midnight in the cold rain downhill towards Tardets-Sorholus and to take the train to Pau.

15

ARRESTED AND IMPRISONED AT DIJON

n the foothills of the Pyrenees on 22 November at Pau, Mary was arrested.[1] She had left three American and one British airmen at Ruffec,[2] but the people there were no longer co-operating with her. Henriette Regeon was supposed to bring them down the line, but when Mary received a telegram which read, 'Quite impossible to come', she sent Ginette Favre to fetch them.

The airmen were to travel as a party of deaf mutes going to an institute at Pau. Ginette, however, did not have the one essential medical certificate amongst the airmen's papers and they were caught in a routine German control on the train from Toulouse to Pau.[3] She might have escaped but she was sitting in the same compartment and held all the tickets, and they were taken to the Maison Blanche in Biarritz for questioning. The German net was already closing in on Mary, but when they found a photograph of her in Ginette's purse they could not persuade Ginette to tell them of Mary's whereabouts.

They did not have long to wait. 'I was a silly arse. I watched the train instead of walking out into my car and back to the hotel. That was stupid. It was like a cow. Cows watch trains – and that was how I got arrested.'[4] Unaware of the earlier arrests, Mary, muffled against the cold and wearing a coat over her Red Cross uniform, was checking the trains as they arrived in Pau. When she was stopped by the German Field Police, they asked for her papers, and when one of them had read her name he checked his notebook and placed his hand on her shoulder, 'You are under arrest.'

Characteristically, Mary took the offensive. 'What for? How dare you? Take your hand off my shoulder.' She opened her coat to reveal her Red Cross uniform, but this only served to confirm her identity.

'Good. At last we meet.'

The Germans also arrested Carlos Lopez, one of her guides. However sure the Germans seemed of her identity, Mary was worried about Lopez, who might not be so quick-witted, 'I don't know why you're arresting me. But why on earth are you arresting this poor devil?'

'You were speaking to him.'

'Of course I was. Or rather he was speaking to me. Do you know what he was doing? He was offering to sell me potatoes. Do I look like someone who would buy potatoes on a railway platform? And to think of the price he was asking!'

Lopez was quicker than Mary had hoped. 'This is most unjust. The lady told me I was asking too much for my potatoes, I tell you I was offering them at a fair price.'[5]

Taken to Biarritz, to the Hôtel de la Paix et Angleterre which had been requisitioned as a German headquarters, Mary insisted that she was the Comtesse de Moncy, the identity that Paul de Saugie had given her. Lopez was taken there too, but stayed closely to the story that Mary had given him and a few days later he was released and was able to give the alarm that Mary had been arrested.

Her version of these events was characteristically idiosyncratic. According to a brief report she made later (to the Americans):

November 43, Left Ruffec after trouble with a Madame La Roche (de St Venant) who double crossed and made Ruffec unhealthy. Took 5 down [they would be McSweyn, Cooper, Martin, Palm and Smith] and sent over via Oloron St Marie etc. 4 others were to follow 4 days later but French in Ruffec got cold feet and asked for fresh orders and help. I sent Ginette Favre to assist but at Ruffec she got no help and took on herself to bring the 4 down, but did not take the necessary precautions. They got picked up between Toulouse and Pau as Ginette had forgotten a necessary Red Cross paper. The men, 1 English pilot, 1 American pilot, 2 bombers, behaved well especially the Englishman who refused any information and was followed by the Americans. Taken to Biarritz and searched, my photo was in Ginette's notecase (heaven know why) and like a fool she when asked who is she, said she did not know; result photo was spread to Gestapo headquarters, Hotel de la Paix. Well treated as I said there was some mistake as I was Red Cross, Pétain etc. And my papers were ok. They asked me to help them find [who] the wicked man was had put Ginette up to escorting the 4 men and I was very nearly let out, but something went wrong and I got taken (a) to a villa in Biarritz and (b) back to Hotel de la Paix, then Maison Blanche [in Biarritz] then Bayonne. Every few nights they moved me around between midnight and 1 o'clock to be sure I could not be rescued.[6]

The final betrayal would come from an unlikely source. Barbé in Paris enjoyed the society of the city's occupiers, including access to Josef Kieffer, the head of the *Sicherheitsdienst* (SD) for all of France. Kieffer was intrigued that young Barbé de Milleville should claim that the Comtesse de Moncy was her mother and it was this that sealed Mary's fate. He took Barbé to Biarritz where, when he entered Mary's cell, he greeted her, 'Good evening, Comtesse de Milleville.'

'I'm afraid that there must be some mistake. I am the Comtesse de Moncy.'

Kieffer stared hard at Mary and left without speaking again, but he left the door ajar, and turning to Barbé who was waiting outside, asked, 'Is that your mother?'

'Yes, it is,' whispered Barbé. It would be the last time that mother and daughter would see each other for the rest of the war.

When eventually Farrell heard of Mary's arrest – from Pauline who had slipped into Switzerland on 22 December – he contemplated ransoming her, but it was already too late: she had been moved, and in any case the Germans had already done well enough financially out of Mary, having taken from her a powder case, her gold cigarette case, a Dunhill lighter, 80,000 francs from her wallet and another half a million francs, which she claimed to have had rolled up in a napkin. So much cash, she argued, was needed for her work as an inspectress of the French Red Cross visiting the region. Mary's story must in part have been convincing, because de Moncy was the name by which the Germans knew her for the next many months and the name she was still using in April 1945.

At midnight on 14 December Mary was fetched from her cell at the Maison Blanche in Biarritz and taken to Bayonne, where she and Ginette Favre were put on the train for Paris. They travelled from there by slow, roundabout trains to Bordeaux where, after a wait of about four hours, both women were put on a train for Paris. Mary put her case plainly. 'As I didn't want to go to Paris, I thought the best thing I could do was get off the train.'[7] The train travelled slowly, and Mary recognised the countryside and the station at Ruffec. A little further north was Châtellerault, where the priest Henri Péan conducted his Resistance network, and where so many airmen had entered the Marie-Claire escape line. That was where she decided she would jump off the train. She had told her guards, two SD officers, that she was feeling sick, warning them by saying she would tap one of them on the knee 'in order not to do it in your lap'. 'So, I hit him on the knee when I got to where I wanted to get off the train, and went into the corridor to go to the lavatory. Unfortunately I walked a bit too quickly because I wanted to get a move on, you see.'

But the guard followed her and began shooting. Mary saw the glass door shatter:

> Oh, the bastard, he's shooting. And I suppose as I turned to go through, he got me in the cheek, I didn't even feel it. I opened the door onto the rail and when you do that you can't jump at once 'cause you have to be careful of a telegraph pole, 'cause if a telegraph hits you, it's nasty.

As Mary balanced on the top two steps the wind tugged at her skirts, but glancing back she saw one of the SD guards raise his gun again to fire. 'As I jumped he fired and hit me twice, which helped of course for getting along a bit. It was a hell of jump.' Mary fell headfirst to the trackside, tumbled over and lay still and unconscious. As the train juddered to a halt, the two SD guards rushed back along the line to find her lying in the undergrowth.

Mary's body, broken once more in the service of her country, was carried to the train and she was taken to the Luftwaffe-run hospital at St-Pierre-des-Corps in Tours. There she was treated by a kindly surgeon who laid her in a body-length plaster cast. When after ten days Mary was no longer drifting in and out of consciousness, she was able to thank her surgeon.

He was, she noted, about her age, and dressed in suitable clothes could easily have passed for an Englishman. His sister was married to an Englishman and her son flew with the RAF. As the surgeon told her, 'My own son flies with the Luftwaffe, so two members of our family might meet in mortal combat, each flying for a different side.' The doctor also thought that she was an Englishwoman, 'It is strange, too, that I have operated on many Englishmen, and now an Englishwoman.'

'If you operated on them as well as you operated on me, I'm sure they were much obliged.'

'Believe it or not, you are the person whom we all admire. Unfortunately there are no German women in England waiting to look after our young airmen and escort them home. Tell me, when did you come to France?'

Sensing a trap, Mary replied cautiously, 'I've been here all the time.'

The doctor laughed, 'We know how you came over. We like to imagine you arriving in one of those little British planes. Do you know, my young pilots have the greatest admiration for the English airmen who fly on those missions, they have a saying "Only the mad English would do such a thing".'

Mary cast her mind back to October 1942 and her farewell from Canadian John Bridger and warmed with pride at the compliment. 'You need have no fear while you are in my hospital. We too hate the SS and we loathe the Gestapo. By the way, several of my young airmen patients have asked if they could come and see you. Do you object?' And that is what happened for the next month: young German pilots came to her room to sit on the bed and practise their English and to talk about any subject other than the war.

However, a month later at five in the morning, two officers of the *Feldgendarmerie* came for her. As the orderly who had cared for her stuffed her pockets with chocolate, fruit and sugar and handed her a large food parcel, he whispered, 'They evidently consider you very important.'

On 15 January she was taken on a twelve-hour journey by car – but not north to Paris, where allegedly she had been tried in her absence and sentenced to death, and where a group of female SOE agents who had also been sentenced to death were being gathered for their final, fateful journey. Instead, Mary was taken by car several hundred kilometres eastwards to Dijon, where she was kept in 'secret' or solitary confinement.

Mary's report on this next part of her saga, read:

> At Dijon still in handcuffs and chains put in 'secret'. They left me alone for 2½ months. In the meantime Ginette had been able to communicate with her sister in Lyon (who later in an endeavour to buy her sister's freedom sold me completely). Ginette remained loyal and because of her sister's messing got sent to Germany (Ravensbrück) in June or July. In the meantime enquiries continued and I was still in 'secret'.

It was not quite the end of the Marie-Claire escape line. When Maurice de Milleville heard of his mother's arrest at Pau, he fled to Switzerland where, in the last week of January 1944 in the British consulate in Geneva, he met Ian McGeoch, a British submariner who had escaped from Italy into Switzerland. McGeoch remembered Maurice at that time as 'aged about twenty, smallish, fine-features, with pale complexion and dark hair, undernourished and clothed in a baggy suit … who … never stopped talking, very fast, mostly in French, but breaking now and then into well-spoken English'.[8]

Maurice had entered Switzerland illegally and had no papers. He was discreet about what his mother has being doing but told McGeoch about his mother's arrest and feared that she would be tortured. He too, he told McGeoch, had been arrested and brutally beaten up but let go by the Germans. Maurice told McGeoch that he needed money – 57,000 francs – to settle debts he had incurred on behalf of the British government in France, and that he wanted British papers so he could go to England and report on his and his mother's activities before joining the British Army. Six weeks later, equipped by Victor Farrell and armed by Maurice with passwords and the addresses of two safe houses in Lyon, McGeoch successfully entered an escape line which took him to Spain.

That same month, March 1944, a Mme Jumard of Lyon and her son were arrested in a joint operation by the *Milice* and the Gestapo and thrown into Dijon Prison. There, Mme Jumard was able to speak a few words every now and again to Mary Lindell while they were having a shower, and when in June 1944 Jumard was released, she smuggled a message from Mary which reached Victor Farrell via the Swiss consul in Lyon.[9]

Meanwhile at Ruffec, Pauline subsumed Mary's escape line into her own, under the code name of Marie-Odile. Under Pauline's leadership many former members of the Marie-Claire shifted seamlessly into helping Pauline. Nicole Lebon continued to convoy escapers in groups of ten to Toulouse, where they were met by Robert and Germaine Thibout, and then sent on to Foix and over the Pyrenees. However, when Pauline moved the centre of her operations to Paris, she and Nicole were betrayed by an unknown informer and arrested near the Madeleine métro station. They were held until 15 August 1944 when they were deported to Germany. There, Pauline, Comtesse de Saint-Venant would once again meet Mary, Comtesse de Milleville, but she would not return from Ravensbrück.

Jumard's information reached MI9 in London on 28 August 1944 and it was logged:

> According to 'reliable information' Mary Lindell, known by her most recently assumed name of Marie de Moncy was being held in cell 108 in the German prison at Dijon, that she had been wounded in the head and was probably charged with espionage.

Mary's life had entered a period of limbo: she was held in solitary confinement, and she was interrogated, but she was not badly treated, and even seems to have reached some kind of rapport with her inquisitor and won the respect of the prison staff, French and Germans alike. She was not beaten because, she believed, there was respect from one professional to another, and they did not send for her children or threaten them:

> The Germans aren't stupid. They knew perfectly well that had they brought Maurice or my daughter and beaten them up before me, I should have said

'Beat away' they wouldn't have got anywhere, and the end result would have been exactly the same in the long run. It wouldn't have saved me. We weren't very mad about the Germans, you know, and we didn't trust them.

Mary's period of being held in 'secret' or solitary confinement came to an end when she was put into a cell with a young Anglo-French woman, Yvonne Baseden. Yvonne recalled:

> We moved to a cell about three doors away which is where I walked in and found Mary Lindell, who I hadn't met before, had never seen before, and realised, of course, that she was English as soon as I walked in, and she immediately looked after me and reassured me, and said that now there are two of us we can chat about these things and so on. Of course she was an older woman who had been in the Red Cross and a nursing sister, and very self-possessed and not at all afraid of anyone whether they were of any nationality or that she happened to be a prisoner didn't concern us at all which was an extraordinary way of looking at it from my point of view. I found it difficult, I personally couldn't see it that way. But it was marvellous to able to be in a cell with someone else there instead of being completely on one's own, well nothing, a bed and a mattress.[10]

Yvonne would have more reason to be grateful for Mary's company …

16

CALLED TO ARMS – OPERATION ZEBRA

Yvonne Baseden had heard de Gaulle's call to arms on 22 June 1940, after the fall of France, '*La flamme de la résistance française ne doit pas s'éteindre et ne s'éteindra pas*' ('The flame of the French Resistance should not go out and will not go out').[1] Yvonne was one of the first to volunteer to help de Gaulle, 'I thought I'd better go and see if I can do anything, I went along to his offices and spoke to his secretary who said that he might be interested and asked me to wait.' After a few minutes he returned to tell her that he was sorry, but as mademoiselle was born of an English father, they couldn't possibly employ or help her and she certainly couldn't join the Free French. This was a grave disappointment for, she told an interviewer later, 'my thoughts and my hopes were already in my beloved France'.

Frustrated in her first choice, Yvonne volunteered for the Women's Auxiliary Air Force and was accepted on 4 September 1940. Her RAF record discloses nothing of her covert life as an agent. However, someone was watching Yvonne's progress and she was invited by letter to an interview on 1 June 1943. As she walked into a nondescript office in a nondescript building – in fact, a dilapidated bedroom converted into an office in the Hotel Victoria in Northumberland Avenue, London – 'I couldn't think why on earth I was there'. The interview was conducted in French and when asked if she was interested in doing something more for France, she was thrilled and answered at once, 'Yes, of course!' She giggled when warned the work wouldn't be easy and might involve parachuting into France and answered, 'Well that all sounds exciting, OK.'

She soon learned that she had made contact with F Section of the Special Operations Executive (F standing for French). She also met the Romanian-born Vera Rosenberg, who had been recruited into the SOE as Maurice

Buckmaster's secretary. Under the name of Vera Atkins she has entered history as the intelligence officer in F Section, or as the power behind Buckmaster, yet Vera served most of the war as a civilian and only in 1944 was she naturalised as a British citizen.[2] Vera also inspired a mixture of fear and distaste in some agents, including Yvonne Baseden, who was frightened by her intensity. By comparison Yvonne found Buckmaster charming and distinguished.

Sent to a basement address which was, she thought, the headquarters of the First Aid Nursing Yeomanry (FANY), she reluctantly exchanged her light-blue uniform for the khaki uniform of the FANY. During training she made many new friends and she also enjoyed the scenery of Scotland, which was new to her. The training was not without its black humour. In September 1943 Yvonne and a new friend, Violette Szabó, were teamed up with a veteran agent, Lise de Baissac who, as 'Odile' in the Scientist circuit, had already accomplished one tour of duty in occupied France. The three girls were sent to RAF Ringway, Manchester, for their parachute training, where the novices, Yvonne and Violette, jumped well but the more experienced Lise broke her leg.

In January 1944 Yvonne was ready to go into the field as a wireless operator and she was introduced to her team leader, the young French nobleman Marie Joseph Gonzagues de St Geniès, whose field name was Lucien (hers being Odette). St Geniès' task was to establish a new circuit in eastern France, code-named Scholar, in an area that Allied intelligence reckoned was already under the effective control of the Maquis. They were told to stand by every third day from 16 February onwards, reporting by telephone to F Section in Baker Street.

Between phone calls they were free and time hung heavy in their hands. They took their meals in Soho and Yvonne recalled with pleasure that they ate well, since St Geniès knew the best restaurants where good French cooking could be found in wartime London and be bought without ration coupons. They spoke French and rehearsed their cover stories constantly, 'We schooled ourselves to forget all that had gone before and to convince ourselves that this masquerade was true.'

In late February she and St Geniès heard from Baker Street, 'We were told that a car would be waiting there to pick us up and take us somewhere, destination unknown. We had to be there at one o'clock.' When they turned up they found:

> Our cases were there, already packed. My three wireless sets, in their innocent-looking fibre cases, had already been sent on. I had a short talk with Colonel Buckmaster and he gave me a farewell present, a precious silver powder compact. The Baker Street headquarters seemed very normal. It was

we, St Geniès and I, who were abnormal. We were conscious of the ordinary daily routine of the office which went on and would continue to go on after we had jumped into the night sky and landed in France. It was rather like looking at a scene from a play, waiting in the wings for the moment when we would go on. Telephones were ringing, doors opening and shutting, people hurrying about with files in their hands, a sprinkling of very odd-looking loafers in civilian clothes and neat, cheerful FANYs who looked jolly healthy as if they'd just come in from swimming after playing squash. And there was Vera.

Through the cold and the drizzle of a typical February day, they drove up the Finchley Road and on to the Great North Road, through Hatfield and onwards. St Geniès sat in the front with the driver, reading poetry, while Yvonne and Vera sat in the back not saying much, until they reached a large and comfortable country house where they were in time for tea. They met several self-contained groups of men and women, each group consisting of two or three people. All of them were drawn irresistibly to a large blackboard over the mantelpiece in the drawing room. On the blackboard was written their field names and, periodically, instructions were chalked in as to when they would be called forward.

Dinner was, in Yvonne's words, magnificent, such as she only remembered from pre-war days, but everyone was living on their nerves:

> There was a strong sense of tension, Conversation were extremely guarded. Nobody spoke of his or her particular mission, remembering those already in the field, knowing that the same silence would be preserved by others when we had gone.
>
> The long day ended. Two groups, each of two men and one woman, had left. They were just no longer there. Nobody had noticed their going. In my heart, I wished them God-speed on their journey and a safe landing. I went to bed but not to sleep.

Three girls shared a bedroom.[3] One talked in her sleep, 'Thank God, she talked in French.' Another tossed and turned as she clutched at imaginary parachute cords. Yvonne's nightmare was a never-ending parachute jump, being perpetually tossed in the slipstream of an aircraft, falling and falling.

The next day was clear and windless and Yvonne looked forward eagerly to the moment of departure. She and St Geniès played long sets of table tennis and between sets rehearsed their cover stories for the thousandth time. The blackboard drew their eyes like a magnet and, 'yes, there we were. We were to leave at five o'clock. Like those who had gone before, we made no farewells. We simply faded out.'

After a false start, Yvonne and St Geniès landed a few minutes before midnight on 19 March at Herré in the province of Landes, some 40km west of Condom, not far from where her mother's family lived. Their destination was Dôle, a small town south of Dijon in eastern France, in the ancient Franche-Comté region of the Jura mountains. St Geniès travelled ahead while Yvonne followed, carrying her codes and papers, on a journey which took four days, first to Marseilles and then up the Rhône Valley before branching off to Dôle. There they took up their headquarters in a château on a cliff over the River Doubs, which was once used as an orphanage and known as *les Orphelins* and was now being used as a cheese depot.

The depot was owned by the Graf brothers who were strongly pro-German, but the Swiss caretaker, Frederick Mayor, and his wife, Gabrielle or Gaby, sympathised with the Resistance and allowed their small apartment in the cheese depot to be used by St Geniès and his team. St Geniès' tasks were to make contact with a French *réseau*, who London called 'Director', based in Annemasse on the eastern border of the Geneva enclave, and pass on new orders to its leader, Jean Pierre Meunier (or Mesnard), who had been communicating with F Section through Victor Farrell's wireless in Bern.[4] St Geniès was also to recruit and train new wireless operators, take stock of what arms the various circuits had, and organise new supplies of weapons. His designated targets were the aerodrome at Salon-de-Provence, German strongholds in the Alps between Col de Mont Genève and Col de Larche, and the night-fighters based in the Bouches-du-Rhône. St Geniès was also to liaise with neighbouring circuits, including the Acrobat *réseau* operating to the north and west of Dôle, in a belt between Dijon and Saint-Étienne.

The most important work, however, was the supply of arms and ammunition to the Resistance, and much of the work of organising the parachutages fell to Yvonne. In three months she was responsible for some dozen night-time drops: three parachutages in March, and five each in April and May, bringing 197 containers of weapons and fifty-eight packages to the Resistance.

However, it was unwise of St Geniès and Yvonne to remain based in one place for so long – other Resistance leaders changed their location frequently. Also, Yvonne seems not to have known about German direction-finding capability and she seems not to have learned the lesson that she should never, ever make repeated transmissions from the same site. Instead, she and St Geniès gambled that, with the owners (the Graf brothers) being so pro-German and with Germans on cheese hunts being such frequent visitors, they could effectively hide in the open.

The warning order for a large drop of arms was given on 13 June, when Special Forces Headquarters submitted a so-called 'Appreciation of the Potentialities of the French Resistance', which set out the current status of the French forces behind the German front line, and requested immediate assistance and increased allocation of aircraft. It was planned that 130 aircraft of the 3rd Bombardment Division, 8th US Air Force, based in England, should drop arms and ammunition to the Maquis in six places in central and south-western France.

The drop, the first ever daylight parachutage, was known as Operation Zebra and was scheduled for Thursday, 22 June, but bad weather in England meant that it was delayed. Yvonne, St Geniès and his team had arrived a couple of days before at their chosen dropping ground across the Doubs near Pierre-en-Bresse and set up their temporary headquarters in a small house where they planned the defence of the site. After two more days of tension, at 7.30 p.m. on 24 June, British double summer time, the listeners heard their message personnel on the BBC, and Yvonne calmly acknowledged on her wireless that the reception committee was ready. The BBC message was repeated twice that evening, but St Geniès' people were already moving into place.

They had recruited neighbouring Maquis groups and a number of vehicles to help them shift the anticipated large number of containers. Yvonne recalled, 'Contact with the Maquis group who helped in the operation was rather difficult and on their arrival at the appointed meeting place we mistook each other for Germans in the darkness and nearly started shooting.' Eventually they assembled some 800 men, most of them, according to Yvonne, gendarmes who had joined the Resistance:

> All were armed and most of them were placed at important points defending the ground. One of the obstacles in this operation was an armoured train which was located a few miles away from the dropping ground protecting a group of German troops working on the railway, but, as it happened, the train moved off a few miles on that day.

In the early morning of Sunday, 25 June, thirty-six Flying Fortresses turned upwind and flew in at 500ft for their dropping run. As it happened, M.R.D. Foot, who would write the history of the SOE, was flying as an observer on this drop and recalled, 'As we got well into central France, we began to lose height. Beyond Lyon, we make a sharp turn to port, and start to fly below the summits of nearby mountains.' Over the drop zone Foot thought he caught a glimpse of St Geniès striding across the drop zone with Yvonne.[5]

Yvonne recalled:

> On the morning of the operation, I was in wireless contact with England and later on with the planes themselves and at the appointed time we saw three bomber squadrons coming in over our ground and delivering the supplies. Not a German was in sight during the whole operation although air raid warnings were sounded in all towns nearby.
>
> It was extraordinary. When the planes came over we could hear the roar of the engines. It was the middle of the morning in beautiful sunlight. We had a lot of lorries and 800 people on the ground to help to move the material as quickly as possible.

Even if Yvonne's wireless transmission had not been detected, the noise of so many bombers at low level must have alerted the Germans to something unusual and, according to Yvonne, they reacted quickly, placing road blocks everywhere. In fact, nemesis was about to fall on Scholar and all its doings, and Yvonne sent one last wireless message, 'Most of big day operations safe but enemy looking all over area.'

The official version of what happened next is that St Geniès and Yvonne left Pierre-en-Bresse by bicycle for the cheese depot where they arrived on Monday, 26 June, feeling self-assured and secure, and they sat down to a celebration lunch with champagne. Meanwhile, according to the accepted account, the Germans captured one of St Geniès' young *maquisards* who was carrying a wireless set, and under duress this boy gave away his destination. The Germans surrounded the château, and their attack developed so quickly that the underground corridors out of the cheese depot couldn't be used for a getaway. St Geniès was killed by a shot through the forehead as he fired from an attic window.

In London, scarcely a month later on 24 July, in an SOE Battle Casualty Report, Vera Atkins wrote, 'Germans surrounded house and St Geniès and his wireless operator were shot whilst trying to escape.' She added that her findings were supported by 'four different sources in the field' and the accuracy of the reports was 'reliable'. From the written evidence in St Geniès' file, now open at the National Archives at Kew, it is difficult to know how Atkins could be so sure of her facts, or indeed what her four different sources were. A subsequent inquiry in 1945 reveals that there was treachery involved and that St Geniès and his people had been betrayed by German sympathisers in the town of Dôle.[6]

Yvonne was arrested and taken to the headquarters of the *Feldgendarmerie* at their barracks in Dôle, where she was placed in a cell with Gaby who was hysterical and Yvonne tried to calm her. The Germans questioned Yvonne roughly, if inexpertly, and her training in how to resist torture and interrogation kicked in. Their questions centred on her identity and her reason for hiding. She was thrown to the ground and beaten and they 'dragged [me] up the stairs past an office full of people in uniforms typing reports. I had a sense of being someone else. The only thing that kept me going was the thought that the job we'd done the day before had been a success.'

Yvonne maintained her cover story that she was Marie Bernier and a nursing assistant to Robert Morel, who was a doctor for the Maquis, which her interrogators seemed to accept. It was a week after the parachutage at Pierre-en-Bresse that she was brought up from her cell and told she was being sent to Dijon.[7]

Yvonne was placed in a small lorry and she recognised amongst her fellow passengers the boy who had been captured with her wireless set, and there were three other prisoners who were accused of black-marketeering and two guards. She was careful to sit near the edge, overlooking the road. She was not handcuffed and was ready to jump whenever the Maquis made their expected attempt to stop the truck. Long afterwards she remembered her disappointment that although some 800 French had been mobilised for the parachutage and the distribution of arms afterwards, not one of them was prepared to rescue her.

In Dijon she was taken to Gestapo headquarters, who took over her interrogation. They glanced at the paperwork that had been sent with her, and she saw their annoyance that the others in the gang had not been sent up, and overheard a telephone call from Dijon to Dôle demanding that they should be sent too. Gradually the cover story of her pretended previous life in Paris began to break down and when she hesitated she was punished by being thrown into a basement cell with an open sewer, but no lights. She felt her way to a bench and kept track of time by listening to the chimes of a church clock.

Next day her captors woke her up and started to call her by her field name, Odette, and spoke a few words in English to her. Yvonne did not react and she was left two or three days more in the black hole of her cell without food, water or any sanitation. On a Sunday, two weeks after the parachutage, she was suddenly ordered up from the basement, climbing the stairs very slowly as she was now so weak.

The Gestapo had obviously made some progress in their investigation: they told her that she was English and she had been parachuted into France, and that St Geniès was also English. Since they seemed to know so much, Yvonne began to talk a little. She had done well: in her training she had learned that about forty-eight hours' resistance to her interrogators would be sufficient to give anyone else in her crowd, or 'gang' as she called them, who had not been arrested enough time to get away. At one stage she was propped against the wall and a German fired his pistol at her feet, but this was the only serious attempt to force information from her.

Now she told the Gestapo her real name, only giving details that they seemed to know already:

> When they saw I had slipped, they had another man in the room who used to come up and stand on my toes shifting his weight from one to one to the other. I pretended to be terribly worried about this and started crying and changed round the details somehow of my story so that it suited their convenience.

She told them she had been parachuted into France near Dôle. But someone was talking to the Germans and next day she was accused of having landed in the south, travelling to Dôle with a man and working a wireless set there. Yvonne maintained her story that she was only the wireless operator and her only job had been to send and receive messages. Now the Germans tried to place her section in London, and she was shown the address and telephone number of Orchard Court – the flat used by F Section – and a book containing about twenty photographs with the names of various agents who were alleged to work at Orchard Court. Yvonne genuinely did not recognise any of these names, but she had time to register that above Maurice Buckmaster's name there was an empty space for a photograph.

It is clear that the Gestapo in Dijon in 1944 did not need her help, for as she remarked in London later, 'obviously the others were telling quite enough'. And eventually she gave them her real name. There was one more test. The Germans wanted to know about the technical aspects of her work as wireless operator. They told her that they had captured sets like hers before; they showed her the codes they had found at Les Orphelins, and told her that they had heard from Berlin that she had been detected by direction-finding 'three weeks ago'. They also had examples of coded messages, including the last one she had been due to send and its *en clair* version. Would she work for them? Yvonne's answer was that she had been in daily contact with London and that by now London must know that she had been caught.

Afterwards she was put into a new cell, 'I was on the top floor, cell number 111.' Though still in solitary confinement, this tiny cell was luxury compared to the board in the basement. It contained a bed, blankets, a bowl and a jug of water for drinking and washing. Twenty-two-year-old Yvonne had successfully resisted all that the Germans could do to her so far. Now she began to rebuild her mental strength, conducting the exercises she had been trained to do before leaving England. Meanwhile, she recalled, 'We knew D-Day had happened but we visualised the armies advancing more rapidly than they were. But it did give some hope.'

She was not questioned again, but from time to time a Gestapo officer, who had been her principal interrogator, visited her with snippets of information that he had gained from others still under interrogation. To Yvonne it seemed:

> They had the whole show fairly well taped and were trying to arrest more people in the south … They seemed rather rushed as the Allies were nearing Dijon and the case was not closed when the prison had to be evacuated. That is why I left Dijon on my way to Germany without having been shot.[8]

Yvonne was beginning to lose track of the date, but after about two months in solitary confinement she was put into a cell with Mary Lindell.

17

ACROSS THE CHARON

The jail at Dijon held hundreds of prisoners, including some French men and women who had been rounded up and were destined for deportation or execution, and although Mary Lindell and Yvonne Baseden were held in solitary confinement, somehow they became aware of each other, separated by only a few doors. Soon the two women began a campaign of resistance.

'You see in the evening we used to whistle "God save the King".' When the Germans rushed up to Mary's door and yelled at her to stop, Yvonne would pick up the refrain, so they would rush to her door, and when she stopped Mary would start again. 'They used to get mad at us, they'd get so mad!'

When the two women finally met in August, Yvonne thought that Mary was obviously English; she thought also that she might be a stool pigeon. Mary's account of how the two women eventually met face to face differs from Yvonne's:

One night she thought that I'd been shot and she burst into tears, and then she couldn't stop. She cried and cried and cried. Mind you she'd been picked up with a radio transmitter set, so she wasn't exactly healthy, and the only thing she had to hold to – she'd never seen me and I'd never seen her – was this whistling.

So hysterical was Yvonne that Mary was taken to the wardress' post to show Yvonne that she hadn't been shot. '"Well," I said, "OK", I was delighted to be going out for a walk. First time I'd been out of my cell without handcuffs. So I said, "Oh yes, I'm all for it".'

Later on Yvonne started another crying fit. Mary, from her prison cell, was still capable of taking charge of a situation:

Now look here, you know perfectly well that I was arrested at Pau and she was arrested at Dôle and we are nothing to do with each other. So, I said, telephone to my SD and telephone to her SD, telephone specially to mine who happens to be an intelligent man and put her into my cell. Like that she won't go off her rocker, otherwise she will go off her rocker. So she was put in my cell.[1]

At some stage Mary and Yvonne were joined in their cell by Gaby Mayor, who was nervous and dispirited. Mary was struck by her doll-like appearance, buttermilk complexion and rose-red cheeks. In characteristic no-nonsense words, Mary reminded Gaby that she represented Switzerland. 'Life is good,' she told Gaby. 'You are going to get out of here one day. It's important not to let anyone see that you are afraid.'

Although, from time to time, the prisoners could hear the rumble of guns and it was easy to imagine that they were getting closer, the Allies were held up temporarily in their advance on Dijon and the city would not be liberated until mid September. Meanwhile rumours swept the prison: the prisoners were all to be taken to Germany; now they were all going to be shot.

Mary had become something of a mascot in the prison. Even the German head wardress was beholden to her because letters from her son, writing to her from South Africa in English because of the censorship laws there, needed to be translated. The French prisoners had placed bets that they were safe if Mary was kept in her cell, but that if she was brought down from her eyrie that would mean they were going to be shot.

Then, on 19 August, the head wardress came to her cell in tears, but could not bring herself to words. Half an hour later she returned smiling. 'Oh, Comtesse, one hundred and twenty five French officers have been waiting in the main hall downstairs since 5 o'clock and their names are on a list for execution. I thought yours was on the list too.' But at 11 a.m. the wardress returned once more, speechless and now with an ashen face, and gestured Mary to follow her. This black comedy concluded in the main hall when the Frenchmen greeted Mary's appearance with groans or cheers according to how they had bet.

There was more comedy to follow. On a trestle table in the hall a group of German Army officers and police were examining the contents of Mary's suitcase. A German turned a ledger towards her and gave her a pen, indicating where she should sign, but Mary, glancing over the entry on the page, put down the pen. 'We British only sign a document when it is accurate and true. When I was arrested I had something over 1,000,000 French francs with me. If you think I am going to sign for only 15,000 francs, you'd better think again.'

'Sign!' one of the Germans demanded.

'No,' Mary countered.

Those in the hall held their breath for a moment before the infuriated Germans began to yell, but the more they yelled the calmer Mary became, until one of them screamed, '*Raus! Raus!*' and ordered Mary to join the waiting Frenchmen. She turned on her heel and sashayed to the end of the room, defying her enemy even in this crisis.

A Frenchman, shaken but approving of Mary's defiance, whispered, 'You do realise we are going to be shot?'

'So what? I'm not going to let those swines bully me.'

After about half an hour, she was joined by others, including Yvonne and Gaby and another Frenchwoman, Reine, and somehow this seemed more hopeful to Mary. The Germans seemed uncertain, and order and counter-order prevailed. Outside the prison the Germans were being driven eastwards and out of France. While Allied troops in the north had temporarily outrun their supply lines, troops from the south were advancing along the Rhône Valley when they were held up by the Germans before Dijon. The only escape route for the Germans was the network of roads and railway lines which led through the narrow Belfort Gap between the Vosges Mountains in the north and the Jura in the south-east. Along this route some 100,000 headquarters, logistics, communications and hospital staff, Luftwaffe ground crew and German men and women – all of little combat value and vulnerable to attack by the Maquis – were fleeing home to Germany.[2]

Lyon was liberated on 3 September and Besançon was liberated on 7 September, but Dijon was held by the Germans until 11 September. Under the circumstances, finding a train to carry their prisoners into Germany rather than shooting them as the French officers expected, must be seen as an act of humanity and orderliness. On 23 August 1944, 190 female prisoners, almost all Frenchwomen, were entrained via Belfort for Germany: one-third of them would die in captivity in Germany.

The prisoners were ordered into trucks, a separate vehicle being reserved for the women. Then Mary was hauled off her truck and a soldier chalked 'KG' on her back. KG, or *kriegsgefangene*, meant she was being treated as a prisoner of war. She was handcuffed and put into a car with two German policemen. The French male prisoners peered over the tailboards of their trucks and watched her go in silence.

In fact, Mary was taken to the railway station, which was seething with German civilians and soldiers. Mary was put into a carriage with Yvonne, Gaby and Reine under the guard of a soldier who stood outside in the corridor. Their hope was for the train to stop so that they could jump off, and it was not long before the train ran into a tunnel to hide from Allied planes. Mary heard the slam of doors and scrunch of gravel as men dropped onto the track, but in the darkness the women could not find each other and soon more guards had been placed outside their door and under the window. A chance of escape had gone.

Here is Mary's version of what happened next:

> With the advance of our armies I was suddenly transferred to Saarbrücken and again because of our advance moved to an unknown destination near Kassel. They tried to hand us over but there were no orders. Also at various other places as I was considered a prisoner-of-war. An English WAAF [Baseden] who had joined me at Dijon etc. was also considered a prisoner-of-war. We got to Ravensbrück and were told we should be sent to Kassel or Konstanz. This however was only noise and never happened.

The Germans had no system for dealing with female prisoners of war and, as Mary would find out, many Russian women captured while serving in the Soviet Army were sent to Ravensbrück. Konstanz was an Ilag or *internierungslager*, an internment camp for enemy civilians, and Mary's hope and expectation was that she would be sent there.

However, on the evening of 23 August Mary and her three companions reached Saarbrücken, a railway crossing between France and Germany, where the women were marched through the bombed ruins of the town to Neue Bremm, a holding camp for prisoners who were on their way to forced labour and concentration camps deeper in Germany. The camp consisted of several wooden barracks built on four sides of a square with a single watchtower on one corner and a rectangular fire pond in the centre. Some of the prisoners were Russian labourers who had been drafted in to work in Saarbrücken, but most were French political prisoners and prisoners of war, victims of the Germans' policy of 'Night and Fog', who were being swept away into official oblivion.

At Neue Bremm the prisoners were stripped and searched and their property taken away, and they had their first experience of the dreaded roll call, or *Appel*, which started early in the morning when the poorly clothed prisoners were made to stand to attention for long hours in all weathers. The diet was so poor that prisoners rapidly lost weight.

In German literature there is an argument as to whether Saarbrücken was a *barackenlager* or a *koncentrazionslager*: the Germans in charge called it a *sportslager*, where they forced prisoners to move always at the double and required others to duck-walk in the crouching position with their arms behind their heads. For the guards' further sport they routinely drowned those who were too weak to compete in the camp's sporting activities in the camp's fire pond.

Periodically the survivors were despatched in cattle trucks to concentration camps whose names live in infamy – Buchenwald, Dachau, Mauthausen, Natzweiler-Struthof, Ravensbrück and Sachsenhausen – but the initiation to these dreadful places began at Saarbrücken. Amongst those who experienced its horrors were Albert Guérisse, who had taken Mary's 'special parcels' off her hands, and Mary's would-be wireless operator, Tom Groome, who witnessed that the conditions at Saarbrücken were extremely bad, the food insufficient and the guards brutal.[3]

A year later, in August 1944, Mary was shocked:

> It was obvious from the appearance of other prisoners that conditions were appalling, The majority that I saw were male prisoners in an entirely sub-human condition, completely apathetic, who shuffled about with their clothes hanging on them and were merely walking skeletons and appeared to be quite aimless [and] who cared little if they lived or died.[4]

The women did not suffer the same harsh physical regime as the men at Neue Bremm, but were held in a large shed across the road from the men's camp, where they were confined in one hut.[5] Yet the women's arrival at Saarbrücken was one more opportunity for Mary to display her reckless bravery and to confound and confuse her German captors with head-on confrontation instead of the meek submission that they expected from their prisoners.

The group having been searched once, Mary and Yvonne were summoned to an office block for an additional search. As Mary's suitcase was rummaged and her things taken out, she replaced them.

'*Was machst du?*' one of her guards screamed.

'In my country people who do not return things are called thieves. I am making sure that I get all my things back.'

Another German took a hot water bottle. 'You have made a mistake, that hot water bottle does not belong to you. It is mine and I intend to keep it.'

As Mary snatched her hot water bottle, the Germans began to shout and the noise brought the Kommandant himself into the room, 'What is the matter?'

'I am a prisoner of war and these people are robbing me. These people are thieves and I have told them so.'

The Kommandant picked up the hot water bottle. 'But this is just the thing for dear little children in Berlin, who are being bombed nightly by your wicked Royal Air Force.'

'We are only giving what you gave us in London, aren't we? The only difference is that in London we stood up to it and did not steal anything from the German airmen we shot down. That being so, I consider you have no right to touch my things.'

The Kommandant ignored her and picked up a block of Swiss notepaper. 'This is very nice. How is it that you have Swiss notepaper?'

'What business is it of yours?' And as he put the notepaper in his pocket, she asserted, 'So you are a thief too!'

'*Raus! Raus!*' and Mary was bundled from the room.

Yvonne was searched next and went into the office wearing a raincoat that Mary had lent her. When she returned without the coat, Mary was so infuriated that she stormed into the office to demand the coat back – and the Germans meekly surrendered it.

Mary and Yvonne were taken to a large, unlit shed full of women. As Yvonne's eyes adjusted to the light she heard a voice call, 'Yvonne, what are you doing here?' Suddenly she began to recognise faces. There was Violette Szabó, who she had trained to parachute with and who she had last seen when she brought her little daughter into the Baker Street offices of SOE. So too, sitting there on their bunks in the gloom, were Lilian Rolfe and Denise Bloch (whom she knew as Danielle). They had been the only three women among a group of forty prisoners of the Gestapo, mainly agents of the SOE and fighters in the Resistance who left Paris on 8 August – all bar six would be executed in Germany.

She learned of four French girls who she had not seen before, and she did not know all their names, but Jenny Silvani, whose real name was Jenny Djendi, would become her close friend. The others were Pierrette Louin,[6] Suzanne Boitte[7] and Marie-Louise Cloarec.[8] All had come, she thought, from Fresnes, and they were in good health and, she understood, had suffered no ill treatment since their arrest, though they had been placed in chains after one of them had tried to escape.

Yvonne looked round the shed, wondering if she would see more familiar faces. It was quite dark now, the crowded bunks full of women, and as she peered she thought, 'My God, the whole of Baker Street is here.'[9] Yvonne told an interviewer many years later:

They were in quite a good state – particularly Violette. There were a lot of people around, and we could not speak easily. And they were very wary of me – suspicious really – because they would have thought 'What is she doing here arriving on another convoy?' And you see, they would not have known the circumstance of my arrest, so they would have been wary of me. And I don't even remember if we spoke English. I doubt it because I didn't want people to know that I was English. You see, as far as the Germans knew, I was just a French woman with the resistance. That is how I survived. They never knew that I was a British agent.[10]

Yvonne's memory was at fault and she had forgotten that she had confessed her real name to the Gestapo in Dijon, who also knew that she was a wireless operator.[11] She continued, with more justification:

But the other girls had been through some sort of process. They had already been put in a different category. They went on in different transport to Ravensbrück from me. They left before I left, and thank goodness for me, I did not go with them.

THE WOMEN'S HELL

After ten days' witness to the curtain-raiser that was Saarbrücken, the four women, Mary, Yvonne, Gaby and Reine, continued their journey towards hell on 2 September 1944. Yvonne remembered that a notice on the side of each truck read '8 horses or 40 men'. They were crammed into a truck which was already crowded full with women who had been several days en route from Rennes. They were packed in until no more could squeeze in and they travelled standing.[1]

The officer in command of the train evidently knew of Mary's presence among the prisoners as the train made a stop-start journey through Germany, north via Cologne and east to Hanover. In both places he tried to place Mary in the town jail, but each was full and so he offered Mary, as a *kriegsgefangene* (prisoner of war), a place in his carriage which was attached to the train. Mary rejected this, 'May I ask with whom I shall be travelling?'

'You will be travelling with me.'

'In that case I'll carry on in the cattle truck!' And the door was slammed in her face.[2]

Eventually the doors of the train banged open. The sign said '*Fürstenberg Mecklenburg*'. The women stumbled out, their legs stiff and numb from being unable to move in the cattle trucks. The welcoming party were men and women of the SS in their field-grey uniforms, with the death's-head emblem on their forage caps. They were armed with whips, sticks and dogs, and as the prisoners fell out of the trucks they were pushed and shoved into rows of five. The dead were left in the trucks or on the ground where they fell.

The train commander beckoned the women from Saarbrücken to one side, while the column of dirty, tired and dishevelled women marched off. Mary contrasted her travelling companions with the tidily coiffured young women in their smart field-grey uniforms who literally cracked the whip.

There was something wrong: the train commander was angry that no car had been sent to pick up his charges and ordered two soldiers to carry Mary's suitcase. Mary and the others in her small group would have to walk to the camp, he apologised, where he would arrange for them to be sent to another camp. 'This place is not for you. It is a concentration camp and a living hell. I shall take you back with me.'

In the late afternoon light of Sunday, 3 September they walked slowly along a sandy track and through a pleasant wood. They passed new, wooden barrack blocks set among the trees on their right and above, on their left, neat, wooden houses on a low ridge. To the right they could glimpse a lake and in the distance the tall spire of a church. There were children at play, flowers planted around the buildings and washing drying in the late summer sunshine. Across an open space, looking like a small mansion, they saw a brick-built office block – this was the *Kommandantur* – and to its left, double doors where guards stood.

Passing through the doors under an arch they passed along a corridor formed by the end of the *Kommandantur* to the right and a row of garages and workshops set at right angles to the left, until they entered another open space and turned right. There they saw rows of identical huts stretching away into the distance and outside each hut were more flowers growing. They were now at the rear of the *Kommandantur* building and another building which ran parallel to it. A few Germans stood on the steps of the building watching them. To their front was another, low concrete building, which they would come to fear, and beyond that, rising above its roof ridge, was a tall chimney.

For so large an enclosure it seemed strangely still, and only a few women wandered between the huts. Mostly they wore similar uniforms: most were in striped grey or blue jackets and dresses and many wore headscarves tied under the chin. Mary's group halted outside a large marquee and peeping inside they could see it was carpeted in straw. But clearly Mary's party was not expected. No one was much interested in their presence, and as the chill and the damp grew they wandered into the tent for shelter, until guards, yelling and snarling, drove them out telling them that the tent was reserved for a party of Polish women who were about to arrive.

The only place to sit or lie was outside and Mary took charge once more:

If we do this in an orderly manner, we may get away with it, though you've seen how the SS behave. I suggest we sleep in pairs. Each of us will go quickly into the tent and fetch one blanket. In this way each couple will have a blanket to lie on and a blanket as covering.

They lay in rows, huddled together in pairs for warmth. Mary was the last to lie down, after checking that all was as well as it could be. She slipped off her overcoat and lay down next to Yvonne, pulling the coat and a blanket over them both. She was barely asleep when the covering was ripped from her and she was confronted by a ginger-haired SS officer, a young blonde SS female who she had seen at the railway station and a party of Germans. 'Who gave you permission to take these blankets?'

The nearest Mary ever came to philosophising about her own extraordinary behaviour, her recklessness and repeated confrontation with German authority was when she recalled what happened next:

> The conditions in Ravensbrück were pretty dim for the general public, but you must remember that I got there in a British uniform [actually French] with a couple of rows of British decorations on, within my identity papers a title which, you know, the Germans love. They were lost at the very beginning, the political officer was completely lost from the very beginning. Of course, when I realised this, I threw my weight about a lot, as you can imagine. They used to call me the arrogant English woman, '*der arrogante Engländerin*'. Actually they were a lot of bastards. I was arrogant, and I considered we had a right to be arrogant, after all's said and done we were winning the war and if ever there were any discussions with them, I used to say right at the beginning, I'd say 'You've lost it, you know perfectly well you've lost the war.' And they knew they had too. It didn't stop them. They were bastards, to the weaker the people, the more beastly they were.[3]

Mary stared hard at the German officer. He was tall, red-haired and ugly-looking with a brutal face: this was Fritz Suhren, Kommandant of the camp. Suhren's house was the last house on the ridge, which she had passed earlier that day. From his front door, or even better, from the balcony of his bedroom, Suhren had an uninterrupted view over the camp including, in the middle distance, half-left from his bedroom window, its tall chimney.

Mary answered Suhren, 'I did.'

'What right did you have to take them from the tent?'

'What right do you have to allow women to sleep out in the open like this? The blankets were in the tent and I gave the order for them to take one each. I alone was responsible. These women have been sleeping in a cattle truck for over a fortnight.'

Astonished, Suhren stepped forward and felt the quality of Mary's uniform and turned to the blonde, who was Dorothea Binz, chief wardress, '*Diese ist schön*' ('This is beautiful'). And turning to Mary he ordered, 'You must put the blankets back at once.'

'Certainly not. We will put them back in the morning, but we need them for the night.'

There was a brief furore from the Germans which Suhren silenced. 'All right. You are responsible and if only a single one of them is not put back you will be punished.'

'Very well. But when the British take something they always hand it back. There are sixty blankets here and you will have sixty blankets in the morning.' With that Mary lay down, and covered herself and Yvonne again. Her arrogance had won them an undisturbed night's rest, and for this once Mary had inflicted a minor defeat on German officialdom.

Next morning Mary heard her name being called. Grabbing Yvonne, she pushed her way through a little knot of women towards an SS officer who, Yvonne recalled, had accompanied them all the way from Dijon. He told the two women that he would forward their request to be treated as prisoners of war or be transferred to an internment camp. Yvonne had already noted that there were other women in the camp in the uniform of the Soviet Army and remembered what she had been told in Dijon – that the Germans did not consider women as prisoners of war but as political prisoners.[4]

According to Mary the conversation followed the lines:

'Are you the Comtesse de Moncy?'[5]

'Yes.'

'So it's true. What on earth are you doing here in this camp?'

'You have a nerve to ask such a question.'

'But you are a *kriegsgefangene*.'

'Yes, and so too is this girl. She's WAAF.'

'But who on earth sent you here? I cannot keep you in this kind of camp.'

'That's perfectly alright. You just have to give permission and we'll walk straight out through the gate.'

'I'm afraid we can't quite do that. But I shall certainly take the necessary action to have you sent down to Lake Konstanz, where there is an internment camp.' The conversation ended with the SS officer writing out a note which he tore from his notebook and gave to Mary. The immediate effect was that Mary and Yvonne were separated from the others and taken to a block where they were given a meal of meat, potatoes and vegetables: it was their last for many months to come.

As anxious outsiders, they observed the camp routine:

SS and women guards moved about and the kitchen fatigue parties presented themselves. Then a whistle sounded the roll call. In rows of five, perfectly ordered, the column of prisoners marched by from the direction of the Lagerstrasse, or Camp Street. This was the muster, whose purpose in theory was to decide the day's work.

From the Punishment Block marched the ranks of the punished, compelled to sing German songs to cheerful airs, followed by ordinary prisoners in their striped dresses. After them … columns of wretched creatures in rags, many of them barefoot, with spades or picks on their shoulders. The sick, haggard and stumbling, returned to their blocks supporting each other … the women guards cracked their whips, blows rained and cries sounded from the laggards. Like Dante's chastised sinners, some were slow in entering Hell.[6]

The other women were marched off to the ghastly indignities of being stripped and deloused, a random, petty process which the Germans used to start the break-up of personality, even before the humiliating entry into camp life. This was a process that many found to be the most gruesome experience of all. They were stripped naked, given cursory medical examinations, which were nevertheless as intimate as they were salacious, and if they had hair lice or the examiner took exception to an individual her hair was shorn off. Jewellery, even wedding rings, was confiscated: it was all part of the German method of dehumanising their prisoners. Then they were told that their clothes and baggage would not be returned and instead they had to scramble among an odd assortment of clothes. One Breton woman wept bitterly when her head was shaved, and wept again when she realised that the Breton clothes she had worn all her life would not be returned to her.[7]

The women were ordered into a column five abreast and, to the barking of dogs and the cracking of whips, they were marched deeper into the camp proper. They had seen flowers at the entrance, but any favourable impression soon faded. Between the blocks on either side of the *lagerstrasse* there was only filth, the flowerbeds were bare, the windows of the blocks were broken and only some had been blocked with cardboard. Here and there women sat in the sun picking their clothes and each other's hair free of lice. Silence hung over the camp and one woman recalled that, in all her time at Ravensbrück, she never saw birds fly over the camp.

Mary and Yvonne were left alone for several hours and the next person to pay any attention to them was dressed like most of the women prisoners they had seen, but was sprightly, moved freely on her own and seemed to enjoy some authority. She wore a red armband, and her message was short, 'You are British and so am I. I have been told to take you to the showers and afterwards you will probably be sent to Konstanz.' Lowering her voice she added, 'If you have anything particularly precious, slip it in my pockets, as the Germans will take everything you have.'

The stranger was Julia Brichta, born in 1895, the same year as Mary Lindell, in Makó, a centre of Jewish culture in southern Hungary. Julia had worked in Britain after the First World War but when she applied in 1932 to renew her visa she was declared 'an undesirable sort of creature who should not be given a visa or allowed to return to the UK', and her name was placed on a blacklist – the reasons why are not known.[8] However, in July 1939 she slipped into Guernsey where she quickly came to the notice of the police.[9]

Employed as a cook, she refused to do any other work and went on strike by refusing to get out of bed. Her strike was broken by a spell in hospital, after which she took work as a maid, but when the Germans occupied Guernsey in 1940 she found new employment as a cook in a German billet. Next she was seen with a German sailor breaking into the White Gables Hotel from where property was reported stolen, then she began to trade on the black market in German rations, and later she underwent a marriage of convenience so that she could acquire British nationality.

Meanwhile the police, prompted by the Germans, had conducted several enquiries into her background. The enquires were sympathetic and concluded that she was a Protestant. Imprisoned and fined in January 1944 she then attempted to bribe the police with silverware belonging to the White Gables Hotel. She was denounced in letters to the German authorities on the island and on 5 May 1944 deported from Guernsey, to join a transport of 552 women who were deported from Paris on 13 May.[10]

Julia Brichta's version of the events, which she told to the *News of the World* in London after the Second World War, was that she had been:

> … caught by the Germans for sabotage in Guernsey and imprisoned there at first and then in many other prisons in France and Germany before being sent to Ravensbrück. I spoke several European languages and the staff of the prisons made use of me as an interpreter. At Ravensbrück, I was made a prison policewoman and given the number 39785 and a red armband that indicated my status … I was handed a heavy leather belt with instructions to beat the women prisoners. It was a hateful task, but in it I saw my only chance to help some of the condemned women.[11]

Julia's red armband denoted that she was a Kapo – one of the camp's functionaries recruited from amongst the prisoners themselves, notorious for their brutality on their fellow prisoners – and rewarded by the Germans with minor privileges, so long as they performed their duties to the satisfaction of the guards.

Julia Brichta's motivation in becoming a Kapo may only have been survival, but her role as she led Mary and Yvonne to the shower block was that of wicked fairy – even though, on this occasion, she did indeed take Mary's valuables from her, guard them and later return them while Mary and Yvonne were taken to the washhouse and ordered to strip. So began, on 4 September 1944, their formal induction into Ravensbrück, as prisoners Number 62940 and 62947.

NOT CALLED TO GLORY

For the moment, Mary was lost. The woman in charge of the showers had no sympathy for Mary and very little sympathy for anyone else. 'Get into the shower!'

'Whom do you think you're speaking to? I'm a British officer.'

'British officer, huh!'

'You have no authority over me. I have just been given orders that I'm to go to Lake Konstanz, where we will be interned with proper treatment.'

'You'll be lucky. Anyway we've got no officers here, this is the beginning of *égalité*. Everyone is equal.'

Mary held out the page torn from the Gestapo officer's notebook, her assurance that she was to be treated as a prisoner of war, which was seized and torn to shreds.

At that moment the doors of hell clanged shut behind Mary and Yvonne. They seemed to have avoided the degrading personal search for hair lice which resulted in the shaving of all hair, but as they came out of the shower they realised that their clothes and Mary's uniform and her suitcase were gone. Instead, they were given an assortment of clothes, so ill-suited that Mary and Yvonne could not help laughing at each other's appearance, and they were led away to quarantine block Number 26, where they found Gaby and Reine. Mary and Yvonne shared a top bunk.

They were kept in quarantine for two weeks. Gradually Mary's hopes fell as it dawned on her that the Germans did not consider captured women as prisoners of war. Then one day, while still in quarantine, Mary heard her name called out and found two Kapos, fellow prisoners who helped to run the camp for the Germans, waiting for her. 'Come along, quickly, you have to go to the *Revier*.'

'What on earth is the *Revier*?' asked Mary.

'The hospital. You are a nurse aren't you?'

'Yes, I was a nurse.'

'Well, come along, this is the best thing that could have happened to you.'

At the camp's sickbay, the *Revier*, Mary met one of the doctors, Percy Treite. Here is Mary's version of events:

> A few weeks after, I was put on to the *Revier* and worked from 12 to 14 hours per day in that hell, but was able there to observe Nazi culture close hand. The head doctor of the *Revier* Dr Trieste behaved very well to me, and did all he could for my compatriots (his mother is an Englishwoman), He kept me in the *Revier* in spite of efforts of other SS doctors and the SS Oberschwester.

Percy Treite had obviously heard of the altercation between Mary and Suhren on the first evening, and he had heard of the Red Cross uniform she was wearing when she arrived at the camp. He made a joke when he saw the ridiculous clothes that had been issued to Mary. 'You have been in hospitals, haven't you?'

Mary told him of her experience of the First World War. 'Very well. You will come and work here in the *Revier*. It's not entirely official yet but as soon as your nomination has gone through you will be transferred from Block 26 to Block 3, which is a clean block where all the prisoner doctors and nurses are living.'

Percival Karl 'Percy' Treite was a gynaecologist as well as an *Obersturmführer* (junior officer) in the *Schutzstaffel*, the dreaded SS. His father, Percival Adolf Treite, was born in England in 1884, and his grandmother, Louisa Foot, was born in England in 1852, and they and all his family were Salvationists. At the end of the nineteenth century General William Booth, founder and leader of the Salvation Army, had made a number of recruits among the large population of German immigrants in East London, and Percy's grandparents had met at a Salvation Army meeting in Whitechapel and married in 1881. The Salvation Army began its work in Germany in 1886, in the face of much opposition.[1] Nevertheless the movement grew, but when one of the English-born Salvationist leaders was expelled from Germany, Booth's solution was to send a German-born Salvationist from his converts amongst the German immigrant community. His choice fell upon Staff Captain Karl Treite who returned to Germany in 1888, taking with him his English wife and their English-born children. There in Berlin in 1911 his grandson, Percival Karl Treite, was born.

By the First World War, despite opposition to the 'foreign heretics', including attempts to disrupt its meetings with stink bombs, alarm clocks and physical abuse, the Salvation Army was bravely established in Germany under the leadership of Lieutenant Colonel Karl Treite. During the First World War more than 200 officers, organised into over sixty corps, did their noble work behind the lines in Germany just as their co-religionists did behind the American, British and French lines. Karl Treite was even allowed to leave wartime Germany to meet William Booth, who travelled from London to Stockholm for that purpose.[2]

In the immediate post-war period the Salvation Army was praised for its social work, which included field kitchens that doled out hot stew, but life became much more difficult for the Salvationists under the Nazis. The Hitler Youth, in particular, sabotaged all Christian youth work. A shortage of news-print was the excuse for banning *Der Kriegsrufe*, the German edition of *The War Cry*, and quasi-military ranks were objected to, collections were forbidden by law, dark enquiries were made about overseas funding of the Salvation Army and demands were made for its network of property to be handed over to the Nazi Party.[3] Eventually, while its religious activities were allowed, its social activities were ordered by Berlin to be handed over to municipal authorities.[4] Another religious minority, the Jehovah's Witnesses, were rounded up and sent wholesale into the concentration camps, but perhaps because of their good works the Salvationists, though harassed, were not arrested.

Raised in a family where his grandparents, parents, aunts and uncles wore uniform and carried military-style ranks, young Percy trained as a doctor. Seemingly he wanted to become the director of the Salvation Army's maternity hospital in Berlin. By 1933 it was impossible to continue his medical education without joining the Nazi Party and, thinking he would gain privileged access to additional medical training, Percy Treite made the tragic choice of uniform and became an *obersturmführer*, the lowest officer rank in the SS. The record shows that he joined the party on 7 October 1933 and that his membership number was 220796. Percy Treite's examination grades in 1936 were good enough to win him a place at the Charité Hospital, one of Berlin's leading hospitals.

Percy Treite worked at the women's clinic at the Charité without promotion within the SS, and he stayed out of the war until April 1943 when he was called up by the SS and sent to a hospital in Szczecin, Poland.[5] From there he was sent on a course in field medicine, after which he was returned to Poland, to an SS hospital in Prague, and then in the autumn of 1943 Treite was sent to the Sachsenhausen concentration camps, where staff for other camps were trained. Treite tried to do a deal: six months at Sachsenhausen in return for an appoint-ment to the front line, but the SS reneged on this. Instead, the SS considered sending Treite to Auschwitz or Mauthausen, but when it was realised that he was a gynaecologist, Treite was sent in September 1943 to the women's camp at Ravensbrück.

Meanwhile, Treite's family had dispersed. His brother, Sidney Bramwell Treite, was a lieutenant colonel in the Salvation Army in Switzerland, where his parents had also fled, and his father died – in the language of the Salvation Army 'was called to glory' – in 1943, and a sister, Lilli, had also taken refuge in Switzerland.

All this Mary would learn later. For now, she hurried back to Block 26 with her news. Mary had not yet experienced the worst of Ravensbrück, but the thought of living in a clean, uncrowded block was almost too good to bear. She was already thinking of others. The three British girls who she had met at Saarbrücken were not in Ravensbrück, but Yvonne, Gaby and Reine, with whom she had travelled from Dijon, were in the camp. Mary told Yvonne, 'I'm going to say that you are a nurse, and somehow I should be able to wangle you into the *Revier* also. They say the work is hard, literally from dawn to dusk, and the food's no better than here but if it's clean we'll have a better chance of survival.'

The response was disappointing. 'I don't know, Mary, they aren't going to make me work here, I think I'll hang on and see what happens. I could always come later. You see what it's like first.'[6]

There was no time to waste and Mary made her quick farewells and returned to the *Revier*. There she was given a choice of two dresses and chose one nearest in colour to her Red Cross uniform, and she found her way to Block 3. On the outside it was identical to the one she had left, but it was not so crowded. The floors were polished and each bed was made up with its own blanket, sheets and pillows. Of the hospital itself, Mary recalled, 'the many advantages were that the hospital was heated, had running water, hot and cold, had a bath and had a door on the lavatory, which was very precious.'

Her fellow occupants, she soon found out, were the prisoner doctors and the prisoner nurses who would work with her in the *Revier*. And for the first time in several weeks, she even had a bed to herself.

Mary Lindell's mother in the uniform of the Young Women's Christian Association in the First World War. Mary's mother was a member of the Trollope & Colls family, London developers, through which Mary inherited financial independence. (YTV)

A rare picture of Mary posing in her French Red Cross uniform, probably at Pau and possibly staged for a post-war camera crew. (Scott Goodall)

Mary Lindell as a nurse in the First World War, aged about 23, wearing her Russian and French medals. (Gabriela Girova)

Mary's First World War identity card, issued by the French Ministry of War, shows her as a nurse using the first name 'Ghita'. (Gabriela Girova)

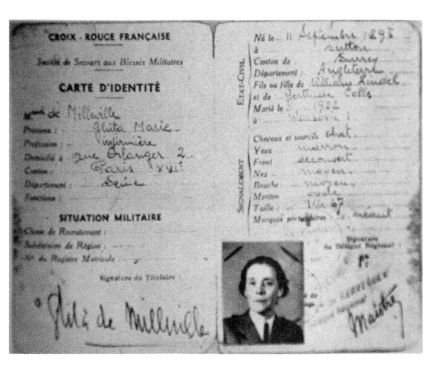

Mary's Second World War identity card shows her as 'Ghita de Milleville' after a marriage in Warsaw in 1922. (Gabriela Girova)

Mary poses with Michèlle Cambards beside a car in which they crossed the German-imposed demarcation line in 1940. (Scott Goodall)

Paul de Saugie, the Swiss agent who helped Mary to cross from Switzerland into France at least twice. (YTV)

De Saugie shows the camera the garden in Switzerland and the wall where Mary, dressed in her Red Cross uniform, let herself down on to the road leading to Annecy in France. (YTV)

lombier Pasquerard, the communist woodcutter who helped Col 'Blondie' Hasler and Marine Bill arks to escape after the Cockleshell Raid, compares notes with Mary Lindell outside Windsor Castle. uthor's collection)

Blondie Hasler (l), Mary Lindell and Bill Sparks (r) at a post-war reunion in 1961. (Ewen Southby-Tailyour)

Armand Blanchebarbe, Lorraine priest, who was born on 16 January 1901 in Lorry les Metz. He was expelled on 13 November 1940 and withdrawn to Foix. He organised an escape line across the Pyrenees with Irénée Cros and Mary Lindell. (YTV)

A scene from the Toque Blanche café in Ruffec staged for the cameras after the war. (Scott Goodall)

Fritz Suhren, whose fresh face and jaunty manner belie the countless deaths and the misery he supervised. (Author's collection)

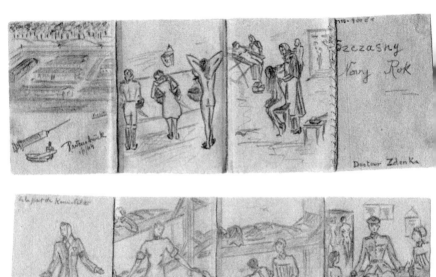

Drawing by Violette Lecoq of the *Revier* and of Percy Treite at work in the hospital block. (Brandenburg Memorials Foundation)

The Red Cross buses were initially painted in camouflage and then hurriedly redone in white by painters who worked through the night. (Nordiska museet)

The body of Eric Ringman, a Canadian and a newly released prisoner of war, was brought back under the Swedish flag. (Nordiska museet)

The train ferry, which had run throughout the war, arrives in Malmö from Copenhagen. (Nordiska museet)

A few fortunate women survived Ravensbrück with their babies. (Nordiska museet)

Mary Lindell (l) in a makeshift uniform is still very much 'the captain of the English' when her group of British and American women arrive at the decontamination tents. (Nordiska museet)

ere she ordered the women to strip and sets an example. (Nordiska useet)

Colonel Nadine Hwang in the uniform she adopted while in the camp … and after she had acquired more fashionable clothing. Karin Blomqvist wrote an account of the women's arrival at the New Museum in Malmö. (Malmöhuset)

Irene Krausz and her mother – Irene became the darling of the American and British women. The Swedish press labelled her 'Shirley Temple'. (Malmöhuset)

page from the guestbook that e women started at the New useum; the proximity of ious names indicates how osely the women were to ch other. (Malmöhuset)

Mary's group on the terrace of the New Museum, from l to r: 1. Unknown; 2. Rachel Krausz; 3. Ma
Lindell; 4. Edith Schimmel; 5. Mary O'Shaughnessy; 6. Magdalen Schimmel; 7. Renée Huyskens
aka Elizabeth Smith; 8. Irene Krausz; 9. Elsie Ragusin; 10. Unknown; 11. Yvonne Baseden; 12. Not
identified; 13.Rosetta Achmed. (Malmöhuset)

Maurice de Milleville talks to the camera post-war. (YTV)

ry's haul of medals on display. (YTV)

Mary in old age. (YTV)

Diagrammatic map of the division of France during the Second World War. (Peter Turner)

THE LIST OPENS

n the first few weeks after her move to the *Revier*, Mary's work was in the treatment room. She cleaned and dressed minor wounds, boils and carbuncles as best she could with the little equipment and materials available. She had time to see how the *Revier* and the camp worked.

There was a small number of German doctors who more or less held themselves aloof. Preliminary inspections of patients were carried out by prisoner nurses who, if necessary, referred new cases to prisoner doctors or to the German staff of the *Revier*. In accordance with German practice, the German doctors' diagnoses were conducted from a distance, the patients standing naked before them while they listened to the verbal reports of more junior staff. Generally a patient needed to have severe symptoms before admission to the *Revier*: only a temperature of 39 degrees was considered severe.

The matron, or *Oberschwester*, of the *Revier* was Elisabeth Marschall: later she would be found guilty of selecting which prisoners would be shipped to Auschwitz, selecting others for execution at Ravensbrück and helping to organise medical experiments.

Most women in the camp were severely weakened by the poor diet, hard work and the lack of rest. Epidemics of dysentery and typhus swept the camp. A major contributory factor that enervated the women was the roll call, or *Appel*, held twice daily. At 4 a.m. the women were roused from their sleep for a meal made of 'a dark liquid resembling coffee' and were issued a bread ration which had to last the day. They were made to stand to attention outside in all weathers while the Germans checked and rechecked the numbers on parade, compared to the number of dead bodies left in the blocks, and reconciled these numbers to their previous tally. After the day's work, the women were made again to parade while their numbers were checked and rechecked. *Appel* could take thirty minutes or several hours, and the punishment for being caught talking or moving was being beaten, sometimes to death, at the whim of one of the guards or of the Kapos. Sometimes the Kapos behaved more violently towards their own, their fellow prisoners, than did the SS guards themselves. Each woman on parade tried to keep still, not even to shiver in the early morning cold, and make no eye contact with a guard or even a Kapo.

As Mary had already found out, even the prisoner doctors and prisoner nurses in Block 3 had to parade and be counted, but because they were fewer in number and the conditions inside their hut were better, there were fewer miscounts and *Appel*, for them, was shorter.

Prisoners who were ill were brought to the *Revier* by their room leaders or block seniors, and that is how Mary Lindell began to understand that, amongst the thousands of women in the camp, she and Yvonne were not the only British. One of the block leaders was a British woman who had already been in Ravensbrück for nearly a year and a half. To the Germans she was prisoner Number 19322, Elizabeth Sheridan, but she went by other names: to the Swedes, when she eventually arrived in Malmö in 1945, she was a pianist, Ann Elisabeth Victoria Seymour de Beaufort, but when she gave evidence to the Hamburg War Crimes Tribunal in 1947, she told the court that she was born in Alexandria on 7 July 1917 to an English father. When arrested by the Germans she was living in Accolay in Burgundy. She gave her mother's address as Mme Seymour, 41 rue Michel Ange, Paris.[1] To her friends in the camp she was known as Ann.

Ann had arrived in Ravensbrück in April 1943, in the company of four other English women: Doreen Verani, born in Liverpool; Suzanne Dubois from London; Edith Certhoux from Dartford; and Rosina Fournier from Wandsworth. The ability to understand orders given in German and to translate them for other prisoners was an essential aid to avoiding casual beatings and for survival in the camp; speaking English, French, German and some Polish, Ann was soon promoted to be a room senior in Block 20. Only Ann Sheridan and Doreen Verani would live long enough to gain a place on Lindell's list.

Each barracks block was run by a female SS officer, the *Blockführerin* or *Blockleiter*, and by a number of trusted prisoners. The senior prisoner official was the block senior, or *Blockälteste*: this was the German title, but as the Poles gradually took over many of these positions the common name for them became the Polish term *Blockova*. The *Blockova* had two or more room seniors under her. Ann quickly became block senior in Block 27, under an SS *Blockführerin* called Rike.

Ann and her fellow prisoner officials had a difficult path to tread if they themselves were to survive. Although their authority derived from the Germans and they had to carry out camp policies and the will of its officers, they were able also to distribute favours and to make life easier for inmates. The block senior, aided by room seniors who she had helped to choose – one for each half of each block – had to wake inmates and take the first roll call at *Appel*. At roll call the status and whereabouts of all prisoners were accounted for, and this gave the block senior an opportunity to cover up for her friends – as, indeed, Ann would cover for another woman, her friend Mary O'Shaughnessy.

Block seniors also helped to choose camp runners, or *Lagerläuferinnen*, who ran messages round the camp and assisted in fetching and distributing the meagre food ration. The block senior and her coterie of minor officials enjoyed first place in the food queues, had their own rooms where they usually did not share bunks, lockers for their meagre possessions and wore green armbands which allowed them to go anywhere in the camp. An unsympathetic and unscrupulous block senior could terrorise the inmates of her block, beat them and, worse, denounce the inmates by writing a report to the camp administration which would lead to punishment, including formal beatings, incarceration and stoppage of rations.

The first block seniors were chosen from uneducated German criminals in the camp, and in the dog-eat-dog environment that developed the inmates suffered. Later the Poles and Communists took over these roles. A few block seniors rose to the occasion and displayed great leadership under difficult conditions. For example, a prisoner could be put on the sick list and the block senior could arrange for light duties, and the camp runners would be helped to carry news around the camp.

Ann Sheridan ran her block as fairly and as decently as she could, and was left to do so by *Blockführerin* Rike. But Rike was temperamental; she would usually be kind, but sometimes she would go wild and slap anyone who came within her range. However, since she left Ann to get on with running the block, Ann was unwilling, later, to testify against her as a war criminal.

Ann visited the *Revier* daily and in whispered instalments she told Mary what she knew of the camp. When she had arrived in the camp in the spring of 1943:

> We had a lovely batch of sadists as SS doctors, but they were all cashiered during the following summer and the hospital staff was changed at the end of August '43. The new doctors [this included Percy Treite] were mostly overworked, due to the overcrowding of the camp.[2]

In Ann's Block 27 there were mothers with their children; at one time as many as forty children aged between 2 and 13. Most block seniors made the children stand

Appel with their mothers, but Ann, after asking once for permission, took it as a matter of course that the children of her block would stay inside. She also tried to keep them out of sight whenever there was any danger of a selection – when the camp staff would chose prisoners for death – although in the end she could not prevent the children of her block being sent, she thought, to Bergen-Belsen.

In her block the children got a better diet and were given the thicker soup made for hospital patients and, when it was available, a ration of milk. Ann got these extra rations because the Pole in charge of the camp kitchen, 'Kazia', knew that they would reach the intended recipients. Sadly, Ann recalled, some other block seniors took the milk for themselves and even some mothers drank the milk intended for their children.

After Ann had been made to stand naked outside the *Revier* in order to have her throat examined, and on another occasion to see the camp dentist, she realised that the Kapos were being overzealous when they ordered prisoners on sick parade to strip bare. 'My own policy was to have everybody in line clothed, and to tell them to be ready to undress quick as hell should it be necessary to do so.' She also made sure that whenever a naked parade was ordered, the Kapos would clear the passageways and rooms where the women were to be examined so that any embarrassment was minimised.[3]

Newborn babies were kept in Block 11, but Ann did her best to ensure that their mothers could visit them and were at hand to feed their little children. She also ensured that, in her block, pregnant women and newly delivered mothers received double rations, again though her friendship with 'Kazia'. There were up to sixty pregnant women in Ann's block; they were fortunate to be there; in other blocks the block seniors kept the extra rations for themselves and their friends.

Mary learned other things about the camp, and the coloured triangles worn by the inmates were explained to her: black for the mainly German prisoners who the Nazis lumped together as asocial – lesbians, prostitutes, pacifists, Gypsies and the mentally ill; green for criminals; red for political prisoners, who included socialists, trade unionists, and Communists. If they were Jewesses, their badges were superimposed on a second, yellow triangle, point downwards, to make the star of David.

There were not many yellow stars because in 1942 all prisoners from the Jewish block had been put on a transport and had disappeared. However, the number of Jewesses was growing again, and according to Ann's friend, Hermine Salvini (an Austrian political prisoner who had been at Ravensbrück since 1940 and worked in the camp administration) by the end of 1944 the number of Jewish women exceeded 6,000. There were 1,600 Gypsies and 150–200 NN (*nacht und nebel*, or political) prisoners kept apart in Block 32. Amongst the 123,000 women who passed through the camp there 'were 20 or 22 British women and 2 American'.[4] (The designation '*nacht und nebel*', or 'night and fog', was a direct reference to Richard Wagner's *Rheingold*, originally applied to anyone in German-occupied territories accused of endangering German security, but by 1944 extended to include almost anyone who was taken into custody. It was meant to deter and intimidate oppressed people by denying the friends and families of the disappeared any knowledge of their whereabouts.)

The working day lasted until 5 or 7 p.m., with only thirty to forty minutes for lunch, which included the time needed to march back to camp. Lunch was a bowl of thin, watery soup made of cabbage or turnips and any bread kept from that morning's issue. Red Cross parcels, which might have helped feed the women and alleviate their agonies, were delivered to the administrative building where they were ransacked for the benefit of the SS guards. All medicines, vitamins, tonics and malts were stolen too. This pilfering explained to Mary, who was a heavy smoker, why she was tantalised by the smell of the guards smoking American cigarettes.

Punishments were commonplace and random. At the lowest level, a prisoner could be beaten for not understanding orders given in German. Head shaving was another punishment, not just for women with head lice, but also for women accused of having sexual relations with a foreigner – although eventually nearly all internees had their heads shaved to prevent the spread of lice. The camp guards, the female overseers and the Kapo were not supposed to harm prisoners, but in fact they beat anyone at will and for the slightest perceived offence. They boxed ears, slapped faces and pulled hair, and they struck prisoners with whips, sticks and belts, and when they fell to the ground they kicked them. Some of the female SS paraded with Alsatian dogs and dog bites were one of the commonest injuries to prisoners. No one, not from the German staff nor the Kapos, was reprimanded.

Formal punishments were issued after a report on a prisoner, and if an overseer took a dislike to a prisoner there was always the risk of a malicious report. The most common form of punishment was *Strafstehen* – being made to stand still for long periods, which varied from hours to days. Sometimes *Strafstehen* was awarded to whole blocks, usually by an extension to the evening *Appel* or over a weekend: no talking, no eating, no movement was allowed, and sometimes internees stood barefoot in the snow and ice. A minor punishment was the movement of a prisoner from a work detail involving light work to one requiring hard labour.

The distribution of mail was sporadic, but another punishment was the deprivation of the right to send and receive mail – or to buy from the canteen, where stamps, paper and pencils were occasionally available.

More serious punishments were ordered by the camp leadership:

> One could be punished for any trivial matter as everything was forbidden. Sometimes a button might have been torn off or the dress was not buttoned up properly or the bed was not made up properly, or because the internee, owing to her weakness caused by undernourishment, could not arrange to do the prescribed amount of work.

The punishment was twenty-five or fifty thrashings, or confinement to the punishment block and the stoppage of food.[5]

Ann had learned much of what she knew about the camp from two long-term inmates who had both found office work in the camp administration. One was Hermine Silvani, a Roman Catholic housewife from Vienna, and the other, Elisabeth Thury, an Austrian newspaper editor. Eventually Mary would make her own impression on Thury, who recalled after the war, 'There were 16–20 English women in the camp, amongst them a woman holding officer's rank called Mary, who was working in the hospital and acted as spokeswoman for her fellow sufferers.'[6]

The death rate in the camp had been four to eight per month in 1940–41, but by late 1944 this was climbing to towards that many per day. The causes of death were malnutrition, tuberculosis, typhus, diarrhoea, gassing and injection.[7]

Ann also told Mary about the working parties that were made up daily: the older women knitted pullovers, vests and socks for issue to the *Wehrmacht* soldiery; the younger women worked at the Siemens factory next door to the camp and the tailor's workshop at the eastern end of the camp; and daily working parties were marched in and out of the camp to perform hard labour in the forests, carry out road building, reclamation and coal shovelling and to help with the potato harvest.

The working parties varied from a few prisoners, who local farmers came to fetch for work in the fields or who went to small handicraft works and manufactories in Fürstenberg, to several hundreds, who disappeared for weeks at a time and sometimes did not return. When they did come back to Ravensbrück they told of a network of sub camps – a score around Fürstenberg and tens more in locations throughout Germany.[8]

It was a complex, bureaucratic system and keeping track of the labour and personnel needs of the empire of slaves required numerous office workers.

In Teutonic style, the camp administration tried to keep track of the movements of prisoners between camp and sub camp. Elisabeth Thury and Hermine Silvani, who both became clerks in the camp administration, did their best to keep Ann, and thus Mary, informed.

Mary also made her own friends inside the camp. The *Revier* was well equipped but poorly stocked; every kind of medicine was scarce and a precious item to be traded on the camp's black market for food or favours. When a woman came to the *Revier* begging for aspirin she found Mary with a stock of stolen medicine, which Mary administered in return for a promise. This was Mickie Poirier, from Alsace, who worked in the office of Hans Pflaum, one of the more brutal Germans at Ravensbrück and the director of labour. Mickie told Mary, 'I work in Pflaum's office. If you ever need help don't forget to ask for me.'[9]

Another friend was Nadine Hwang,[10] a 40-year-old Sino-Belgian who had arrived on a transport from Paris in May, six months before Mary. Nadine was exotic because she was Eurasian, a lesbian and a colonel in the Chinese Air Force. Sometime in 1934 Nadine had met the American heiress Natalie Clifford Barney, a doyenne of the Parisian Left Bank literary circle, and became her part-time secretary, chauffeuse and lover.[11]

Then in her thirties with cropped hair and wearing a black-satin costume or a military uniform, Nadine was strikingly handsome, and one homosexual salon guest flirted outrageously with her, only to be disappointed when he discovered that she was a woman. Barney wrote about the precise yet sensuous way in which Nadine moved, or even ate an orange, and in Nadine's coal-black eyes, Barney 'learned to read every nuance of joy or distress'. She entertained Barney's guests with a wild sword dance by firelight when she would slice the air over the guests' heads.[12]

In the summer of 1940 Barney fled the German invasion of Paris to another lover in Italy, from where she shuffled money between bank accounts in England, Switzerland, the USA and France, sending large sums of money to girlfriends who had stayed behind in occupied France, including to Nadine. Quite when Nadine was arrested by the Germans, and whether it was for being asocial, an enemy alien, or non-Aryan, is not clear, but she was among the 515 Frenchwomen and thirty-seven other nationalities deported from Paris on 13 May 1944, including Julia Brichta, Mary O'Shaughnessy, Marie-Germaine Tonna-Barthet (married to a Maltese) and Sylvia Rousselin from Mosley, Lancashire, who would all later appear on Mary Lindell's list.

Curiously, although Nadine stood a head taller than most women in Ravensbrück and her Asian appearance was distinctive, there is no reference to Nadine in any of the literature about the camp. What role Nadine played in the camp, where she worked, what coloured triangle she wore to indicate her status – none of these things are known about her, but clearly she was able to move freely around the camp and soon she became Mary's messenger.

In her turn Nadine made friends with English-born Rachel Krausz. Rachel had married a Hungarian-born Jew who was living in Holland, and when the family were arrested by Dutch Nazis, Rachel, her son and daughter, Irene, had been interned in Ravensbrück, where they had been since February 1943. Little blonde Irene – she spent her eighth and ninth birthdays in the camp – became something of a favourite in the camp and Rachel, fearing that she might be kidnapped and brought up as a Nazi, protected Irene by taking her everywhere with her and hiding her by day under her worktable in the Siemens factory.

The Krausz family were listed at Ravensbrück as Hungarians, but many months later when Nadine learned that Mary was making up a list of the British women at Ravensbrück, she would arrange for Rachel to meet Mary, who told her, 'Now your name's on my list and let's hope we're going to be freed and sent to Sweden.'[13]

Mary also learned from Ann Sheridan about the *Transportuntersuchung* (special inspections) that she had to attend, when women were selected for transport to other labour camps. Only the healthier women were sent to the sub camps, and for these inspections the women paraded naked, their hands and feet were inspected and their bodies examined – at a distance – for scabs, itches or any sign of infectious disease.

Mary asked what had happened to the British women who she had met with Yvonne in Saarbrücken. Ann did not know, but several large parties had arrived from the Paris region in late August when, Ann told her, at the end of their fortnight in quarantine and only two days after Mary had arrived in the camp, a large party of them had been sent to Torgau, south of Berlin. She had heard on the grapevine that amongst them were American and British women.

PARIS – THE FEAST OF THE ASSUMPTION

Mary discovered that the month before in Paris, the Feast of the Assumption had been celebrated by the Germans by herding some 2,000 men and women into cattle trucks destined for Germany. All had been imprisoned at Romainville in the eastern outskirts of Paris, where the Germans had used Fort de Romainville as a prison and transit camp since 1940. Among them were several American and British women who arrived at Ravensbrück on 21 August. Slowly Mary pieced together their story from scraps of information that she had learned then and from what she learned after the war.

The American women were Virginia D'Albert-Lake, Toquette Jackson and Lucienne Dixon, who had all been active in the Resistance in France.[1] Another American by birth was Sadie Loewenstein-Zdrojewski, the New York-born wife of Daniel Zdrojewski, who was chief of a Polish resistance organisation called Struggle for Independence. Sadie also had a code name in the Resistance, 'Lilian Lefèvre'. In the same transport were two agents of SOE: Yvonne Rudellat and Eileen, or Didi, Nearne, who had both clung on to their false identities of Jacqueline Gauthier and Jacqueline Duterte.[2] One other was Jeanine Alex Dilley, who gave her next of kin as Walter Dilley of Catford in south London and who may have been the 'Janette' mentioned in Virginia D'Albert-Lake's memoirs.[3] The names of most of them, but not all, would appear on Lindell's list.

Also among them were three women who had worked on the Marie-Claire escape line: Ginette Favre, who had been arrested with Mary, and Pauline Barré de Saint-Venant and Nicole Lebon who had afterwards run the Marie-Odile escape line. There were also the sisters Maisie and Isabelle Renault, who for much of the war had run the secretariat for the French *réseau*, *Confrérie Notre-Dame* (CND), coding messages and prioritising them for transmission to London by sea, air and wireless.

One of the Americans was Lucienne Dixon. Although born in New York, she had been brought up in Paris by her grandmother, and in the First World War she had worked for the French Red Cross. Lucienne returned to the USA in 1918 as a nurse escorting wounded American soldiers, and she had married an American mining engineer.[4] She maintained strong family ties in France and between the wars she crossed the Atlantic several times, once on her honeymoon, once to show off her newborn baby, Frank, and again in 1931 when Frank was 6 years old. Frank was named after his uncle, Frank M. Dixon, the Governor of Alabama from 1939 to 1943. In the new world war Lucienne joined the *Section Sanitaire Automobile* (SSA), and the spring of 1940 found her driving an ambulance among the refugees and defeated British and French troops after the evacuation at Dunkirk. It is possible that during this period Lucienne may have met Mary Lindell.

Like Mary, Lucienne was dismayed by the German invasion of Paris, but instead of joining the general exodus of Americans from war-torn Europe after the fall of France, she joined the *Organisation Civile et Militaire*, or OCM, an arm of the French Resistance, which sprang up in the occupied zone to oppose the invader.[5] The OCM was penetrated by the Germans in late 1941 and its leaders and many members were arrested, but Lucienne avoided arrest and joined the remarkable Renault sisters and their brother, Gilbert, in the CND, helping to code and decode messages and to courier them across Paris.

Lucienne was arrested in April 1942 when she was held incommunicado for five or six weeks by the *Feldgendarmerie*, but she gave nothing away and was released for lack of evidence. She was arrested again in October 1942, this time by the Gestapo, but again gave nothing away and was set free in January 1943.

When her son Frank reached 18 he was interned at Compiégne by the Germans: at first his mother visited him with his younger sister, Françoise, but when his French grandmother came instead, Frank realised that his mother had been arrested for a third time.[6] The CND had been betrayed. Lucienne had had the opportunity to flee, but was determined to stay in France while Frank was there, so Françoise was put into the care of family friends while Lucienne passed a warning about the arrests to London, and, inevitably, a few days later in December 1943 she too was arrested. It was third time unlucky:[7]

> I was taken to rue des Saussaies [this was the Gestapo interrogation centre where she calmly prepared for that worst of all tortures, waterboarding which she had heard rumours of]. I feared the ordeal of the bathtub and I trained myself often at my house by putting my head under water. I wasn't bullied.

I did hear someone being put to torture of that kind. It wasn't very reassuring and it was naturally meant to demoralize me.

But once more the brave Lucienne had nothing to say to her captors: after two short spells in cells at Fresnes and Compiégne, she was sent to Romainville. There was no further interrogation, but there was no trial and this time, no release. At Romainville, however, she found her friend Toquette Jackson, who was also married to an American. They had met while working for the Red Cross in the First World War and afterwards when Toquette was a nurse at the American Hospital in Paris. There Toquette (born on 3 August 1889 in Colombier, Switzerland), whose full name was Charlotte Barrelet de Ricou, had met and married Sumner Waldron Jackson, known as Jack, who had come to Paris with the US Army in the First World War. Jack had been a volunteer in the Harvard Surgical Unit at British General Hospital No 22 in northern France, until the USA entered the war and he was recruited into the US Army Medical Corps.[8]

Toquette's widowed mother lived in a large house on the lake at Enghien, north of Paris, and to make ends meet she took in foreign students who were learning French (one of whom was the future Count Stig Thott, from Skabersjö in southern Sweden). They had a son Phillip, known as Pete, who was born in 1928, and Jack rose through the ranks of the American Hospital, and by 1940 was chief surgeon. The Jacksons became mainstays of respectable American society in Paris.

When the Germans arrived, Sumner became involved in helping British servicemen to escape from occupied France. One of the first of these was Private J.F. Baron of the 1st Battalion Black Watch. Baron had been wounded and captured at Saint-Valery-en-Caux with the remnants of the 51st Highland Division on the morning of 12 June 1940. He escaped and made his way to the American Hospital in Paris, which he reached on 29 June, and where the doctor on duty ordered a hot bath and bed. Baron was a gardener by profession and he stayed for six weeks, doing odd jobs around the hospital, until on the night of 5–6 August he heard that the Germans were going to conduct a census of all foreigners in Paris. The doctors and nurses gave him some money and he was taken by ambulance 200km to Montargis, from where he walked to Vierzon, on the line of demarcation. A café owner showed Baron out of the back door, which happened to open out into unoccupied France.[9]

By 5 December Baron, who became the first documented case of an evader being helped by the people of the American Hospital, was back in England.

For the next two years Jack Sumner brazenly forged patients' records to ensure that a steady stream of downed aviators evaded capture.

Meanwhile, Toquette started her resistance to the German occupation by joining the Goélette *réseau*, which gathered intelligence for the Free French. Soon the Jacksons' apartment at 11 avenue Foch, at the opposite end of the broad boulevard to the Gestapo headquarters, became a post office, a bank and a safe house for the Resistance. One of the covert visitors was Michel Hollard, whose Agir *réseau* gathered intelligence on German rocket-launching sites in northern France. Hollard made frequent journeys by train from Paris to the Jura, crossing the mountains into Switzerland, sometimes at night and in the snow, to give his drawings to the British military attaché in Bern. Post-war, Pete Jackson was proud that these drawings had passed through his parents' home on the avenue Foch.[10] When Pete returned from a holiday in St Nazaire with photographs of the effects of British bombing on the harbour and port facilities, the photographs were given over dinner at 11 avenue Foch to Hollard, who also smuggled these to Switzerland.[11]

In May 1944 the Jackson family were arrested: Jack and Pete were sent to the notorious Neuengamme Concentration Camp and Toquette was sent to Romainville. At Romainville, Toquette found Lucienne Dixon and met a third American, Virginia D'Albert-Lake.

Virginia, from Dayton, Ohio, had been travelling in France when she met and fell in love with Philippe D'Albert-Lake, the son of a French father and an English mother, and they married in 1937. After the fall of France, Philippe repeatedly urged Virginia to flee to the USA, but she refused and instead the couple were drawn into helping evaders.[12] Philippe and Virginia helped more than sixty aviators along the escape lines, until on 12 June 1944 Virginia, who was escorting some American aviators to safety in the forest of Fréteval, was stopped and arrested by a French-speaking German officer who recognised her American accent. Although she was assured that as a belligerent she would be treated as 'a woman and a patriot', she too was sent to Romainville, where she arrived on 1 August.[13]

With the Allies only 40km from Paris, Raoul Nordling, the Swedish Consul General in Paris, was trying desperately to obtain their release as well as that of Jewish prisoners held at Drancy, through his contacts with the German commander of the city, General Dietrich von Choltitz.[14]

Raoul Nordling was a Swedish businessman and diplomat, whose father, Gustav, had settled in Paris in the 1870s. He was born and went to school in France, and although Swedish by nationality, Nordling described himself as a citizen of Paris; he spoke French better than Swedish – at least until he had been to Sweden to complete his military service. He would be remembered for his part in persuading von Choltitz not to carry out Hitler's orders to destroy Paris.

By mid August the hopes of the women at Romainville were high. They could hear the distant sounds of artillery from the advancing Allied armies who had reached Rambouillet, and nobody believed that the Germans would have time to move their prisoners before the Allies came. The women had been promised a Mass for the Feast of the Assumption, but on 15 August they were woken to cries in German and broken French, '*Nicht Messe, nicht Messe! Morgen. Alles transport Deutschland. Tous mourir. Tous mourir.*'[15]

The Germans were busy taking away as much loot as they could carry and, in a monstrous act of cynicism, this included their prisoners. Instead of going to Mass the women at Romainville were ordered to pack and carry their baggage into the courtyard where, realising that they were about to be transported, the women cried to those in the cells above to tell the Resistance. In the courtyard they were pushed into alphabetical groups, but when an air raid interrupted this process, they were herded into tunnels dug into the bund around the fort.

The women hoped that the raid had interrupted their transport, but at about 4 p.m. they heard the grind of Paris city buses as they came down the incline to stop by the tunnels. The SS crammed them into the buses so tightly that they could hardly breath and the buses could not climb the ramp, so farcically they were made to get out again and walk beside the buses until they could reach the top. While the SS pushed and shoved, friends linked arms with friends so they would not be separated.

Boarding a bus for the second time, Virginia D'Albert-Lake struggled to be beside the driver of her bus: she had a fistful of messages to give him. He was on her left and an armed SS guarding the open door was on her right. Virginia pleaded with her eyes until the driver nodded, and she slipped her messages and a bundle of francs into his hand. In a low voice he whispered, 'This job make me sick, All day long since early morning I've been driving prisoners form Fresnes and Cherche-Midi to the station at Pantin.'

'Then all the prisoners are being evacuated?'

'*Oui.*'

'And the Allies? Where are they? Are they advancing?'

'Sure, they're doing fine, they're at Rambouillet!'

Virginia's message to her husband Philippe read:

The entire prison is being evacuated to an unknown destination. Thank you for the parcel which arrived yesterday. It was a lovely one and brought me great pleasure. My fifteen days here passed very agreeably. It's very sad to be obliged to leave when others are so near, But what can we do? The morale is high and I'm in good health. We are three hundred women leaving the prison. My love to all, especially to my darling, See you soon! Virginia.

It would be the last time for many months that she would be able to say she was in good health. Months later she would be pleased to share a piece of tendon that she found in the bottom of bowl of watery soup.

Others smuggled messages to the bus drivers – some were words of farewell, others were pleas for rescue.[16] Even while they were on their way to Pantin, Nordling was at the German headquarters in the Hôtel le Meurice in talks with von Choltitz. The long line of overladen green buses wound in single file through the streets of Paris, passing pavements crowded with holidaying Parisians who stared back at the women who pressed their faces to the windows. The holiday-makers knew what was happening; they pitied the women but they did nothing.

Most of the railway stations of Paris had been destroyed by bombing but the small, suburban station of Pantin, normally only a goods yard, was still untouched and jammed with rolling stock, including long lines of cattle trucks. From every truck as far as Virginia could see, from each crack in the door or tiny ventilation window, she could see anxious faces. The trucks, left over from the First World War, had stencilled on their sides, '40 men or 8 horses'.[17] On that hot August day, 1,654 men and 542 women were crammed eighty and ninety to a truck. Among them were 168 Allied airmen who had been shot down and arrested; the Germans were determined to treat them as criminals rather than as prisoners of war.[18]

The best place in the truck was under a ventilation window or near the door, but the door was where the *tinette* had been placed – a 10lb jam tin which was their only toilet. The women at the ends of the truck, rather than fall and stumble over the others, urinated in smaller cans and emptied them out of the ventilation windows, to the annoyance of the women who were defending their places there. Tired, sick and nervous in the hot August weather, in a railway wagon which soon began to stink and which lacked light and a through draught, the journey was to become a nightmare for the women.

The train did not depart until after dark on that summer's evening, and because Allied bombing had so disrupted the railway network, it travelled slowly eastwards towards Germany. Before the doors were finally slid shut and locked, a young Red Cross worker gave them drinking water and an encouraging message, 'Don't worry, you'll never get to Germany. It's impossible: you'll be liberated before then.'

All the while they were in France, Virginia and her fellow passengers were full of hope. By morning they had only reached Lagny-sur-Marne, less than 40km from the centre of Paris. East of Meaux, an Allied air raid brought the train to a halt in a tunnel, where it stuck for several hours. In the heat and darkness of the tunnel, in a truck ventilated only by four high, narrow windows, the women suffered. All Virginia heard was the tramp of guards' feet on the gravel outside, their guttural calls to each other and the echo from the walls of the tunnel as people called out, 'Water! Water! Give us air! Give us air!'

When, after three and a half hours, the train backed out of the tunnel, the return of light and air was greeted with joy and a return of courage. Everyone was made to disembark and now Didi Nearne made the first of her many escape attempts.

Beyond the station was a field bordered by trees and although her legs felt stiff from having been standing for so long, Didi thought that she might reach the trees if she ran fast enough. However, a guard easily ran her down. He grabbed her arm and hauled her back to her group of frightened women, threatening that he would shoot without warning if any of them attempted something similar.[19] One woman, also an agent of SOE, Alix d'Unienville, did manage to hide during a melee around the drinking fountain in Méry-sur-Marne,[20] but the other prisoners were beaten into a column of twos and marched off across a road bridge over the Marne.[21] In the next village, another woman, Nicole de Witasse, attempted to escape by hiding under a hay wagon, but she was hauled out and horribly beaten about the head by one of the female SS guards.[22]

At last, after a march of about 8km, they emerged onto the railway line opposite a broken bridge where another train waited for them. So too were the Red Cross, who provided a meal of boiled potatoes and milk. The train remained stationary for two or three hours while the prisoners were allowed to sit on the embankment, and it was only when climbing into her truck that Virginia recognised someone she knew among the male prisoners. It was an English airman, Wilfred Marshal, who only a few weeks before she had helped to escape and who she had last heard of on the Franco–Spanish border.[23]

On 17 August the train reached Bar-le-Duc. So many women were ill that one truck was converted to a hospital, staffed by two women prisoners, a doctor and a nurse. Its only facility was a thicker layer of straw than the other trucks. The same day Raoul Nordling, after protracted negotiations, reached a formal agreement with the Germans in Paris that all prisoners, including deportees, were placed under his protection.

Apart from Nordling's noble efforts and the protests of a few individual Frenchmen, it is difficult to see why no greater efforts were made to stop this transport. It had taken all of one day to assemble and fill the train while it stood at Pantin, while the convoys of buses were driven by Frenchmen through the streets of Paris, and while the cries of the women went unheeded. The train travelled slowly enough across France, and the Resistance was well aware of its movement. They were too busy fighting among themselves about who was going to rule Paris after the Germans had gone. The Allies too were – or should have been – deeply concerned about this transport, not just for the large number of Resistance fighters who were on board but also for the sake of the airmen who were being deported.

When the train reached Fürstenberg (the station for Ravensbrück, 80km north of Berlin) on 21 August, the women disembarked, gasping for fresh air. While stretching their limbs they had time to admire the pretty, well-tended cottages by the lakeside. Within eight months one in four of them would die under the most miserable conditions in the coming harsh winter from malnutrition, forced labour, beatings and gassing.[24]

TORGAU

B y September 1944 Ravensbrück, perhaps designed for 15,000 prisoners, held more than double that number, with more transports arriving nearly every day. The Germans were being forced to retreat in the east and the west, but were not giving up their prisoners easily. As the prisons of Europe were emptied and their miserable inmates were shipped into Germany, camps like Ravensbrück became more and more crowded.

The large tent where Mary Lindell had commandeered blankets for the women on her first night at Ravensbrück, and which had been erected as temporary accommodation, now became permanent accommodation where some of the most horrible deaths would occur from neglect.

While Mary and Yvonne were still on their way to Ravensbrück, the newcomers on the Assumption Day transport were held in quarantine in a single block. It was crowded with rows of three-tiered bunks, separated by narrow alleys. The bunks were barely 3ft wide and two bunks were shared between every five women. Friends who had worked together in the Resistance formed little groups, whose camaraderie in the coming weeks and months would make an essential difference to their prospects for survival. They learned to co-operate even while crowding round for their midday soup, which they drank while standing outside in the sun. At first no one asked what the dust was that filtered down from the smoke, which hung over the camp on still days.

Then, on a September day, word spread among the women who had come from Romainville that there would be a selection for an *Aussenkommando* (working party) at one of the sub camps which was supplied with slave labour from Ravensbrück. It seemed to the American, British and French women that nothing could be worse than staying at Ravensbrück and they were keen to be selected.

All were ordered to parade outside the *Revier* for the *Transportuntersuchung*, the petty, ritual humiliation that routinely and mindlessly accompanied every change in fortune and location, even, as they were yet to learn, the gas chambers. Ordered to undress and leave their clothes on the damp ground, they were left to wait naked until they were called forward, when nurses examined the women's hands and teeth while doctors looked on from a short distance. Next morning those who had been selected were sent once more to the showers, robbed of their clothing and even the meanest possession (which they had succeeded in bargaining against their meagre bread rations), and issued with other clothing, but no coats or jackets to keep them warm against the coming autumn.

Just two days after Mary arrived at Ravensbrück, on Wednesday, 6 September, the three agents who she had met at Saarbrücken and women from the Assumption Day transport from Paris left from Fürstenberg for a labour camp at Torgau, 160km to the south of Berlin, travelling in the depressingly familiar cattle trucks, crowded fifty or more to a truck. Torgau was a prison town, known as Stalag IV-D, where French prisoners of war were housed in old factory buildings near the railway station. Virginia d 'Albert-Lake recalled:

> The town seemed to harbour hundreds of French prisoners of war. They were on the streets; they hung out of windows; they stood in barbed wire confines. We called out to them as we marched along … We were happy to see them … We learned that the Allied armies had crossed the frontier in to Germany! We remarked on the good state of health of the men and their gaiety. We were happier than ever to have left Ravensbrück![1]

They were marched for thirty minutes to a camp in the woods, where the blocks were new, and even though the bunks were in three tiers, the palliasses were fresh, the floor was made of concrete not mud, there were steam pipes by which to keep warm and everything was clean. They were called to an *Appel*, where a German officer addressed them in good French:

> I wasn't expecting you today. In fact I counted on only half your number, and was expecting Polish women, not French. However we will make the best of it. You may lack sufficient food this evening, but from tomorrow on, you will have what you need. After the roll call, blankets will be distributed and you will begin work on Monday morning. The morning *Appel* will be held at 6:00. You will be awakened at 5:30.[2]

This was a whole two hours later than the *Appel* at Ravensbrück.

That evening it seemed to the American and British women that they might be treated as human beings: they were given two clean woollen blankets, sauerkraut, a piece of sausage and fresh bread – not the black sawdust that they had had at Ravensbrück. They even had a bunk each.

Next morning, the German Kommandant had even allowed them to attend *Appel* in the chill of early morning with blankets draped over their shoulders. Though they had no means of knowing it, life at Torgau was easier than at other places. The drawback was that they were in a munitions factory and there was a brief attempted revolt among the Frenchwomen, who argued amongst themselves for and against assembling ammunition that might be used against their own people.

The women, among them Pauline Barré de Saint-Venant, took a vote that they were belligerents and they proposed a bill of rights under which not even the Nazis had the right to expect them to work in the factory. But the revolt ended when the Kommandant's patience ran out, 'Of course it can be arranged. Those of you who refuse to work in the munitions factory will simply be sent back to Ravensbrück.'

The Kommandant divided the women into three groups: those who were willing to work in the factory by the front gate, those who wanted to work in the camp kitchen on the right, and those who were willing to do the camp housekeeping by the back gate. He added a significant rider, 'English and American women stay together!'

Virginia D'Albert Lake recalled:

> The Anglo-Americans, of whom there were seven, were relegated to the kitchen work. We prepared vegetables. Eleven and half hours a day we peeled potatoes. Our fingers, hands and arms ached, and then became numb with fatigue. But I won't complain about the job, because it had its advantages. We were permitted while working to eat all the raw vegetables we wanted. We were forbidden to carry any back to the camp, but we did it all the same, hiding as many as we could in our clothes to give to the factory girls, who needed vitamins even more than we.[3]

From early in the morning the American and British women sat on crates in a long, narrow cellar built half underground and lit by electric light, but once the sun had chased away the dew and damp, they dragged their crates and vegetable baskets into the fresh air where they were able to see and be seen by the French prisoners of war and to call out to the men. Supervision was light:

the female SS guard was 'not unkind' and, if satisfied with their progress, the women were allowed to roast potatoes in a fire. However, the infirmary was always crowded and the first death occurred at the end of September, and the second a day later.[4]

Then, in the seemingly random way in which working parties were shipped to and fro, rumour spread that the working parties at Torgau were to be split up. Virginia wrote:

> This breaking up of our group was painful. We had left Paris together and we had been together ever since. Already a strong attachment, born of the same ideals, the same suffering, the same hopes, had made us one. Small differences could not ruffle its grandeur. We wanted to stay together.

Many of the Frenchwomen working in the munitions factory were moved to another site, and this included one other Englishwoman, Eileen 'Didi' Nearne. Didi and her siblings had been brought up in France and, like her older brother and an older sister, was recruited into SOE and she landed in France on the night of 2–3 March 1944 to work as wireless operator for the Wizard network.[5] Arrested in July and subjected to torture by waterboarding, Didi never gave away her secrets.[6]

Didi was in the ill-fated transport on the Feast of the Assumption, 15 August 1944, that Raoul Nordling had tried to halt. At Ravensbrück in early September she and Yvonne Baseden, who she had met under training in England, recognised each other but maintained their French personae and not their British SOE identities. At Torgau, while the other American and British women worked in the kitchens, Didi worked in the underground ammunition factory. Nevertheless, she also recognised Denise Bloch (they had flown from Tangmere in Sussex to France by Lysander on the same night), Lilian Rolfe and Violette Szabó. When Didi met Violette she found her 'in good health and fine spirits and planning to escape'.

While Didi had explained her quandary, Violette was horrified to hear about Didi's torture in Paris, and she urged Didi to admit that she was British. After all, Violette told her, when she had admitted to the Germans she was English she had not been mistreated, and she was sure this was because they feared reprisals once the war was over. Didi refused to drop her disguise, but she did agree that if there was any possibility of escape she would join the others.

However, a part-formed escape plan failed at its first test. Somehow Violette obtained a key for one of the gates. Didi was all for going immediately, but

Violette wanted more time to plan what they would do once outside the camp walls, and while the women were discussing this they were overheard and betrayed. Warned of this treachery, Violette threw the key away before a search could be mounted by the guards, with all its possible consequences if the key was to be found. Then, on 3 October, Didi went to Abteroda with a party of Frenchwomen who had acquired skills in the ammunition factory, and when Abteroda was evacuated, Didi and her French companions were taken to a work camp at Markkleeberg in the suburbs of Leipzig, where they were put to work on finishing parts for Junkers aircraft.[7]

There was yet another SOE agent at Torgau who remained under her pseudonym. Yvonne Rudellat, born in 1897, was one of the first and oldest of the female agents to land in France.[8] She also proved to be one of the most successful SOE agents during the war, who would be commended for her outstanding courage and devotion to duty. She worked for several circuits and travelled widely, sometimes passing through German checkpoints while carrying explosives hidden in the basket on the handlebars of her bike. Her work was as a courier, but she also reconnoitred landing zones and received parachutists from England.[9]

However, in June 1943 she ran out of luck and, while with Pierre Culioli and escorting two recently landed Canadian agents, she was shot and severely wounded by pursuing Germans.[10] Yvonne too was in the transport that left Paris on the Feast of the Assumption. Yvonne was sent to Torgau, where she was recognised by Didi Nearne, but after three weeks there she was sent back to Ravensbrück as unfit for work. There she was placed in Block 17, the block for NN prisoners, and she was given light duties like cleaning and knitting, but she also received a pink card – which would become a sentence of death.

Little is known of Yvonne's last few months. Renée Rosier[11] was with her when they were transported from Ravensbrück on 28 February to Bergen-Belsen, where they arrived on 2 March. They were together in Block 19. Yvonne was 'not in bad health, suffered occasionally from loss of memory, but she remained in good morale and she looked neither particularly drawn or aged'. However, Yvonne soon contracted typhus and dysentery and was transferred to Block 48.

The British liberated Bergen-Belsen on 15 April, when they found thousands of people dying among the unburied bodies. There were so many sick at Bergen-Belsen and conditions were so chaotic that some 20,000 people died there after the liberation and were buried in a mass grave. Yvonne had the opportunity to say that she was a British agent, and the last time Renée Rosier saw Yvonne alive was on 22 April. When a new roll call of the survivors was taken on 27 April 1945, Yvonne's name, Jacqueline Gauthier, was not there.

Meanwhile, Virginia and the other American and British women at Torgau were not needed once the harvest was over. There was one last orgy on the Red Cross parcels that had been given to the French prisoners of war and hoarded in the German Kommandant's office. The women were left to their own methods to divide up the contents and did so, organising themselves into groups of ten and appointing one representative from each group to take turns in distributing luxuries that they had not seen for months.

Almost all of the contents had come from the USA. There were familiar names and brands which had not been seen in war-torn France since 1940: Klim milk, Kraft cheese, Sun Maid raisins, Jack Frost sugar and more. Each woman received at least quarter of a chocolate bar, a dozen crackers and a handful each of raisins and sugar cubes. They were not to know that this was the most food they would see for many a month, through the bitter winter and into the spring of 1945.

On 6 October the Americans and British were searched, and they helped to carry the sick into cattle trucks lined with fresh straw. The train rolled away to Ravensbrück, where their reception was depressingly familiar. They were stripped and robbed of everything, showered, some were shaved, and they were issued with a new assortment of garments, but no warm, outer clothes against the approaching winter. The first supper consisted of sweetened milk and barley soup, and they were quickly assigned to a block, where they were no sooner asleep than the siren sounded for *Appel* and they were forced out of the block to stand still on parade in the bitter-cold darkness of early morning.

At Torgau the American and British women had been relatively well treated and so, at the end of the harvest when they returned to Ravensbrück on 6 October, they were shocked to find that there were even more women in the camp and that the conditions had deteriorated. They were stripped of their clothes, subject to the degrading showers and inspections in the nude, and the unlucky ones had their heads shaved. *Appel*, they found, was at the unaccustomed and unwelcome early hour of 4 a.m. and they were driven out of their hut by a Kapo who was, Virginia wrote:

> … a witch, she never missed a chance to strike a prisoner or do her a nasty turn … and shove us through the door, not even allowing the time to swallow a bowl of coffee. To go out the door was like diving from a high platform into icy water.

There were slow queues for the latrines and many women failed to reach the end of the queue before they were made to stand for long hours during roll call, without stockings or any warm outer clothing. Then, while they stood, the SS woman in charge of their block beat them with her stick, pulled their hair, seized their miserable possessions and spilled them on the ground, and kicked the women when they bent to retrieve their few precious things. 'She threatened us, she punished us, and she deprived us of what meagre rights we had as human beings.' And instead of quarantine, which at least would have meant a period of enforced rest without work, the women were given the task of draining the swamps near the camp, shovelling sand into trucks which they pushed to the lakeside and emptied.

At Torgau when work was done they had been allowed to sit in the sunshine, but at Ravensbrück they were confined to their blocks where there was nothing to do except lie on their crowded bunks.[12] So, when the women heard that another *aussenkommando* was being assembled, for Königsberg, they were keen to volunteer. Surely anything was better than staying at Ravensbrück?

LINDELL'S LIST GROWS

Mary Lindell reckoned that while the population of Ravensbrück varied between 25,000 and 45,000 women, only a tiny fraction – between a score and about two dozen – were British by birth or marriage, and gradually she learned more about each of them. She also noted the deaths and disappearances of others including Cecily Lefort and the Scots nurse, Mary-Helen Young.

First on Lindell's list was Mary O'Shaughnessy. She had been working as a children's governess in Angers when the Germans took over the local hospital in 1940, and she turned her knowledge of France and French language into helping British soldiers and airmen to escape. For several months in 1940 she visited Sergeant E.H. Hillyard, whose wounds were so serious that he could not travel. Hillyard had been wounded on 14 June 1940 and taken to hospital at Le Mans where his right arm was amputated. Three days later the hospital was evacuated to Angers, and there Mary O'Shaughnessy began to visit him with a friend, a Scottish governess known only as 'Miss S'. Mary felt considerable empathy with Hillyard because she already had a prosthetic arm.

The ladies brought Hillyard civilian clothes and when the German doctor told him that he would soon be fit enough to go to a prisoner-of-war camp, Hillyard decided that he should make his escape. 'Miss S' hid him for two days until Mary smuggled him into the attic of her employers' house, under the near perfect cover that they were on the best of terms with the German forces of occupation. It was time for Mary to make contact with the nascent Resistance and they conducted Hillyard over the demarcation line. By 3 November he was in Marseilles and on 12 November a medical board at the Michel Levy Hospital passed him unfit for further military service and he was repatriated, arriving in Britain by the end of March 1941.[1]

Mary O'Shaughnessy enjoyed a remarkable period of a further four years of liberty in occupied France, but was eventually betrayed and arrested. Taken first to Lyon and then to Paris, she was forced into a cattle truck on 13 May 1944 with several hundred other prisoners and commenced a five-day journey to Ravensbrück.[2] Mary shared the same soul-destroying experience on arriving at Ravensbrück. The women were forced to strip naked and shower, their clothes were taken from them and they were issued with a prison uniform which, in early 1944, consisted of chemise, knickers and a thin cotton dress.

Mary could not understand the method by which the women were chosen for the indignity of having their heads shaved, as it seemed to her to be haphazard and not governed by any standards of necessity or hygiene. She somehow managed to keep her greying locks. When she reached her allocated block, Block 31, she found that there were between 600 and 1,200 women who slept two, and sometimes three, to a foul, lice-ridden mattress in three-tier bunks. The diet was ersatz coffee for breakfast, half a pint of soup at midday and another half pint in the evening with a quarter of a loaf that had to last all the next day. Those who were working were also given two or three potatoes.

At first the guards were not armed with whips, but still they delivered summary punishment with their fists, boots, sticks or anything else that came to hand. Later in 1944, both men and women guards started to carry whips. The punishments were random, and on one occasion Mary was beaten for no more reason than that she did not understand German. When she did not respond to some spoken command, the guard struck her left and right to the face, breaking her teeth, and when Mary remained on her feet the guard struck her a third time with her fist, breaking her nose.

Mary ceased to take note of how many beatings she witnessed, but one she remembered was of an elderly Polish woman who was dragged by her hair and kicked by two SS men, who were joined by two SS women until the victim was unconscious and dying. She also witnessed women returning to her hut after they had been sent to the bunker for formal punishment – twenty-five strokes of a stick or a whip delivered to the naked back by a Russian inmate.

Mary O'Shaughnessy remembered Dorethea Binz well: aged 22, height about 5ft 7½in, medium figure, thin, longish face, lots of light hair always well done under-curled and bobbed, quite good-looking, and always accompanied by a little white terrier. Mary recalled that despite her youth, good looks and her pet dog, Binz was notorious for her cruel, bestial treatment of the prisoners and was feared by the prisoners and guards alike.

Besides Mary O'Shaughnessy, another Irishwoman was Kate McCarthy, who as a nun had taken the name Marie Laurence.[3] Like Mary Lindell she had been a nurse in the First World War, when she had been awarded the British Red Cross medal. Kate had stayed in France after the war and in 1940 she was serving in a civilian hospital at Bethune, in the Pas-de-Calais in north-eastern France.

As the Germans crossed the border from Belgium, she found herself with several British and French soldiers in her care. As they recovered, she smuggled them out of the hospital, and some of her earliest patients made it through the lines to the beaches of Dunkirk and were evacuated with the British Expeditionary Force. Later she found a way to hand over her patients to fledgling resistance groups and this is how she came to be associated with *Musée de l'Homme*, a group of resistants in Paris who distributed their own newspaper and sent evaders across the line into Vichy France.[4]

Kate was arrested at Bethune Hospital in June 1941, tried (at a time when the Germans still bothered with such formality) and sentenced to death. Despite being categorised as a special enemy of the German state, her sentence was commuted to deportation and she spent the next four years in various concentration camps. She must have been a tough lady because she survived them all: Anrath in the Ruhr, a forced labour camp for NN prisoners; Essen, where she was forced to work for Krupp's arms manufacturers; the cluster of camps at Neuengamme near Hamburg; Lübeck-Lauerhof; and Cottbus, a transit camp to Ravensbrück, where she arrived in December 1944 and was welcomed into Mary Lindell's circle of American and British women.

There was another Franciscan nun, Agnes Flanagan, who belonged to a convent at Tournai in Belgium and who was working as a nurse in Paris in 1940 when she was arrested.[5] Little is known about Agnes, who arrived in Malmö on 26 April 1945, two days before the women on Lindell's list. When the British authorities arrived to collect evidence from the survivors of the camp, she was already being cared for at a convent at Drottingholm, outside Stockholm.[6]

Mary-Helen Young, who had trained as a nurse in London and worked in a hospital in France during the First World War, became a private nurse and was in Paris when the Germans took the city. As a Briton she was interned during the general round-up of aliens in 1940 but released about six months later, presumably on grounds of her age (she was nearly 60). In the interwar years Mary-Helen had visited her hometown in Scotland, the last time being for three months in 1938, and now she had an opportunity to leave France altogether. However, for whatever reason, she never applied for the necessary exit papers. She did send cryptic postcards to her married sister that she was well, one of which was dated November 1943 and simply read, 'From Marie-Hélène who is well and sends her love.' The card was probably sent when she was already under arrest for a second time.[7]

According to Simone Saint-Clair, a French journalist and former inmate at Ravensbrück,[8] Mary-Helen had assisted a resistance group in France which helped downed British airmen to evade capture. Other reports said that she had allowed her house to be used by SOE agents as a wireless base. However, Saint-Clair did not know exactly what the little Scots lady had done because 'although I saw her often in the camp, we made it a rule never to talk about what we had done in the underground'.[9]

Mary-Helen was transported from Compiègne on 31 January 1944 in a transport of 959 women. Slightly over 900 of these were French, and the remainder represented some fifteen nationalities, including seven Americans and three British women. One in five of all of these women would die in exile in Germany, but among the four North American survivors were two rare cases of women who were returned from Ravensbrück to internment in France: Elizabeth Arden's sister, the Canadian-born Gladys de Maublanc, who would be liberated from Vittel on 12 September 1944, and Germaine (or Francine) Johnston-Sebastien, who would be liberated from Fresnes on 17 August 1944. Germaine's mother, Jeanne Sebastien, would also be liberated on the German–Swiss border on 9 April 1945. Both mother and daughter had been active in Pauline Barré de Saint-Venant's escape line in north-east France before Pauline fled to Lyon in 1944.[10]

The third American was Janet Comert from Chicago, who would survive when the camp was overrun by the Soviet Army and who emerged into freedom on 11 May 1945. The fourth survivor, and the only one of the group on Lindell's list, was Elisabeth Smith. Nothing is known of Elisabeth's fifteen months in Ravensbrück, except her number in the camp (27825) and that she seems to have avoided being sent on any working parties outside the main camp. She would also prove to be an impostor.

Five others died: the unfortunate and entirely innocent Rose-Marie Jones, who was murdered at Ravensbrück in February 1944; Mary Chevignard, born in South Dakota, who reached the German–Swiss border on 9 April 1945 but died shortly after crossing into Switzerland; Renée Noirtin, one of the oldest deportees (born on 5 August 1879) from Hoboken, New Jersey, who disappeared in Ravensbrück in February 1944; the SOE agent Cecily Lefort who, having given up the will to live, was murdered in the *Jugendlager* in mid February 1945; and, finally, Mary-Helen Young, who would die with Cecily.

When, post-war, Simone Saint-Clair told the *Aberdeen Press and Journal* that Mary-Helen had 'died as she lived, a brave Scotswoman. Right up to the very end nothing could break her. She would smile, even in this hell that the Germans had made for us, she was a brave woman, the bravest of the brave', the newspaper had summoned an icon and proudly acclaimed her as Scotland's very own Edith Cavell.

Another British woman who Mary Lindell noted was Barbara Chatenay. They may even have chanced to meet in the First World War, when Barbara and a number of other well-bred American and British girls had been volunteer ambulance drivers. Barbara married Victor Chatenay, a French war hero, author and politician, and in the Second World War the Chatenay family were all engaged in resistance to the German invader.

Barbara's brother, Douglas Stirling, was a general in the British Army who soon put Victor in touch with the British Secret Intelligence Service. Victor led a resistance group called *Honneur et Patrie* until 1943 when he was betrayed while making a rendezvous at a Paris café and, though bleeding from a shot in the leg, he escaped through the Paris métro. Victor eventually reached England where he joined de Gaulle.[11]

Meanwhile, Barbara was arrested, tortured and deported to Ravensbrück where her strength of character and inventiveness were appreciated by her fellow prisoners. Her particular contribution to survival in the camp was to teach the women to rub brick dust into their cheeks so that they appeared healthier than they were and at parades were able to avoid being selected for the gas chamber. Barbara would owe her life to Percy Treite, who treated her several times in the camp's *Revier* and who called her 'my English rose', but this did not deter Barbara from giving evidence against him after the war.

Mary O'Shaughnessy added other names to Lindell's list. The names she recalled, besides her friends Ann Sheridan, Kate McCarthy and Barbara Chatenay, were Sylvia Rousselin, Janine Dilly, Marie Tonna-Barthet, Anne Marie Roberts, Pat Cheramy, Doreen Verani and Rachel Krausz. It was a tribute to the skill with which Rachel hid her daughter from sight that Mary O'Shaughnessy could not recall seeing Rachel's daughter Irene.[12] All these, apart from Pat Cheramy, would appear on Lindell's list.[13]

Pat Cheramy was born Eleanor Maud Hawkins in Aldbourne, Wiltshire, on 21 March 1906. Pat, a lady golf champion, had married a French engineer, Charles Cheramy, and lived in Montauban in the non-occupied zone of France. They were soon recruited into work for the Pat line, sheltering escapers. They came to the attention of MI9 in the summer of 1942 after a Spitfire pilot,

John Misseldine, had knocked at their door. Misseldine had been shot down over St Omer and, though burned in the face, had made his way through Paris and south in the company of a young Belgian to Montauban, possibly looking for Donald Caskie who had been exiled there.[14]

Pat sheltered Misseldine while a carefully worded telegram was sent to his parents announcing the birth of a baby. The cable was sent on 9 July and when it reached Misseldine's parents, his mother had the sense to take it to the Air Ministry, who contacted MI9 and a few days later an agent called at the Cheramys' house and asked for Misseldine by name. That very night he was on his way by train further south and on 15 August he was collected from the beach by HMS *Tarana*.

The Cheramys were arrested in January 1943 when the Pat line began to be rolled up, and Tom Groome and Edithe Reddé, who were hiding in their home, were caught while transmitting a wireless message.[15] All four were led away in handcuffs. Little Michel Cheramy, only 18 months old, was taken away too, but the Germans allowed his grandparents to come and collect him.

This was a lucky group, who would all survive the war: Groome survived Dachau, Charles Cheramy was sent to a concentration camp but also survived, and Edithe Reddé, known as 'Eddie', would escape and cross the Pyrenees with Blondie Hasler and Bill Sparks, to be trained in Britain and fight again in France.

A different fate awaited Pat Cheramy, who, together with Ragna Fischer, was deported in October 1943 from Aix-la-Chapelle to Ravensbrück. While on a working party building roads outside the camp, Pat was brutally attacked by a guard who smashed a heavy stick over her head, leaving her with a useless left hand and impaired sight and hearing. In this condition, and having lost more than 50 per cent of her body weight, she was sent to Mauthausen, but escaped in the general dissolution of that camp and was found near death on the roadside by an Australian soldier who fed her and helped her to cross the border into Switzerland in April 1945.[16]

24

LIFE AND LESS IN THE *REVIER*

Mary learned so much about the camp from her relatively safe and advantageous position within the *Revier*. Her network of informants included Micky Poirier, who worked in the camp labour office; Ann Sheridan, who visited the *Revier* from her block regularly; Elizabeth's friend, Mary O'Shaughnessy; Nadine Hwang, who continued to move freely around the camp; and Ragna, who was in charge of a sanitation team that visited the blocks daily.

Much of the work within the *Revier* was done by prisoners like Mary. The hospital itself was well equipped but crammed with patients who lay on bunks and in the corridors, and medicines of all kinds were in short supply. Mary recalled that the weekly ration for the consulting room where she worked was 350 aspirin and ¼ litre of methylated spirits and that while drawing these from the camp store, she and a Russian prisoner colluded in stealing whatever supplies they could.[1]

The horrors of Ravensbrück did not end at the hospital door. Outside there was overcrowding, inadequate clothing, malnutrition, endless *Appels*, hard labour, casual beatings, lack of hygiene, lice and disease. A patient needed to have a temperature of 39°C before admission to the hospital, and inside conditions were only a little better. The German staff of the hospital seemed not to have been interested in or capable of improving conditions. Several women witnessed that when Percy Treite arrived at Ravensbrück as an assistant doctor in September 1943, he did try to improve the arrangements within the hospital and to improve the sanitation,[2] but there was little he could do to improve conditions or the supply of medicine, and he was weak. Other women lumped all the doctors together.

And to add to the horrors of Ravensbrück, the Germans were capable of adding one more repulsive act: the new dreadfulness that was medical experimentation.

Fewer than 100 women were experimented upon, most of them Polish, but the memory is seared into the minds of the survivors from Ravensbrück.

The sanatorium at Hohenlychen, 8km from the camp, was an orthopaedic hospital run by the SS during the war. There, between July 1942 and around September 1943, doctors – principally Fritz Ernst Fischer and Herta Oberheuser – worked under Karl Gebhart to test the efficacy of sulfanilamide, a synthetic antimicrobial agent, in curing wounds. They did so by deliberately wounding healthy women and infecting their sores with foreign bodies such as ground glass and wood shavings.

Before these trials were concluded, Gebhart began a second trial in reconstructive surgery, from around September 1942 to December 1943, using muscles and bones taken from healthy women, which he attempted to transplant into wounded German soldiers at Hohenlychen. The victims of these inhumane practices suffered pain and permanent disability.

The doctors at the *Revier* at Ravensbrück, including Treite, were responsible for the palliative care of these women. Surprisingly, of the seventy-four Polish victims, only five died as a result of the experiments, which says something for the standard of post-operative care that was achieved despite the lack of facilities. However, six victims with unhealed wounds were executed and several of the survivors testified against the monstrous perpetrators. The grotesque nature of these experiments was made no less odious by the cold, clinical terms in which Fischer confessed to what he had done.[3]

A third monstrous experiment was the mass sterilisation of women. Sterilisation was legalised in German law in 1933 in order to purify the Aryan race of anyone deemed to be genetically defective or inferior. The Germans wanted an easy and cheap way to sterilise women and they experimented with injections to the uteruses – without anaesthetic – of Jewish and Gypsy women, which caused side effects such as vaginal bleeding and severe abdominal pain. They also trialled X-rays, usually administrated stealthily, and this left many of its victims with radiation burns. Percy Treite arrived in September 1943 and undoubtedly sterilised some Gypsy girls: his defence in 1947 at the Hamburg War Crimes Tribunal that these were officially authorised actions under pre-war German law would be dismissed.

The care of the victims fell largely to the prisoner doctors and prisoner nurses like Mary Lindell. One case was that of the teenage Belgian Hortense Daman whose leg had been cut open and deliberately infected. She was carried on a stretcher into Block 9 where she met Mary Lindell, 'whose forceful personality,' Hortense recalled, 'made her a figure who could not be ignored'. The tiered bunks of the block were a dumping ground for those too weak to withstand the rigours of the camp, for the dying and the dead, whose emaciated bodies were carried out daily and lay discarded on the earth outside the block until they were eventually carted away.

Mary was kind and found Hortense a bunk near a window where her mother could visit her and smuggle her a few extra rations, and found her a stool to sit on in the sunshine during the day. But Mary could be blunt too, and one day Hortense overheard a conversation about her. 'If that girl doesn't get off her backside and learn to walk again, you know where she'll end up. Up the chimney.' The remark was intended to be heard – Mary had a loud voice, 'like a foghorn over the sea', and a bossy tone – and it had the desired effect of motivating Hortense. When Hortense protested, Mary snapped, 'At least I pulled you off your seat, didn't I?' And when others criticised Mary for her apparent callousness, she was unrepentant, 'I do not apologise for the intention.' She and the other nurses knew that Hortense had to learn to walk if she was to survive.[4]

By October 1944 Mary Lindell and Yvonne Baseden knew only that the female agents who they had met in Saarbrücken in August had been seen in Ravensbrück, but that they had left on a transport with a batch of Frenchwomen for a camp elsewhere in Germany. One afternoon Yvonne was delighted to see Denise Bloch (whom she knew by one of her code names, Williams) and Violette Szabó. They told her that Lilian Rolfe was with them and about the working party which had been to Torgau, where, when they had refused to work in a munitions factory, they had been set to work in the kitchens.

They told her that they had been in touch with some French prisoners of war who had a wireless link to the outside world and that they had passed on a list of names of everyone in their transport. (No evidence has been found that this information reached London.) Having 'been lucky' on the Torgau transport, Denise told Yvonne that they hoped to be lucky again and were keen to leave on the next transport. Yvonne thought it was her duty to join her colleagues and thought of volunteering too, but as soon as Mary heard of it she put a stop to any such idea. Thereafter, Yvonne decided to remain at Ravensbrück with the Frenchwomen, to be as inconspicuous as possible and work in the fields in preference to doing enforced war work for Germans.[5]

By encouraging Yvonne to make this decision, Mary Lindell probably saved her life. One witness, Jacqueline Bernard, recorded that of the 250 friends and comrades who left for Königsberg on 16 October, less than thirty survived. After the war Jacqueline, trying to comfort grieving parents, wrote:

I sincerely believe that death through excessive fatigue and starvation is not painful. One simply grows weaker and weaker and I've rarely seen a dying girl in those circumstances realise that she was dying. She would often be talking quite normally or making plans for when she would be back home. Most of those who died in this way were never admitted to the hospital huts, and were compelled to stand up every morning for at least an hour during roll-calls. Many died before the roll-calls ended.[6]

Toquette Jackson, Denise Bloch, Lilian Rolfe and Violette Szabó were among the women who thought they might 'be lucky' again, and who took the risk of leaving Ravensbrück.

Lucienne Dixon escaped this fate. She had found Isabelle and Maisie Renault, who she had worked with in Paris, and she decided to stay with them. Lucienne joined Maisie on daily working parties and they were marched out from Ravensbrück in the early hours to dig up tree roots in the pine forest and did not return until late in the evenings. The tall trees hinted of beauty and freedom, and once the sun was up and the cold had gone, the friends talked of music and books, and fantasised about the food they would cook and the menus they would prepare in France. While the female SS guards toasted bread on a bonfire, the prisoners shivered in their wet clothes and drank their midday soup huddled together in a derelict hut.

In the evenings they carried back sticks and branches for fuel to warm their hut.[7] They wore clogs, but once the rain turned to snow they had to stamp their clogs every few steps to shake off the packed snow. The pines in their white coats now looked as mournful and as oppressive as their guards. There were casual beatings, senseless searches and petty theft, while the women grew thinner and greyer and developed purple blotches under the eyes. And the cold bit most in the dark hours of *Appel*, when the women in their thin clothes waited, dizzy and numb, in the frosty air whilst the Germans counted and recounted their prisoners and the dead were carried out from the blocks. One morning as Lucienne marched out of the camp she noticed that the temperature gauge at the main gate showed -30°C

Christmas brought the dismal news of a German counter-offensive in the Ardennes and the season was celebrated apathetically: many began to fear that they might not see the New Year. As if it were possible, as the year of 1944 drew to a close conditions in Ravensbrück worsened. With a promise of rest and recuperation, the Germans had already started to issue pink cards to anyone considered unfit for work for whatever reason – age, sickness or infirmity.

At first tired women would ask for one of these cards, hoping for a respite from the hard labour of the camp. Their names were taken and periodically they would be called from parades and sent to the *Jugendlager* – a former youth reform school – adjacent to the main camp. But soon the realisation came that no one returned from the fabled 'rest' camp and that holding a pink card was a sentence of death.

Simone Saint-Clair told the readers of the *Aberdeen Press and Journal* about the diet of ersatz coffee and soup made of mangel-wurzels and potato peelings, and the 4 a.m. parades which lasted for hours outdoors in winter and summer, when many women collapsed and died on the spot. She also told them that Mary Young had become too feeble to do any of the heavy work like carrying coal, felling trees and reclaiming marshland, which went on until seven in the evening. 'Unfortunately, Miss Young had white hair. The Germans knew what to do with women with white hair or women too exhausted to work or even had swollen legs. For them it was the gas chamber.'

Mary O'Shaughnessy had an artificial arm and she was inevitably given a pink card, though for several months her name was not called. Slowly the realisation dawned on the women that the promise of an easier life at Uckermark was a cruel joke: no one returned from the youth camp, which had become no more than a marshalling yard for the gas chamber. When eventually Mary's name was called at the beginning of February 1945, she and about seventy others were made to trudge a mile and half through the snow and ice to Uckermark.

The journey took over an hour because they had to carry their sick companions with them. Mary was more fortunate than most because she had been given a pair of stockings and a pair of wooden-soled open-backed shoes. Once there they were made to stand for three or four hours in front of one of the huts. When they were let in out of the cold, they found themselves crammed into a space with no room to lie down and they had to sleep sitting with their feet drawn up beneath themselves. They were locked up for a night and a day, with no food and water or sanitation. Two women died on the first night. On the fourth day the survivors were let out into another hut and given straw palliasses which had been filled in the snow. As the straw was dried by the warmth of the women's bodies they discovered that the palliasses were crawling with lice. No blankets or other bedding was provided.

Life was easier in the *Jugendlager*, in the sense that there was no work, but the day was spent at *Appel*, or waiting for the next roll call – in fact, waiting to die.

Starting at the first roll, selections for the gas chambers began. SS guards stomped in and out of the ranks of women selecting those who looked ill or listless. Those selected were ordered into a third circle of hell, another hut where again the women were deprived of all facilities and were allowed out only for further, endless roll calls. These took place morning and evening and at unannounced intervals during the day, for the sole purpose, that Mary could fathom, of making further selections for the gas chambers. Any coats or blankets were taken from the women and, Mary recalled, they were made to stand to attention wearing only their thin dresses in 24°F (-4.5°C) of frost. It mattered nothing to the camp staff whether the women died of hunger or exposure, fell to the floor of their huts, collapsed while at roll call, or were savagely beaten by the SS woman in charge. If they did not die by these means, they would eventually be loaded onto lorries and driven away, never to be seen again.

Somehow, luckily, Mary O'Shaughnessy received an urgent message from Mary Lindell urging her to return to the main camp when, in the second week of March, she and 1,000 other women were suddenly ordered back to the main camp. This was not humanity offered by the Germans, only a change in policy. Apparently the gas chambers at the *Jugendlager* could not cope and the women were not dying of other causes fast enough.

They were made to trudge twice through the snow between Uckermark and Ravensbrück before the survivors were readmitted to the main camp. There, Mary was placed in Block 29, where Ann Sheridan was the *blockälteste*, and about 1,200 women were crowded into the block containing 250 three-tiered bunks. The women shared at least two to a bunk with one disgusting latrine between them all.

Mary's new day consisted of *Appel* and then being marched out of the camp in the early morning for heavy duties, which included shovelling sand, a midday return march for half an hour's break for soup, and work again from 12.30 to 7 p.m. Mary did not know how she managed to shovel so much wet sand from one pile to another with her artificial arm. As far as she could tell, the main purpose was to reduce her and her companions to a state of exhaustion and ill health. She did know that if she paused in her work for moment she would be struck or slashed with a stick by one of the guards.

Mary owed her life to Ann Sheridan, who smuggled her into the block and hid her under a bed. While she hid there, the bodies of women who had died overnight were stripped and placed in the wash house of the bock until they were loaded, as many as sixteen at a time, onto a handcart and wheeled away to the crematory, with its all-pervading stink, as smoke and often flames vented from the crematory's 30ft-high chimney. When the wind did not blow, a pall of blue smoke hung over the camp. The smell was filthy and revolting.

DEATH OF A HEART BROKEN

There were many ways of dying at Ravensbrück, but Cecily Lefort is probably one of those whose death was caused by a broken heart. She was born Cecily Margot Mackenzie, in London on 30 April 1900, into an Anglo-Irish family. She grew up fond of sport and particularly sailing, and at the age of 25 married a French doctor, Alix Lefort. They lived in an apartment in Paris and enjoyed their summers in a villa near the fishing village of St Cast, west of St Malo.

At the fall of France, Alix Lefort insisted that his wife should leave for England while he remained behind. In London, Cecily joined the WAAF, where eventually her knowledge of some French was noted – she was yet one more agent whose French was not perfect, despite nearly a score of years married to a Frenchman. Even Bunny Rymills, the pilot who would fly her to France, noted that 'her French did not seem to me to be all that hot'.[1]

Nevertheless, in 1943 she was recruited into the SOE and on 16 February started her training at the SOE's school at Wanborough Manor, Guildford, in the same class as other female agents like the Indian Noor Inayat Khan and the Swiss-born Yolande Beekman. From Wanborough, Cecily went to Beaulieu where she was joined by Diana Rowden, a graduate of another class at Wanborough.[2]

Cecily's instructors doubted whether she had the initiative to achieve very much, and she was described as 'very ladylike and very English'.[3] This was an opinion repeated by Rymills, who described her as 'looking like a vicar's wife'.[4] However, even before she had left for France, Cecily proved useful to the DF (escape) section of SOE. Hearing that someone was looking for safe houses on the French coast, Cecily offered her house at St Cast and advice on the sheltered bays and beaches along the coast. She also offered an ancient Irish ring which could be shown to the caretaker proving her authority,[5] and 'in this curious way the "Var" escape line of DF section was successfully established, unknowingly using the same route as the Scarlet Pimpernel of the French Revolutionary era'.[6]

Cecily was landed near Angers, France, in the early hours of 17 June 1943, in a double Lysander lift, with her new friends Noor and Diana. Given the precautions usually taken to segregate agents, it seems odd – at least a breach of SOE's own best practice – that these three women, who knew each other well and had presumably learned a great deal about the organisation and purposes of SOE, should have travelled at the same time.[7] The capture of one of them would surely lead to the downfall of the others. Furthermore, arrest was highly likely because Henri Déricourt, SOE's air operations officer in France, was a traitor and the Germans knew about these landings. Cecily was followed from Paris to Montélimar in south-eastern France and her movements watched to see if she would lead her followers to other members of her circuit.[8]

The circuit that Cecily joined was Jockey, run by Francis Cammaerts, whose area of operations was the left bank of the Rhône Valley.[9] After just three months in the field she was arrested on 15 September. Cammaerts tried to find her and asked F Section to bribe the Gestapo, but the first definite news of her whereabouts came from a Belgian woman who had been in prison with her in Toulouse.

On 31 January 1944 Cecily was put on a transport of 959 women to Ravensbrück. Travelling in the wagon with her were the American Gladys de Maublanc, Mary Chevignard, Janet Comert, Germaine Johnston-Sebastien and Renée Noirtin; the British Rose-Marie Jones and Mary-Helen Young; and the mysterious Elisabeth Smith.

While under training with SOE in 1943 Cecily had sent messages via the Red Cross to her husband, Alix, signing herself with '*affectueuses pensées*', and Alix certainly knew where she was because he sent food parcels to her at 'Frauen-Konzentrations-Lager, No 27962, Bloc 13, Ravensbrück bei Fürstenberg, Mecklenburg'.

Sometime after her arrival at the camp Cecily fell ill and was diagnosed by Percy Treite as having stomach cancer. This fell within Percy's medical expertise and surprisingly, given the lack of facilities in the *Revier*, he operated successfully on Cecily, 'making a very god job of it'. For two or three months afterwards she received an enhanced diet, but she was never very strong after that.

Then, amidst her privations, Cecily received a letter from her husband. Alix was asking his imprisoned wife for a divorce. Cecily had made friends with Barbara Chatenay and it was Barbara who would recall that Cecily had no prior inkling of this and the shock was so great that 'Cecily was unable to defend her-self' and she doubted whether Cecily would survive the ordeal of Ravensbrück.

Forty-four years old, but thin, haggard and seemingly much older and feel-ing too feeble to work, Cecily accepted her pink card and went on 13 January 1945 with other elderly and exhausted women to the *Jugendlager*. She struggled through the snow with Mary O'Shaughnessy and Mary-Helen Young, in the hope of respite and rest.

All three women were on Mary Lindell's list, and when she heard where they had gone she sent urgent messages for them to return to the main camp. Mary O'Shaughnessy heeded Lindell's advice, but Cecily preferred to remain with her friend Mary-Helen, and two or three weeks after their arrival at the *Jugendlager*, Cecily and Mary-Helen were called out of their block and taken away in a lorry, never to be seen again. There were differing reports of whether she was murdered by gassing or injection, but in truth Cecily had lost the will to live and she died of a broken heart caused by her husband's desertion in the hour of her greatest need.

DAUGHTERS OF LIBERTY

For much of her time at Ravensbrück Yvonne Baseden lived in Block 15, where she was befriended by a Frenchwoman of her own age who she knew as Jenny Sylvani (her real name was Eugénie Djendi). Jenny was one of the four captured *parachutistes* who were being held at Saarbrücken between 17 and 26 August 1944, when Mary Lindell and Yvonne arrived there from Dijon.

In January 1943 in Algiers, Jenny, Marie-Louise Cloarec, Pierrette Louin and Suzanne Boitte joined the Free French Army, where they were trained as wireless operators and dubbed the 'Merlinettes', after the name of the French head of signals, Colonel Lucien Merlin. The girls were given the French military rank of *sous lieutenant*. After qualifying as wireless operators, they were sent to England to learn to parachute.[1]

Marie-Louise, Pierrette and Suzanne were parachuted into France 24km north-west of Haute Vienne on 5–6 April 1944 (on the same night that Lilian Rolfe and Violette Szabó were being landed by Lysander near Tours) and Jenny was parachuted into France on the night of 7–8 April 1944 and arrested on 9 April.

It is not known why Jenny was arrested so quickly, but the three other French women reached Paris. Their personal security was not good: all three went to the same safe house belonging to a cousin of Pierrette, who she had not seen for some seven years, and they were quite open that they had arrived in France by parachute and had been helped in reaching Paris by the local police. The girls made little effort to be inconspicuous. They smoked noticeably better cigarettes than were available in France, were conspicuous in a local black-market restaurant and upset the regular customers, and soon young men were calling at all hours. All had baggage, including heavy cases in which they carried their wireless sets. Pierrette had a large parcel of cash which she needed to hand over to someone in the Resistance, and Marie-Louise sent a telegram to her sister openly announcing her arrival in Paris.

Within a month all six of these women would meet again as prisoners of the Germans, and on 17 August 1944 the four Merlinettes were moved to Saarbrücken and from there, after a two-day train journey, they arrived on 26 August at Ravensbrück where they were placed in Block 15, set aside for '*nacht und nebel*' (or NN) prisoners. As NN prisoners, they were not sent on outside work parties, but even without forced labour, conditions were still bad and they became markedly worse as the winter of 1944–45 wore on.

In November the four Merlinettes were summoned to the camp office of the SS where they were interrogated about their identities, and Suzanne, the self-appointed leader of the small group, protested to the Germans that they should receive Red Cross parcels and better treatment. As officers, they should be transferred to a prisoner-of-war camp. The Germans interviewed Suzanne, putting on a show of great courtesy and promising that her case would be referred to Berlin. After a second interview, Suzanne told Jenny that she had seen the Germans studying a telegram on the table before them which seemed to hold orders about the Frenchwomen.

Excitedly Jenny told Yvonne Baseden that they had all been summoned to appear the next day at the SS office, and at *Appel* on 18 January the Merlinettes were placed under curfew in their block. Later, Yvonne heard that her friend Jenny and the three other women had been seen standing in their striped dresses in front of the SS office surrounded by guards. A German woman, Ruth Neudecker, who frequently attended executions, was present and the road to the Siemens factory, which ran past the crematory, had been cordoned off. No more was seen of the four Frenchwomen.

All assumed that they had been hanged because they knew that there was a gallows by the ovens, but the only proof of death was when they searched a pile of clothes that had belonged to the dead of the camp and Suzanne's grey coat with her name in the pocket was found. Others thought that the four had been shot, but the Norwegian Kate Johansen, who worked in the clothing store and was a friend of Mary Lindell, told Mary that she had received into the store four sets of French clothing without having been given any civilian clothing in exchange, and that these clothes carried no trace of bullets or blood on them. When asked, a German whose name Mary did not know brought a hand to his neck to indicate that these women were hanged.

When Yvonne Baseden heard this, she too felt convinced that they had been hanged. She felt that she owed her own escape from this fate to the fact that, unlike the others who had come to Ravensbrück via Paris, any paperwork about her had not followed her from Dijon, and she was more than ever determined to keep a low profile while in the camp. She remained Marie Bernier, a little French girl who had worked on the edges of the Resistance but played no important role.

Meanwhile Mary Lindell, who had appointed herself captain of the English – and of anyone she considered English enough – had already noted Danielle (or Lin) Williams,[2] Lilian Rolfe[3] and Violette Szabó, one of the best known of the female agents.[4] She had met them at Saarbrücken, and she knew that they had been sent on two working parties, first to Torgau and then to Little Königsberg.[5] Marie-Thérèse Henry, who was on the same working parties, recalled that on about 25 January the order had been given for all American and British women to parade the next morning at 6 a.m.

The women quickly convinced themselves that they were going to be taken to Switzerland as part of a prisoner-of-war exchange and said goodbye to their friends joyfully.[6] However, further enquiries elicited different dates and conflicting versions of what happened next. All agreed that the three SOE girls had been executed. One thought that they had been hanged at the end of January, another gave the date of their murder as between 27 January and 5 February. Someone else thought that the women had been marched out of the camp sometime in February 1945 'and it was generally accepted that they were shot on the usual execution ground. It was common gossip that their personal clothing etc. had been handed in to the camp store shortly after.' Some were adamant about what they knew, even if they were self-contradictory:

No internee was permitted to witness the executions, but from the manner in which they taken away, we at once realised that executions were imminent. We recognised already the faces of certain SS-men, who were usually present, though their names remained unknown to us. Frequently we heard the shootings during the evening parades, from which we deduced that most of the executions, perhaps all of them, were carried out by shooting … one evening at the end of February or the beginning of March, a group of ten internees were executed. We heard no shooting at the time. Amongst them were 3 British women. All three of them came from the Punishment Block.[7]

None of them witnessed the actual executions. 'We only saw how our fellow-prisoners were led out of the camp – usually in the evening shortly before roll-call, and during roll-call we heard the shots.'[8]

Mary Lindell's memory was quite clear. The women returned from Königsberg towards the end of January 1945 and were placed in the *Straffblock*, and sometime at the beginning of February they were moved from there to the bunker. When Mary heard about the poor state of their health she organised clean clothes and extra food to be smuggled in for them. Jacqueline Bernard, who remained longer at Königsberg, believed that the women would be 'looked after better in Ravensbrück where the conditions in the hospital huts were not quite so bad as in Königsberg, and where they had small supplies of medicine whereas we had none', but she was wrong.

For a year there was no clearer news of what happened, until Vera Atkins was allowed to interview Johann Schwarzhuber and obtain a deposition from him dated 13 March 1946. Atkins immediately reported to London. Schwarzhuber recalled that towards the end of January 1945 he had received an order from the Gestapo, countersigned by Suhren, to locate the three women. Schwarzhuber had found from camp records that they were at Königsberg and ordered their return to Ravensbrück. There, one evening (he did not give the date) towards 7 p.m. they were taken to the courtyard by the crematory. Present were the camp Kommandant, Suhren; the chief camp doctor, Schwarzhuber; Trommer; SS Sergeant Zappe, SS Corporal Schenk and SS Lance Corporal Schult; and the camp dentist, the despicable Martin Hellinger, whose job it was to rob corpses of their gold fillings.

By coincidence, only a day or so after Atkins' report reached London, on 17 March 1946 the *News of the World* published a picture of 4-year-old Tania Szabó holding a photograph of her mother. The accompanying story told the readers that Violette Szabó had been 'marched to the German concentration camp at Ravensbrück in February 1945, since then nothing has been heard of her'.

The story brought forth a letter from, of all people, Julie Brichta, who agreed to be interviewed. It was the closest to a confession of her own role at Ravensbrück that she would ever come to. Her claim that she had been sent there by the Germans for sabotage of their war effort on Guernsey was a travesty of her actual role as a black-marketeer and collaborator who had been denounced as a Jewess and deported via various prisons in St Malo, Rennes, Paris and Romainville until she reached Germany. There, because she spoke several languages, she soon ingratiated herself with her captors and made herself useful as an interpreter and voluntarily became an enforcer of the camp's bitter discipline. She wore a red armband to show her status as a Kapo and went armed with a heavy leather belt which, she admitted, she used to beat her fellow prisoners.

Brichta reckoned that there were 50,000 women and children in a camp built for 7,000. There were also, Brichta knew, a few Englishwomen in the camp, although, apart from her first meeting with Mary Lindell, Brichta was not admitted to their circle. All the women were dirty and starving and beaten daily, and Brichta confessed to the *News of the World* reporters that she used to accompany the camp Kommandant and two doctors as they made their selections, translating for them:

> 'You go to the right, you go to the left.' 'To the left' meant the gas chamber; 'To the right' meant a temporary reprieve. It was a hateful task, but in it I saw my chance to help some of the condemned women. Altogether I was able to save the lives of more than 100 women – pitifully few, I know. It was only on such occasions that I used the belt, not heavily, on the shoulders of the condemned. My object was to confuse the Germans. With a great show of indignation I made it appear that some of the women had made mistakes, then, at the right moment, I was able to drive them past the ranks of the condemned.

Quite how by this dissimulation she saved any lives at all, other than her own, is not clear. Brichta was fortunate: at the Hamburg War Crimes Tribunal some were tried for their lives for lesser crimes than those to which she confessed.

Her declaration of guilt continued:

> Defenceless women were kicked and beaten as they lay on the ground. Once when going through the huts with the commandant and the doctors, the guards were ordered to drag exhausted women from the beds where they lay naked, on to the floors of the huts ready to be carried away, piled on top of one another.

Since Brichta was one of those guards, she could not distance herself from this activity.

But far the most startling and prejudicial statement that Brichta made was when she admitted that she was the last person to speak to Violette Szabó. Brichta had recognised Violette, Denise Bloch and Lilian Rolfe when they returned to the camp from Königsberg. She told the newspaper that they 'were in rags, their faces black with dirt, and their hair matted. They were starving. Only Mrs Szabó could walk. The other two were on stretchers.'

She claimed, 'I saw them in their last hours' and when the order came for the three women to go to the Kommandant's office, Danielle and Lilian were carried on their stretchers, but Violette walked unaided. 'I,' said Brichta, 'was the last person to speak to her.'

Schwarzhuber had told Atkins that a woman had accompanied the murder squad but had been turned back when they reached the crematory. Schwarzhuber had such little regard for the inmates of Ravensbrück, whether they were miserable prisoners or prisoner guards like Brichta, that he did not know her name. He thought that the woman was a Czech: it seems likely that this woman was the Hungarian-born Brichta.[9]

The women, said Schwarzhuber, were brought forward singly by Schenk. Suhren read out the order for their execution, Schult shot each one through the back of the neck and Trommer certified them dead. The corpses were then removed one by one by prisoners working the crematory and they were burned in their clothes. For added shock for the readers of the *News of the World*, Brichta recounted how the bodies went straight into the furnaces and their bones were afterwards ground into dust and used as fertiliser or fed to the pigs.

At least Schwarzhuber had the grace to add that all three women were very brave and that he was deeply affected. Suhren too, Schwarzhuber wrote, was impressed by the bearing of the women, but he was also annoyed that the Gestapo had not done their own dirty work and had ordered him to supervise the executions instead.

Clearly, however, neither Atkins nor her colleagues read the *News of the World*, and Brichta was not called as a witness to the War Crimes Tribunal in Hamburg, nor as an accused.

There is one curious incident concerning the date of Lilian Rolfe's death and that of her companions. Her twin sister, Helen, was another who took a dislike to Vera Atkins, telling an interviewer, 'I remember I disliked her. She smelled.'[10] Vera Atkins had told her that the date of the execution had been established, with some uncertainty, as being at the end of January or early February. However the twins, Lilian and Helen, often had premonitions about each other. Lilian had come to Helen in a dream: she was dressed in brown and in terrible distress and she was crying, and Helen knew 'something awful had happened to Lilian. It was on 11 February 1945, not long before I saw Vera Atkins. I now know that was the night she died, although Vera Atkins gave a different date later, but I know that she was wrong.'[11]

VIRGINIA'S WEDDING RING

The American Virginia D'Albert-Lake's patriotism shines through her memoirs, written soon after her liberation although not published until many years later. Other memoirs are filled with political agenda, and it is curious that reading, for example, Lanckorońska,[1] Germaine Tillion[2] or Sylvia Salvesen,[3] one could be forgiven for thinking that there were only Polish, French or Norwegian women in the camps.

Virginia herself reflected on the differing natures of these groups. The French were proud and aloof and the Germans despised them as stubborn, arbitrary troublemakers of a defeated and prostrate nation. The Russians were far more pliable and co-operative, and they were even respected and feared because of their victorious armies. The Poles were tolerated amicably because they were good fighters and workers. The French, Virginia noted, liked to lash with their tongues, whereas the Russians and Poles preferred their fists.

When asked how she had survived in the concentration camps, Virginia answered, 'It was a question of will. You could never give in. The women who cried at night were usually dead in the morning.' Virginia herself never gave in, but she learned very quickly one principle: 'If one refused to collaborate with the Germans, one should be as self-effacing as possible. It was neither the place nor the time to be aggressive. The least one was noticed, the better.'

Virginia survived being sent on working parties to Torgau and to Königsberg, and gave a grim account of a winter building an airfield, in inadequate clothes and on a scanty diet, before she and the survivors were evacuated when the Soviet Army was only a few kilometres away.

Virginia's third arrival at Ravensbrück on 5 February was unlike the others. Discipline and routine in the camp was beginning to break down. There were no showers, no changes of clothes, no examination for lice, and her accommodation was a cold, damp, airless tent where some 600 women, most suffering from dysentery, were crammed. Her part of the tented accommodation was run by a particularly brutal Polish *Blockova* who, with her cronies, fawned over their SS *Blockführerin*. The camp's sanitary system had also broken down: at first women were made to climb into the latrines up to their knees and dig out the manure which was spread in the surrounding fields, and then they were forced to dig pits about 3ft in diameter between the huts, with women squatting round these pits in the open.

Three days after Virginia's return to Ravensbrück, at *Appel* the Germans began to select sixty women at a time for new working parties. Virginia and her friends felt too weak even to lift a spade. It was not difficult to feign illness and so avoid *Appel*, but one morning an SS woman entered the tent and, using her stick, she began drive them out. Virginia lay on her stomach and the blows fell on her back and head until it was so painful that she clambered to her feet and went outside into the cold. But the selection, for that was what it was, for the alleged working party was done. Only later did she learn that this was a selection for a 'black convoy' – a transport of women, mostly those too weak to work, to the gas chamber where, in the early weeks of 1945, 5,000–6,000 women were murdered.

Thefts from the prisoners continued, meagre as their possessions were. They were robbed of soup bowls, blankets and what little food they had somehow hoarded. One day the *blockführerin* spotted Virginia's wedding ring. Her knuckles were so swollen by the cold and hard labour that she could not take it off, but the German, who normally beat prisoners with a heavy rod so that they would not come near her and give her lice, now trapped Virginia in the washroom and gave her a scrap of ersatz soap and insisted she should take off the ring. She took her time, hoping to escape, while the German goaded her. She was cruel and Virginia hated her. Tears ran down her face – this was all she had left of Philippe and the world outside the camp – and in desperation she cried, 'I am an American. Do you steal the wedding rings of Americans too?'

The effect was stunning. 'Are you American?' The woman looked at Virginia as though she had seen her for the first time, 'You may keep your ring'.

On 16 February – she remembered the date forever – Virginia suffered the ignominy of having her hair shaved. She felt she had reached the lowest depths, the final humiliation; she was hairless but still covered in lice. For several days she was too weak to leave her bunk, until on 25 February the *Blockova* asked, 'Will the American who was at Königsberg, come immediately?'

Without explanation she was ordered to undress and given anti-vermin powder to dust herself with, and a whole new set of clothes including a coat.

Three days later she was summoned again. This time it was, 'Madame D'Albert is wanted at once!'

'Hurry,' the *Blockova* used her name again, 'Madame D'Albert, the office doesn't like to be kept waiting.'

In the office she met two prisoner clerks and an SS woman. Strangely all were smiling at her and unexpectedly she was led out of the gates and into the pine trees. As she passed the kitchens and shower block everyone stared at her. Two more SS women turned to stare at her and Virginia fell back in amazement when one spoke to her in perfect English, 'You are Mrs D'Albert? You are an American?'

'Yes,' she murmured.

'Give me the place and date of your birth!'

As one of the SS wrote these down, she said, 'Tonight you will be very happy. You are going away.'

What Virginia did not know was that Philippe had escaped from France to London and raised the alarm about her arrest. Her mother had written to the US Secretary of State, Cordell Hull, to ask if Virginia could be exchanged for a German prisoner and a request for information had gone from Washington to its embassy in Switzerland. On 23 February Virginia's mother heard that her daughter was 'alright' and 'in good health'. Clearly whatever approach the Americans had made had had some effect.

Virginia left Ravensbrück with Geneviève de Gaulle, niece of the Free French leader. Geneviève had been arrested as long ago as July 1943, suspected of working for the French Resistance movement *Défense de la France*. She had been held in the bunker for many months and though thin had benefitted in recent months from a better diet.[4] Virginia, however, weighed only 76lb compared to her normal 126lb.

They were taken by train and on foot to Libenau, a Red Cross camp on Lake Konstanz from where she was repatriated in May 1945 and reunited with Philippe. Virginia wrote, 'If I had spent one more week in Ravensbrück I would have died like my friends.'

28

PINK TICKET TO THE YOUTH CAMP

One of Virginia's friends was her fellow American Lucienne Dixon, who on 13 February 1945 was unexpectedly included in a selection of Frenchwomen for an *Aussenkommando* at Rechlin, where labour was wanted to build and repair barracks and runways after it had been repeatedly bombed by the USAAF.

Once more the women were made to strip and shower while their meagre possessions were stolen, and the Frenchwomen began to lose their cohesion. It was unsafe to shirk any job because Gypsies informed on them and robbed them, and a simple thing like a stolen bowl meant nothing to drink out of, and therefore no soup.

At Rechlin, Hungarian Jews were in charge of soup distribution, which was so thin that rations at Ravensbrück seemed generous by comparison. The midday meal did not arrive until 4 p.m. and then they had to fight Russian prisoners for their bread ration. In the prison blocks at night they fought the Poles for space in a bunk. Here, Lucienne met her friends, Maisie and Isabelle Renault, with whom she had worked in the Resistance in Paris.

Work was organised erratically. One day they would dig a trench or an underground shelter, another day they would turf the Kommandant's garden, and on others they would be marched several kilometres into the forest to carry timber back for construction. Not least, some danger came from the air: the USAAF bombed the airfield from high level and the RAF strafed and dive-bombed. They were allowed shelters, but as soon as a raid was over they would be ordered out to fill in the craters.

Just as unexpectedly as the selection for Rechlin, on 13 April it was announced that Rechlin would be closed and, amidst rumours that the Frenchwomen would be freed, they returned to Ravensbrück. The now familiar but still vile reception procedure, stripping and showering, did not augur well, but otherwise they were left alone for several days.

Much had changed at Ravensbrück where, throughout the early months of 1945, conditions grew worse and worse. Besides the cold and the lack of clothing, there was less food, more disease and the killings increased in tempo, in detail and in general. In early 1944 the *Jugendlager*, or Youth Camp, adjacent to Ravensbrück proper, which had been a detention camp for young, unruly German women, was ordered to close. On 20 January its occupants were either parcelled out to SS personnel as household servants or sent into the main camp, and it fell fully into the evil realm of Ravensbrück.[1] At first, rumours spread that the *Jugendlager* had become a *Schönungslager*, or convalescent camp, where conditions were better than in the main camp, and some women looked forward to going there. The women in the typhus and tuberculosis wards were the first to go, and then all the women holding pink cards, indicating that they were too old or too sick to work, were rounded up and sent to the *Jugendlager*.

Mary Lindell quickly saw through this ploy, though not before some of the women on her list – Mary O'Shaughnessy, Mary-Helen Young and Cicely Lefort – had gone to the *Jugendlager*. When nobody returned restored to health by a stay at the *Jugendlager*, several of the wiser and more sympathetic block leaders reported that everyone in their blocks was fit for work, while others used the opportunity to ease the congestion in their blocks by reporting many more women who held pink cards. Soon the sub camp was even more overcrowded than the main camp and held some 3,500 women, mostly the frail and sick.

The four French parachutists, the Merlinettes, were shot in January and the three British agents of SOE, Denise Bloch, Lilian Rolfe and Violette Szabó, disappeared in February. Individuals like Virginia D'Albert-Lake and Geneviève de Gaulle were sent away to internment camps, and the prognosis for the thousands of women suffering in the main camp was not good.

New prisoners continued to arrive daily, mostly from camps in the east and some after long marches, while in February a number of women and most of the children in the camp were sent to Bergen-Belsen: most of the children died en route. Also in February there was a transport to Dora-Mittelbau, near Buchenwald, which included most of the NN prisoners, but a few weeks later many of these women returned. On 28 February there was a transport to Bergen-Belsen and on 2 March nearly 2,000 women were transported to Mauthausen, but while Suhren, the camp Kommandant, was sending his surplus prisoners to other camps, they were sending theirs to him.

When SS Obersturmführer Johan Schwarzhuber was posted from Auschwitz to Ravensbrück, as *Schutzhaftlagerführer* or 'protective custody camp leader', he attended a meeting with the senior SS doctor, Richard Trommer, at which

Fritz Suhren passed on Himmler's orders that all women who were sick or incapable of marching were to be killed. Rations were stopped – or stolen – from the women at the *Jugendlager* and many died, and yet they were not dying quickly enough to satisfy Suhren. Trommer distributed a white powder to his nurses to administer to the victims and next morning they were found dead. Schwarzhuber gave orders to one of his staff who had also come from Auschwitz, Otto Moll, to shoot the survivors. When even these methods did not satisfy Suhren, he ordered the construction of a gas chamber.

Schwarzhuber took responsibility for the selections: from around 5 February, each afternoon he would go to the *Jugendlager* and organise lists.[2] The women on each list would be told that they were being transferred to another camp called Mittwerda – a place which did not exist – and they were crowded into a barrack block, from where they were taken by truck to a workshop on the service road which led to the main camp. The journey only took five or ten minutes. The workshop had been converted into a gas chamber.

At the Hamburg War Crimes Tribunal, Schwarzhuber admitted to having been at one such mass murder:

> I was present at a gassing. There were always 150 women who were forced into the gas chamber at one time. Hauptscharführer Moll ordered the women to undress and that they were going to be deloused. They were thereupon sent into the gassing room and the door was closed. A male prisoner, wearing a gas mask, climbed onto the roof and threw a canister into an opening, which he immediately closed again.

Schwarzhuber claimed that he heard only groaning and whimpering from inside, but death for the women was agonising and not quick. There were screams, not whimpers, from inside the gas chamber, screams which even the SS guards found unbearable, and for the next few minutes they revved the engines of their trucks to drown the horrendous cries. Then the room was cleared of the dead and dying, who were thrown into the furnaces.

Even this was inefficient and the gas chamber was closed down in early April 1945 after it had been in operation for no more than two months. Instead, a mobile chamber known as 'the bus' made its appearance on 2 April in a wood near the *Jugendlager*. A hundred women would be invited to take their seats, then a little chimney would start to revolve. Afterwards their bodies were buried in mass graves. The mobile chamber continued in use until the end of April, when, to destroy the evidence for their foul deeds, it and the gas chamber were blown up by the SS.

It is not known precisely how many women were killed by gassing, but the methodical Germans invented a fictional camp called Mittwerda, where women who had been gassed were supposed to have gone. The only surviving list of women sent to Mittwerda on one day in January 1945 contains 450 names.[3] Suhren acknowledged that 1,500 women were gassed at the camp while he was in command, other estimates range from 4,500 to 6,000 and the actual number is likely to have been much higher. This is besides the number of women who died in the *Revier*, where the given figure for the first three months of 1945 was 3,858. Others died at work or around the camp. Often there were so many bodies that they were stacked outside the blocks to await collection, and the frequency of the collections had to be doubled to twice daily.

Women were still being forced to work in the factories around the camp, but fewer and fewer women were being sent to factories further away, and now there were thousands of women with no work to occupy them, and there was growing anarchy in the barrack blocks. There was increasing chaos in the camp, beginning at the end of February and continuing throughout March and April 1945. There were a growing number of incidents of theft between the prisoners, and lesbianism, which hitherto had been frowned upon, was now flaunted.

Unmarked by most and as result of negotiations between Professor Carl Burckhardt, president of the International Red Cross and SS Brigadeführer Walter Schellenberg, on 4 April a convoy of trucks from the American and Canadian Red Cross arrived. Some parcels reached the prisoners, but the SS pilfered or stole many.[4]

Amidst all this misery, unexpectedly the Red Cross arrived to rescue many of the women. On 5 April a transport of 300 women left, not for some other hellhole in Germany, but for Kreuzlingen in neutral, free Switzerland. The transport consisted of 299 Frenchwomen, and one Polish woman, the Countess Karolina Lanckorońska, who Burckhardt had asked for by name.

The outlook for the remaining women at Ravensbrück was grim.

29

THE WHITE KNIGHT

Unknown to the women there was a white knight riding to their aid. He was Folke Bernadotte, Count of Wismar, a nephew of King Gustav V of Sweden, and he married American heiress Estelle Romaine Manville in 1928. He represented Sweden in 1933 at the Chicago Century of Progress Exposition, and in 1939–40 was Swedish Commissioner General at the New York World Fair.

Bernadotte was brave, even stimulated by danger, brimmed with enthusiasm and self-confidence, and had a unique ability to inspire confidence in others. Though rarely seen with a book in hand, he had the knack of analysing any problem quickly and of reducing it to its essential components. By 1944 his most important war work was as vice chairman of the Swedish Red Cross when he supervised the exchange of disabled British and German prisoners of war – work which necessitated frequent visits to London and Berlin. He spoke both languages near perfectly.[1]

At the end of October 1944 Folke Bernadotte visited the headquarters of the Allied commander-in-chief, General 'Ike' Eisenhower. His visit was at the invitation of US General Curtis LeMay to thank him for the part that he had played in caring for a US airman who had been crash-landed in neutral Sweden and had been interned there. It was also an opportunity for Bernadotte to enquire on behalf of his government how and where Sweden could most effectively assist with humanitarian aid in post-war Europe.

Then, on 3 November at lunch at the Bristol Hotel he met the Swedish Consul General, Raoul Nordling. He knew already that Nordling had played an important role as an intermediary between the French Resistance, Allied forces and the German Army of occupation. Over lunch, Nordling entertained Bernadotte with his adventures in the days immediately before the liberation of Paris. Bernadotte was especially thrilled by Nordling's account of how he had persuaded the

Germans to prevent large numbers of men and women from being deported to Germany. Nordling's enthusiasm was as irresistible as it was inspiring:

> As I listened to him I became infected by his enthusiasm. I asked myself if I couldn't do something similar for those who were languishing in German concentration camps. Thus a seed was sown in me which was to grow into the expedition of the Swedish Red Cross into Germany in the spring of 1945.[2]

Bernadotte returned to Sweden via London where he held a meeting with representatives of the World Jewish Congress. A plan to evacuate Norwegians from German prisons had been mooted in 1943 by the Norwegian professor Didrik Arup Seip, who had been held in a concentration camp and was then being held under house arrest in Germany. His plan was adopted by Niels Christian Ditleff, the Norwegian minister in exile in Stockholm.

Through the advocacy of the Danish Admiral Carl Hammerich, this plan was extended to cover Norwegians and Danes in prisons in Germany, and a Red Cross mission was already in Berlin attempting to collect and send home Swedish-born women who had married Germans. Then in February 1945 the Swedish Foreign Ministry approved a plan under which Bernadotte would visit Germany, ostensibly to check on the progress of the Red Cross mission. His real reason was to meet Himmler and see if he could do, on a larger scale, what Nordling had done in Paris.[3]

In Berlin, Bernadotte met Austrian-born Ernst Kaltenbrunner, who was chief of the *Reichssicherheitshauptamt* (RHSA or Reich main security office), and Walther Schellenberg, who was head of foreign intelligence, and then the German foreign minister, Joachim von Ribbentrop. After careful negotiation, on 19 February Schellenberg drove Bernadotte to Hohenlychen Sanatorium where he was greeted by the head doctor, Karl Gebhart, who gave Bernadotte a description of his work at the clinic for German refugees. Presumably he did not tell Bernadotte of his other ghastly work, the experiments that he had performed on women from Ravensbrück.

That evening Himmler, Schellenberg and Bernadotte had a two-and-a-half-hour meeting about transferring the Danish and Norwegian prisoners in German concentration camps to Sweden. Himmler did not agree, and a compromise was reached that these prisoners should be gathered at Neuengamme, the concentration camp east of Hamburg.[4] The two sides disagreed about the number of people involved – whether it was Himmler's estimate of 2,000–3,000, or 13,000, a number which Himmler dismissed as greatly exaggerated.

Bernadotte found Himmler vivacious, inclined to sentimentality in matters affecting Hitler, and enthusiastic, but he noted in his diary, 'Nothing can exonerate Heinrich Himmler from the terrible guilt which rests on his shoulders.' Himmler did agree that the sick, mothers with children, and Swedish women married to Germans might be evacuated to Sweden. He insisted that the agreement should be kept secret: both he and Folke Bernadotte feared that if Hitler found out what was happening, he would veto the Swedish plan.

Bernadotte returned to Stockholm to inform his government and make preparations for what was to become one of the most remarkable rescue missions of the age. What the Swedish Red Cross lacked in manpower and resources was made up for by the Swedish Army, which allowed both career soldiers and conscripts to take leave of absence and volunteer to join the Red Cross. They joined up at Hässleholm in southern Sweden where they formed four transport platoons (three of twelve buses each and one of twelve covered lorries) and a supply platoon. All told, there were seventy-five vehicles and 250 men and women. In the midst of their move to Malmö on 9 and 10 March, the Swedish Foreign Ministry decreed that each vehicle should be painted white and be marked with prominent red crosses. Every painter in Malmö was called in to help, and painting continued through the night and finished aboard the ferries to Copenhagen.

Meanwhile, the steamer *Lillie Mathiesen* sailed to Lübeck laden with fuel, spares, food and first-aid material. On 12 and 13 March the overland expedition reached Friedrichsruh, the home of the Bismarck family, where the Swedish and Swiss consulates had taken refuge from a bombed-out Hamburg. This decision may have been influenced by the Swedish-born Ann-Mari Tengdom, now Princess von Bismarck, who was a former classmate of Bernadotte's. There, while plans were drawn up for the evacuation of prisoners, a shuttle service ran between Lübeck and Friedrichsruh to unload the *Lillie Mathiesen.* (Bernadotte's mind may have been stirred by knowing that the *Lillie Mathiesen* was named after Lillie Ericsson, a revue artist with whom he had once been deeply in love.[5])

From Friedrichsruh the convoys of 'White Buses' travelled over Germany, as far afield as Dachau and Schömberg in southern Germany, and Mauthausen in Austria. Typical of the drivers was 24-year-old Sten Olsson, a bus driver from Klippan in southern Sweden. One of his colleagues had turned down the chance to drive a bus to Germany and, without knowing what was involved, Sten had volunteered. 'I didn't know anything, and to do it I was either an idiot, stupid or something in between. But it was a way to get out in the world.'[6]

Olsson had been at the wheel when, in great secrecy on 12 March, the first convoy of buses and trucks rolled over the border from Denmark into Germany. The next few weeks filled Sten Olsson with a sense of injustice as he drove between various concentration camps, through bombed-out ruins and across the mangled landscape. The Soviet Front was not far away and frequently he heard the growl of guns. He noted that there were Allied prisoners of war on the road and he hated the stench of bloated, rotting animals.

However, Kaltenbrunner was trying to disrupt their operations, and Bernadotte's forceful presence was again needed in Berlin, where he flew on 5 March. Kaltenbrunner told him bluntly, 'I do not intend to assist you.'

Bernadotte showed his steel. 'And I am not going to [tolerate] one of Himmler's subordinates trying to sabotage an arrangement agreed between him and myself.'

Bernadotte went to Friedrichsruh to await the arrival of the White Buses, and during the course of the next few weeks, and notwithstanding Kaltenbrunner's opposition, over 4,000 Scandinavians were gathered at nearby Neuengamme.

The scale of the operation staggers the imagination. Between 15 and 30 March, seven convoys of buses ran to Sachsenhausen, returning with 2,200 passengers, and another convoy of thirty-five buses made the 1,100 mile journey across war-ravaged Germany to Dachau and back carrying all its own fuel and supplies and sufficient food for 600 people. When the operations seemed about to stutter for lack of resources, the Danes lent a hand with resources that they had prepared under their own plan to rescue Danish nationals. Its success was due to Bernadotte, Colonel Gottfrid Björk (the commander of the expedition), the bravery of the individual members of the Swedish expedition, and to the reliability of the Volvo buses.

Meanwhile, another Bismarck estate, Schönhausen, had been brought into use by the Swedes, this time as a temporary sanctuary for the Swedish embassy. It was while driving between Berlin and Schönhausen that Bernadotte saw, for the first time, women prisoners from the concentration camps. It was, he wrote, simply 'a dreadful sight'.

On 22 March he returned via Copenhagen overland to Stockholm, but a few days later he was in Germany on his third wartime visit. On Good Friday, 30 March 1945, Bernadotte was given the first opportunity to visit Neuengamme, becoming the first representative of a neutral, humanitarian organisation to visit a concentration camp. He was greeted by the Kommandant, Max Pauly, who showed him round the Scandinavian section, where he had had two or three weeks' notice to tidy up.[7] Pauly was courteous, helpful and reasonable, and yet Bernadotte boiled with anger at what he saw. The discipline was evidently barbarous and the overcrowding appalling, and he caught glimpses of other parts of the camp where there were thousands of unhappy human beings, or rather human wrecks, wandering aimlessly, apathetic and vacant-minded.

On Easter Monday Bernadotte held a second meeting at Hohenlychen, where he found Himmler both nervy and solemn. During the four-hour meeting attended by Schellenberg, Himmler admitted that Germany faced a crisis but denied that the war was lost. Himmler told Bernadotte, 'I am ready to do anything for the German nation, but the war must go on. I have given my oath to the Führer, and that oath is a binding one.'

Bernadotte answered, 'Don't you realise that Germany has lost the war?'

Himmler did not answer, and Bernadotte was not deterred from his purpose. The conversation became surprisingly frank and he told Himmler that he should be considered a war criminal because appalling cruelties had been committed under his command. It was at this meeting that Himmler proposed to Bernadotte that the German armies in the west would surrender and that the Allied armies could then, jointly with the Germans, halt the westwards advance of the Soviet Army. Bernadotte's response was that he was unwilling to act as intermediary with Eisenhower since that might be taken as sign that he, Bernadotte, believed in the possibility of a separate peace. Bernadotte also learned of Hitler's orders that the concentration camps at Buchenwald, Bergen-Belsen and Theresienstadt were to be evacuated by marching the prisoners 305km westwards.

Despite all the difficulties, Bernadotte obtained the permission he sought to collect all sick prisoners – some 100 Scandinavian female prisoners and two Frenchwomen – from Ravensbrück to Padborg in Denmark. On Saturday, 7 April the first Danish and Norwegian women were assembled to begin their journey to Sweden: the number is imprecise, but may have been as many as 125. The order came from Suhren himself, '*Achtung! Achtung! Alle Skandinavische Fangen vortreten!* [All Scandinavian prisoners forward!]' It was the first signal for the stoppage of work since the camp had opened. The Scandinavian women went straight to their block, packed their meagre possessions and were then taken to the bath house where they were given civilian clothes and told to wait. On Sunday at 1.30 a.m. they left Ravensbrück in the famous White Buses. Suhren stood at the gate and wished them goodbye, '*Gute Heimfart!* [Have a good trip home!]' Later that day 5,000 Swedish food parcels that had come on the buses were distributed in the camp, though only a fraction of their contents reached the starving inmates.[8]

On 9 April Bernadotte flew from Tempelhof to Sweden to report not only to his government, but also to the ambassadors of the UK and USA.[9] Bernadotte took the opportunity to smuggle Didrik Seip and his wife onto his plane – order in Germany was breaking down so quickly that the bribe to the guard was only one packet of cigarettes. On 15 April, Gemma la Guardia Gluck (sister to the outspoken anti-Nazi Mayor of New York), her daughter and her grandson, who had been held separately for nearly a year at Ravensbrück, were put on a train to Berlin and given their liberty. By mid April most work had stopped due to a shortage of raw materials, while the White Buses continued to visit every few days.

Then, between 18 and 20 April the Red Cross base at Friedrichsruh was repeatedly attacked by the RAF. Following reconnaissance flights on the first day, a dozen Red Cross vehicles were blown up, and four Danish drivers and a nurse were killed. Even while plans were being drawn up to evacuate Friedrichsruh, the castle was attacked by a wave of bombers, killing the Swiss Consul General and his wife. The British had convinced themselves that Himmler and the SS had set up their headquarters at Friedrichsruh.

Hitler's birthday, 20 April, was marked by a tiny extra portion of meat in the soup, and in an amnesty on 21 April a group of about sixty German political prisoners at Ravensbrück were given loaves of bread and released. Still in prison clothes, they alarmed the good citizens of Fürstenberg by banging on their doors to demand more food and clothes, but eventually made their way to the railway station and left by train.

Then, over breakfast at Hohenlychen on 22 April, Himmler agreed that Bernadotte could begin to evacuate all women at Ravensbrück and to do so not via Neuengamme but direct to Denmark and on to Sweden.[10] Now Bernadotte drove to Lübeck via Friedrichsruh where he made arrangements for a convoy of fifteen Danish ambulances, under the command of the Swede Hans Arnoldsson, which departed Friedrichsruh later on 22 April to collect the women from Ravensbrück. Eventually Arnoldson was told he could take away all the French, Belgian, Dutch and Polish women – about 15,000 souls – a responsibility which he accepted, even though this was more than three times the capacity of the White Buses.

All this occurred while Bernadotte was being pressed to carry Himmler's peace overture to the Allies. At a final meeting in Lübeck in the early hours of the morning of 24 April, Bernadotte told Himmler, 'It is in my opinion quite impossible to carry out a surrender on the Western front and to continue fighting on the Eastern front. It can be looked upon as quite certain that England and America will not make any separate settlements with Germany.'

Himmler insisted, 'I am well aware of how extremely difficult this is, but all the same I want to make the attempt to save millions of Germans from a Russian occupation.'

Bernadotte replied, 'I am not willing to forward your communiqué to the Swedish minister for foreign affairs, unless you promise that Denmark and Norway shall be included in the surrender.'

Himmler insisted on driving his own car from the meeting, but became entangled in barbed wire from which Bernadotte and the members of the Swedish delegation extracted him with great difficulty. The Swedes agreed that this incident was highly symbolic.

At Ravensbrück working parties were no longer being sent out and the routine of the camp came to a halt. On 24 April all Frenchwomen were ordered to muster on the *Appelplatz* and Fritz Suhren appeared in person to make a selection – this time the selection was for a place on one of the White Buses. Lucienne Dixon had spent the previous night sharing a bunk with Maisie Renault and her sister Isabelle, where they had made plans for the future. They talked about the families they would have and they swore to each other, 'We shall never quarrel again, we shall make pilgrimages, we shall devote our lives to the happiness of others.'[11]

On the *Appelplatz* Lucienne Dixon, hoping that this was her turn to board a White Bus and hoping that her nationality would not be checked, joined Maisie. Mickie Poirier, from the camp labour office, assured them that this was a genuine evacuation and not a black transport, but Lucienne was ordered to stay behind: as an American, her name had been removed from the selection. Lucienne, suffering from an unsteady heart, was lucky to be supplied with drugs through a friend in a kindly Polish block, but the Canadian food parcel she had shared with the Renault sisters had aggravated her dysentery. She knew that the Allied armies could not be far away, but would the Germans want to exterminate the last remaining witnesses to their atrocities?

Also on 24 April there were two last columns of White Buses making their way to Ravensbrück. For long distances the Swedes were alone on the highway and passed many German vehicles which were abandoned or burnt out by the roadside. Only when they got closer to Berlin did they meet refugees from the city who were fleeing in fire engines, horses and carts, on bicycles and pushing handcarts. Åke Svensson urged his drivers to keep bumper to bumper so that no German vehicles could slip between them, and at last they reached Ravensbrück on 25 April.

Again Mickie Poirier was on hand to assure them that other nationalities would be released later. That night Maisie celebrated by drinking coffee that she had found in a Canadian Red Cross parcel, but next day was a disappointment. The Germans had agreed to a certain number of releases; they had a list and neither Maisie nor her sister were on it. In any case, the sisters agreed that they would not be parted, but Suhren apparently intervened to say that they were to consider themselves on parole and would be on the next convoy. As a gesture of this intent he allowed each of them another Red Cross parcel.

A large party of Frenchwomen, among them the Renault sisters, had waited all night outside the camp but the suggestion that they go back into the camp for shelter had been met by a storm of protest. Even so they were not sure of their fate until the group had marched along the road by the side of the lake, with the gas chambers to the left, to be pointed to the right away from the gas chambers and were told, 'You are free'.

There, by the lakeside, they sat on the verge and ate the Red Cross food. Shortly afterwards the first White Bus stopped and Sven Frykman climbed down, to be mobbed by the women. When he freed himself from the throng he looked around and simply said, 'Now you no longer need be hungry'.

The confusion and delay over Maisie's liberation was caused by order and counter-order amongst the Germans. On 24 April, when Hans Arnoldsson, the senior Swedish medical officer attached to the White Buses, arrived at Ravensbrück the Germans told him that on orders from Hitler all evacuation of prisoners was to cease. In any case Suhren had become uncooperative and told the Swedes that the camp's records had been destroyed.

The ovens of the crematory had been used to burn almost all the official records at Ravensbrück. Suhren's latest orders were that the so-called 'guinea pigs', the unfortunate women who had been used in medical experiments, were not to be handed over and to liquidate all prisoners as soon as enemy troops approached. It took at least a day to reach Himmler by telephone so that he could assure Suhren that the orders had been changed again – the evacuation was to continue. There was even a freight train put at the Red Cross' disposal and, against the tide of refugees and military units trying to escape the oncoming Soviet Army, with some 4,000 women crammed into fifty wagons, it travelled via Lübeck to Padborg in Denmark. The train was lost for four days and when found by Hans Arnoldsson on 29 April with a broken-down engine, he feared the worst, but only two women had died and a dozen needed to be rushed to hospital. This 'ghost train', as it came to be known, saved 3,989 women.

Other buses arrived, but Frykman was clearly in charge and the women crowded around him to tell of their woes. In the camp there was turmoil, and as confusion grew the Swedes stopped negotiating with the Germans and took everyone they could without asking. In the second to last convoy of White Buses, consisting of Danish ambulances and lorries, Gösta Hallqvist and Eric Löthman took 706 French, Belgian, Dutch and Polish women.

Gradually, as the crowd thinned, Maisie managed to speak to Frykman, 'Monsieur, are you also going to rescue the American and British women?'

Astonished, Frykman stared at Maisie, 'The commandant has assured me that there is no one else in the camp other than Poles and German nationals. The former will be bussed out tomorrow.'

Maisie gave him the names of her friends, including Lucienne and Toquette, and the numbers of their blocks.

Smiling, he thanked her and added, 'We will fetch them.'[12]

The Swedes Hans Folke and Åke Svensson had also learned that there were Englishwomen in the camp, and had made up a list of eight English women. When challenged, Fritz Suhren denied this, but then a Dutch prisoner nurse gave the Swedes the name and number of Mary Lindell. An SS officer, Danziger, attached to the Swedish column as liaison officer, was sent to find her.[13]

Inside the camp Mary was ill, she had lost even more weight and her resistance to illness was much reduced, and for the third time she went down with pneumonia. This time she had been put to bed in the *Revier* where she was cared for by the German nurses Else and Erica. One night after Erica had taken Mary's temperature she sent for Percy Treite, who arrived ten minutes later with an Austrian prisoner doctor. For the first and only time Mary saw Treite smile. 'Now, Queen Mary, what have you done?' When he listened to her breathing, his only comment was, '*Mein Gott*', and he left the room to fetch sulphonamide tablets stolen from one of the Canadian Red Cross parcels.

Pills in Ravensbrück were frequently given for the wrong purpose – to kill and not to cure – and Treite could see the fear in Mary's eyes. 'It's quite alright, Queen Mary, can you read this? See, the seals are intact, you may break them. Trust me,' he whispered, 'trust me.' Then he asked for the syringe and another medicine.

Erica told him, 'We don't have that here, it's in Fürstenberg.'

'Then send a despatch rider on a motorbike to fetch it. Tell him to go quickly.'

Half an hour later, Treite returned, 'Do you trust me?'

Mary replied faintly, 'I do trust you.'

A little later, Treite's secretary came to see her, 'Treite has told me to give you a message. He has done everything that medicine can do to save you, all that is left is to offer a prayer and he is going to do that. What shall I tell him?'

'Tell him to go to hell!'

When Treite heard this he burst into laughter, 'She'll live. She'll live.'

Mary was still in her sickbed when she heard about the White Buses. Her first thoughts were, 'Well, the first who should have left were the British.' Mary protested to Percy Treite, asking him if he could do anything about it: Treite returned with the news that the Americans and British women were to be held as hostages and to be exchanged against German officers. Next day Treite tried again, when Mary heard that the camp authorities had denied to the Swedes that there were any British there:

> Now I was the captain of the British, had pneumonia and was dying, so I could do nothing. One or two of them used to come and say 'What the hell are you doing!' And I would say 'Well I'm trying not to die, as far as possible.'

When, at last, Mary could get up and go to Schwarzhuber's office she demanded to know, 'What about the British? On what authority do you keep us here?'[14]

Schwarzhuber stared at her stonily, 'I didn't know there were any.' Of course he knew that Mary knew that this was a lie. Their conversation grew heated, until Schwarzhuber shouted, 'Do you know I can still have you shot?'

'Of course you can have me shot, but that does not alter the fact that I should not be here. After all, I am a prisoner of war and it is quite contrary to the Geneva Convention to keep me in this camp at all. Now, what do you propose to do about it?'

Schwarzhuber looked at her with some admiration, 'Have you a list of all the Englishwomen in this camp?'

'Yes.'

'Perhaps you will let me have it then?'

Mary paused, 'Certainly not. I will give you a copy of the list at the same time as you hand me a written authority to leave the camp with these women, and not before.'

To her surprise, Schwarzhuber took a sheet of paper and wrote out an authorisation for her and for the American and British women to leave the camp, leaving a blank space for Mary to fill in the names. 'If you come here at 6 a.m. tomorrow, individual passes will be available, and you will be free to go,' and with that he wished her goodbye.

The first person she told of this apparent good luck was Yvonne Baseden, but a little later Mary received an urgent message not to gather up her friends. 'If you do, you will never be seen again.'

Overnight Mary thought about this warning and by the next morning had stoked up a fury. She stormed into Schwarzhuber's office, 'In England our word is our bond, obviously you have a different code in Germany.'

'I am sorry, I apologise,' he interrupted, 'but orders came from Berlin after you left that you were not to be released.'

Mary raged, 'I see, and what do you intend to do with us?'

'You must remain here. I am sorry, but those are my orders,' and opening a cupboard, he showed Mary a stack of Canadian tinned food. 'To show you my good faith, you may take this food for the Americans and British.'

Mary's sarcasm knew no bounds, 'And how do you expect me to carry so much?'

Mary was surprised when Schwarzhuber ordered several washing baskets to be filled and a guard of camp policewomen, without whom it would not have been safe to move about the increasingly disorderly camp, to carry the baskets. As they turned to leave, Mary took out several tins, 'You may need this food yourself before very long.' Now it was Schwarzhuber's turn to be surprised.

He was stunned for a moment, 'Only an Englishwoman would have thought of making such a gesture.'

'It was not for you. It was for England.'

There was greater drama the next morning. The cry went round the *Revier*, '*Die Engländerin Marie! Die Engländerin Marie!*'

Yvonne, who was with Mary, begged her not to move.

'Don't be silly, Yvonne, they'll find me if they want to.'

She was escorted to the *Appelplatz*, where she found Schwarzhuber leaning on his bicycle. Without preamble he demanded, 'Do you trust me?'

'No, as a matter of fact, I do not.' Mary was still afraid that perhaps Schwarzhuber only wanted the women on her list brought together so that they could be eliminated.

When he saw the doubt in her face he leaned forward, 'You must, you must. Dr Treite agrees and told me to come and see you. Go and get the Englishwomen at once, and the Americans as well, and bring them to my office.' He was, Mary recalled, frightfully ashamed of himself. 'It was beyond my control,' he offered. 'Now get your people together and I personally shall see that they get away.' For the first time, Mary realised that he was not arrogant but tense and strained.

Mary had only a moment to make her decision, and decided that this time Schwarzhuber was serious. There was one other person in the camp she could trust and Mary turned to her friend, Nadine Hwang, to help her to assemble the people on the list. Mary had adopted her, even though she was neither American nor British.

At what must have seemed like the last moment, Lucienne received a message from Mary. Her name was on Mary's list and she was to go to the main gate where there was a bus waiting for her, a bus painted white and emblazoned with the Red Cross and the Swedish flag, and in large letters the word '*SVERIGE*'.

As Nadine moved swiftly from block to block, the women gathered quickly, made hasty farewells to others, and soon Mary led her little group up to Schwarzhuber's office. Even there the drama was not complete – the Germans could not reconcile the women's camp numbers with their names.[15] 'Never mind,' snapped Schwarzhuber. 'We will accept the Englishwoman's numbers. Just take the names.'

With Schwarzhuber riding his bike slowly alongside, the women marched off towards the gate, where Yvonne Baseden stood by Mary while she counted them out by touching each on the shoulder – there were twenty-two women on Lindell's list. They stepped through the gate and waited for Mary. Now Schwarzhuber touched her on the shoulder, 'I am sorry, but you have to remain behind.'

Mary's heart seemed to miss several beats and she felt suddenly quite nauseated. Yvonne, who heard these words, turned back too, 'Then I shall remain behind also.'

'Don't be so stupid, Yvonne, get out quickly.'

'No, I'm going to stay with you, Mary.'

Mary recovered from her shock quickly. 'Don't be such a fool, Yvonne. Get out and tell the world. You're the only one who can do anything. Go on, for God's sake, before it's too late.'

With tears streaming down her face, Yvonne joined the others and was led off towards a column of White Buses. There she found a Swedish officer and explained what had just transpired. 'Do you mean that Marie-Claire is in the camp? My God! The British have been asking us to find her. We were not even sure that she was alive.' But he added ruefully, 'She'll be rescued before long, but there's nothing I can do just now, I must get this convoy going.'

Mary wandered back into the camp, her heart in her mouth, wondering if yet again she was going to be tricked by the Germans and she was destined to lose her life on the eve of liberation. Two German prisoners were startled to see her return to the *Revier*, 'Good God, Mary, we thought you had gone.'

Mary smiled wanly, 'I am afraid that they love me so dearly that they have decided not to let me go.'

As she wandered disconsolately along the *lagerstrasse* she met Percy Treite, 'But what are you doing here?'

She told him her tale. Treite was furious and insisted that Mary should join the very last group of women, mothers with babies and some of the sick, and he added her name to the list as one of the nurses. Treite escorted her to the bus – the last White Bus to leave Ravensbrück.

A SPELL IS CAST

For one woman, the experience of the White Buses was unique. Somehow Elsie Ragusin had passed through Ravensbrück oblivious to its many dangers and thinking that she, and one other, were the only Americans.

Elsie was born in New York on 4 November 1921 to first generation immigrants from Pola in Italy. Her father was a seafarer in the great tradition of Venetian seamen, and as a young man had served in the Austrian Navy. However, her parents had brought her to Italy in 1939, ostensibly to see Elsie's grandparents, but more probably to find her a suitable husband from the old country.[1] Her family lived in a villa in considerable luxury on the island of Lussinpiccolo, like the patricians they were in that corner of the world. Elsie settled into a pleasant life of music, festivals and theatre, and she found work as a court interpreter.

Contemporary pictures show a vivacious, attractive, brunette girl with luxurious hair, sitting on the rocks and wearing some very non-Italian shorts – and she did indeed become engaged to a handsome naval cadet. The war largely bypassed Lussinpiccolo, until 1944 when it was invaded by the Germans, and in the late spring of 1944 Elsie and her father were arrested and deported.

Elsie was sent to Auschwitz, but as the Soviet armies advanced from the east, the Germans began to concentrate their source of slave labour by transporting their female prisoners to Ravensbrück, where Elsie arrived sometime in late 1944. Like others before her, Elsie noted the careful ranking of the prisoners, in their blue and grey striped uniforms with their coloured triangles, and when she was given a red triangle her spirit was not broken and she defiantly sewed the letters 'USA' onto hers. Despite the depraved conditions all around her, Elsie was proud 'to display my origin and my country with the burning love and desire to once again set foot on my beloved native soil'.

One day, while hiding from a selection for a working party to go into the forest, she escaped through the window into the next block and there she had the extraordinary experience of meeting Gemma La Guardia Gluck. Across the generations the two fellow Americans struck up an instant friendship, calling each other 'my little camp daughter' and 'Auntie Gemma'. Emboldened by contact with Gemma La Guardia Gluck and her renewed sense of being an American, Elsie demanded to know of the authorities why she was being made to suffer so. Other women, fearful of the consequences, tried to dissuade her from making any protest and tearfully kissed her goodbye when, two days later, she was marched off. When interviewed she blurted out, 'How would you feel if you had a son and he was held for no good reason and mistreated and you couldn't help him?'

Her reward was to be given a waitress' uniform and the job of serving food and cleaning the guards' canteen. The work was dry and warm, but Elsie quickly realised a new danger as she was followed by the men's lascivious eyes. They were tall, lean and intelligent-looking in their uniforms and Elsie's heart pounded. Now she begged to stay in the kitchen and she prayed hard for God to put an end to this madness. Eventually she was interviewed by Suhren himself – over the same period, he interviewed several prisoners, including Geneviève de Gaulle,[2] Gemma La Guardia Gluck and the woman he knew as Odette Churchill, and it seems likely that Suhren was calculating which of these might be valuable to him and useful in his own plans. When he had heard her out, Suhren replied, 'There is nothing that can be done. How can you possibly turn back safely such a long way with bombs falling, shooting and killing everywhere?'

Elsie traded part of her rations for a prayer book and on 20 February 1945 she wrote a prayer, 'O my God, do not leave this little lamb lost among this throng of people unknown to me, but protect her wherever she may be and guide her safely to her beloved Shepherd.'

As the selections grew more frequent the food grew worse and the brutality even more random. She saw planes flying overhead and heard the reverberations of artillery and bombs, and more ominously the sound of small arms fire. Rumours spread that the camp would be set on fire to destroy the evidence of its horrors.

Then one morning at *Appel* Elsie too was selected. But instead of being led off to execution, men in strange uniforms approached her. They were Swedes, they said, with the unlikely explanation that they had come to liberate her and take her to Sweden. Not believing them, and remembering other trucks which had taken women away never to return, Elsie and the women around her became hysterical. But the kindness and sympathy shown by these unlikely saviours soon quelled their panic. The women were given cigarettes, chocolate and packages of food to persuade them to board the buses, and once seated they stared in silence as the gates opened and the buses drew out of the camp. A spell was cast over the women and for the duration of its power there was silence in the bus. They could neither laugh nor cry, but then eventually there was both laughter and tears. Later Elsie wrote, 'Hope and joy entered our hearts again and the Swedish Red Cross became the incarnation of freedom and the love of humanity. Through their help, we had been permitted to go back into life again!'[3]

Now sitting in the penultimate White Bus to leave Ravensbrück, on 23 April 1945, she thought she was the only American. There were other Americans on Lindell's list and, though she did not know, she was sharing the crowded bus with the friends Lucienne Dixon and Toquette Jackson – these two women may have been speaking French to each other – and another American, Anna Bolyos. Elsie's languages were English and Italian and she may not have understood the babble of languages being spoken around her.

Each bus, licensed in Sweden for twenty-five passengers, carried forty to sixty women, and ambulances intended for two people carried a dozen. The main group of American and British women were in the penultimate bus to leave the camp, and Mary was with the sick in the very last bus to leave. For many, the journey passed in a dream, the convoy travelling nose to tail along roads crowded with refugees, through bombed towns, past ruined buildings and through countryside where it seemed that the earth had been ploughed by artillery shells.

They could not travel by night because the *Tiefflieger*, as Germans called the Allied low-flying fighters, shot at any glimmer of light, so they only moved by daylight when their Red Cross markings could be clearly seen, along roads which were chock-a-block with soldiers, prisoners of war and refugees. At first it was thought that the White Buses would be immune from Allied air attacks, but the RAF pilots were increasingly trigger happy and had lost their respect for the Red Crosses prominently marked on the White Buses. 'British fighter planes patrolled the roads and on the slightest suspicion shot up the convoy of buses, nevertheless,' Sten Olsson recalled. 'I was never afraid, not one iota. For me, it was all one huge and exciting adventure.'

West of Schwerin, one convoy of White Buses had halted and the passengers had taken shelter while the RAF flew over without firing; then, believing that the danger was over, Gösta Hallqvist had made preparations to continue the journey towards safety. As he did so, several aircraft attacked, killing at least eleven and severely injuring twenty-six, including Hallqvist. Later Sven Frykman would report that the attacks were deliberate and had been preceded by Allied planes flying overhead. The Swedish government made a diplomatic protest, but the Allies responded that they had never granted nor guaranteed safe passage.[4]

On another occasion when the convoy stopped so the women could go to the toilet, the guards had made them do their business in an open field, but they were compensated by finding the field full of dandelions which they dug up with their fingers and devoured. Sometimes small children ran out to stone their vehicles. When the convoy of White Buses in which Mary and the American and British women were travelling arrived at the Danish border at Padborg on 26 April, they saw the Danish flag, the *Dannebrog*, flying everywhere and the Danish Red Cross was there to meet them.

Denmark was still under German occupation and the buses were still escorted by German soldiers, but the mere fact of having left Germany made the women's hearts feel lighter, and they enjoyed their first decent meal in many a month. It was at Padborg, when Folke Bernadotte visited, that in defiance of their guards the women broke out into singing 'La Marseillaise' and the Swedish anthem 'Du Gamla, Du Fria [Thou ancient, thou free]'. Bernadotte wrote in his diary:

> The salute went straight to my heart. These people were still captives, though they felt that freedom was within reach, but they well knew what would happen if at that moment the German camp discipline were to be enforced. They risked that, desiring to show their gratitude and they could not have done so in a more moving manner.[5]

Bernadotte continued to negotiate concessions from Himmler, and by now he had persuaded the German that the women should not merely go to transit camps in Denmark, but that they should be placed in the protection of a neutral power, Sweden.

Little Irene Krausz, who sat on the front bench of one the White Buses behind a driver she only knew as Sven, turned to her mother and asked, 'This is a dream, this must be a dream, surely it can't be true that we are going to be free?'[6] The dream was so powerful that many were unaware of the route they travelled, but the Swedish records show that the score women on Lindell's list, including eight Americans and eleven British, arrived in Malmö by the midday train ferry (which had run throughout the five years of the war) on 28 April 1945.[7]

In April and May 1945 some 16,000 refugees arrived in southern Sweden, where the civilian population was mobilised, including female reservists, and formed different teams for reception, quartering, sanitary, transport, feeding and clothing. Schools, sports halls and dance palaces were pressed into service as accommodation, and one of the more unusual buildings to be turned into a refugee camp was Malmö Castle.

The sixteenth-century brick-built castle, Malmöhus, had only recently been turned into a museum and it is referred to in contemporary literature as the New Museum, whose director was Ernst Fischer. Fischer was a member of a local branch of *Tisdagsklubben* (the Tuesday Club), the majority of whose members were publishers, writers, journalists and academics.[8] Formally it was a weekly lunch club from which foreigners were excluded, but a secret part of *Tisdagsklubben* possessed hidden wireless sets and printing equipment, studied methods of sabotage and was, in theory, ready to start a resistance movement should Germany invade Sweden. Though this was part-founded by SOE, SOE did not control it.[9]

More overtly, *Tisdagsklubben* became increasingly concerned to counter Nazi propaganda and its members campaigned for better treatment of refugees.[10] It was therefore natural, when Malmö filled with refugees in April 1945, that Fischer should turn his mind to how he could help. At least one member of Fischer's museum staff, Karin Blomqvist, was also a member of the Tuesday Club. Fischer recalled that he discussed with his staff the difficulties there were in Malmö in finding accommodation for a sudden rush of so many refugees, and he rang the local authorities to ask, 'Have you given any thought of using the museum?'

'The museum? No, we haven't given a moment's thought to doing that.'

Half an hour later, he had persuaded the authorities that he had lofty space, which was easy to clean, with plumbing on all floors and the possibility of creating a large washroom; the castle's hall could become a dining room, there were meeting rooms, terraces, even a small chapel, and the grounds within the walls and moat were ideal to protect the occupants from the curious and to enforce a quarantine.

Two hours later, the entire museum staff – curators, guards, watchmen, cleaners and messengers – were at work in the natural history department where small display objects were put into store and larger ones were boarded up. Next morning three more rooms in the art and crafts department on the upper floor were cleared of furniture, glass, porcelain and textiles, and volunteers began to make up 600 beds by stuffing straw into paper sacks. At 6 p.m. all was ready and during the evening a first group of 280 women – Belgian, Dutch, French and several other nationalities – were settling in.

Fischer marvelled at how quickly the refugees transformed themselves, quitting their dirty, slovenly, worn-out clothes and sitting on their mattresses to cut and stitch the replacement clothes they had been given. Rouge and lipstick appeared as if from nowhere and the women made paper cut-out ornaments for their hair. Fischer also noted a phenomenon which had occurred previously in the camps in Germany: months of fighting for survival had reinforced the women's national pride, or rather, their national prejudices. The Polish Catholics looked down on the Polish Jews, the French would have nothing to do with any Pole, the English – and he meant Mary Lindell – looked down on everyone, and Mary fell out with Nadine Hwang.[11]

In her two weeks of quarantine in Malmö Castle, Nadine caused something of a sensation and she attracted the attention of the press – Chinese colonels were few and far between in peaceful Sweden, still less female colonels. Rumours swirled around Nadine: she had been the colonel of a regiment of Chinese women warriors; she had been captured while on a secret mission in France; under interrogation not even the Gestapo had been able to persuade her to say a single incriminating word during five years' captivity. The truth was only slightly more prosaic.

Nevertheless, Nadine impressed people. Like the other women who recuperated at Malmö Castle, she was undernourished, but she was still tall and slim even after two weeks of good Swedish food when she had put on 7kg of weight. She was neat and tidy in the striped camp uniform, which somehow she had preserved, she appeared smartly dressed even in the grey overall with which she was issued on arrival in Sweden, and before long she found herself some civilian clothes in which to appear *à la mode*.

At first Nadine kept close to the little group of British women who were organised and led by Mary, and she shared a bed space with Mary Lindell and Yvonne Baseden. The Swedes had worked out that both Mary and Yvonne were British secret agents, even if they did not understand that they worked for different agencies. However, Nadine and Mary fell out over their cigarette ration (both were then heavy smokers): the Englishwomen received a generous cigarette ration from their consulate, while Nadine received none from hers. During the quarrel Mary was heard to shout, 'You, yellow dog!', and that was the end of their friendship. While Mary and her group signed the visitor's book together at Malmö Castle, Nadine signed alone and on a different page.[12]

The women's stay was not entirely without humour. Karin Blomqvist recalled that Julie Brichta's English was so accented that when asked where she came from, all that could be understood was 'cha-laisle' and Karin needed an Englishwoman to explain that she meant the Channel Islands. And when one of the Irish sisters was asked if she had children, Karin became confused whether the answer was 'None' or 'Nun'.

***

The women who landed at Malmö possessed nothing other than a few items they had saved from Red Cross parcels, and in a few cases the precious, small things which they had hidden in the seams of their clothing. One girl's most valued possession was a piece of thread around her wedding finger, which replaced the golden band that had been stolen.

The Germans had taken away the women's names and reduced them to numbered pawns in the grotesque and evil empire of slave labour that supported the German war machine. One of the first priorities for the women who filled in their landing cards on arriving in Sweden in April and May 1945 was to reclaim their identities. In German bureaucracy each prisoner was allowed only one given name: now they could claim second and third given names, and for a few it was possible, perhaps, to create another truth about themselves.

In no case was the transformation so great as that of Elisabeth Smith, who had been deported on 31 January 1944 from Compiègne in northern France. To the Germans she was prisoner number 27825, born on 22 November 1915. When she arrived in Sweden on 28 April 1945 she blossomed into Elisabeth Mary Rose Smith, born in Quebec, Canada, and gave her profession as 'pilot'.[13] She even told the Swedish newspapers that she had been taken prisoner after flying to France on a special mission in 1942. However, a search in Britain of the archives of the Air Transport Auxiliary, the Women's Auxiliary Air Force and the Special Operations Section reveals no such person as Elisabeth Smith.

Elisabeth was among a small group of former inmates of German camps, all claiming British nationality, who reached Gothenburg on 5 June 1945. There she gave the additional information that her next of kin was her mother, Mrs Mary Rose Smith of 42 Washington Street, Quebec.[14] The British consular authorities recorded that there was no evidence of her nationality, British or Canadian, and that she had no known relative in the United Kingdom. The women were flown to Prestwick in a Swedish aircraft on 8 June, but before they left they were interviewed in greater detail. The interviewer noted that Elisabeth, '[had] made a very bad impression and was accused of being a renegade by many of the refugees. She wished to marry a Swede whom she has met. The evidence regarding the accusations against her have been reported to the Passport Control Officer.'[15] Whatever evidence was given to the SIS, it does not seem to have survived.

Who, then, was Elisabeth Smith? Mary Lindell had accepted her as worthy of being on her list of American and British women, she had made friends with Yvonne Baseden in the camp, and Elisabeth and Yvonne had stood close to each other when they landed from the train ferry in Malmö in April 1945. A year later, Vera Atkins gave Yvonne as Elisabeth's point of contact, implying that they were still in touch,[16] but after 1946 Elisabeth Smith seems to have walked out of the pages of history.[17]

* * *

The departure of the White Buses did leave several thousand women at Ravensbrück, many too ill to travel, and amongst them at least two other British women. One of them was Josephine Zborowsky, Canadian by birth and married to a Canadian citizen. Josephine had been placed in Block 4 and left with other stretcher cases in the hope that there she would be looked after.[18]

The second woman is best known simply as 'Odette'. Born Odette Marie Céline Brailly in Amiens, she had left her three daughters to go to war to avenge the death of her husband, Roy Sansom. She trained in May 1942, along with Lise de Baissac, Jacqueline Nearne and Mary Herbert. Her reports under training were less than flattering: she was 'impulsive and hasty in her judgements, excitable and temperamental' and 'her main weakness is a complete unwillingness to admit that she could ever be wrong', but she was also very energetic and likeable.

She was landed on the Mediterranean coast near Port Miou on 3 November 1942, with Tom Groome, the wireless operator who Mary Lindell had rejected.[19] There, she met the charismatic Peter Churchill, head of the Spindle circuit, and, seduced by the remains of the good life still available through the black market on the Côte d'Azur, Odette agreed to stay on, and Churchill made her his courier. Soon they were lovers.

On 11 November the Germans invaded the unoccupied zone of France, and Churchill and Odette took refuge in the Italian-occupied part of France at the Hôtel de la Poste in St Jorioz. Post-war audits agree that Spindle, in general, and Churchill and Odette as individuals, achieved relatively little and, worse, Odette and Churchill were well known to the *Abwehr*'s Hugo Bleicher who, posing as a Colonel Henri, was spinning a story that he wished to defect to England and had already penetrated several circuits.

Churchill visited London, and on 15 April was parachuted back to France with orders to break contact with Bleicher and with Odette, but disaster was only hours away.[20] She was part of the reception committee and easily persuaded Churchill to come back with her to the hotel. That night there was a knock on their door and Odette went downstairs in her dressing gown where she was greeted by Bleicher; she and Churchill were arrested. Both were taken to Paris where their solitary confinement was relieved by visits from Bleicher and regular food parcels.

Worse still, before the war was over and the extent of the *Abwehr*'s and the SD's penetration of F Section was widely known, Churchill's friendship with Bleicher came under some very sceptical scrutiny.[21] Churchill was imprisoned with a group of very important special prisoners, known as '*die Prominenten*', who were moved through several concentration camps until on 4 May 1945 they were liberated by the US Army at a lakeside hotel in South Tyrol.

Meanwhile Odette was interrogated in Paris, though controversy exists about the degree of violence used against her, and she made no claim of having been tortured by near-drowning in a cold bath, which had been the ill fortune of other female agents. However, she did persuade her interrogators that she was married to Peter Churchill and that he was a nephew of Winston Churchill. After more than a year of imprisonment, she was taken in May 1944 to Avenue Foch to join a score of women who were packed into a train and sent to prisons in Germany. Among them were eight other female agents who were killed, either by lethal injections and thrown into the ovens at Natzweiler on 6 July 1944, or executed by shots to the back of the head at Dachau on 13 September 1944.

Odette was preserved from either of these dreadful fates and sent to Ravensbrück, where her special treatment continued. Like Geneviève de Gaulle and other important prisoners she was kept in solitary confinement in the cell block, but excused the hard labour and the disease-ridden crowding of the other blocks. Like other VIP prisoners she received monthly visits from Suhren, and when she complained about the lack of natural light she was moved from a basement cell to one on the upper floor, where she had a sprung bed and enjoyed the same scale of rations as her guards. Suhren also authorised twice-weekly visits to the *Revier* where she was treated for hair loss and swollen glands. The worst aspects of her treatment seem to have been her inability to control the temperature in her cell, and that the wardress, Margarete Mewes, stole her rations.[22]

Odette's own account of what happened after Mary Lindell and the White Buses left Ravensbrück was given on 4 May 1946. On the night of 27 April 1945, when the other British women had reached Denmark, at about 12.30

Suhren came to the door of her cell and made a gesture indicating a throat being cut. She thought her end had come. Suhren told her to get her things together and be ready to leave the camp early the next morning.

Odette was escorted to a prison van outside the main gate. Inside the van were a mound of medical stores and several other VIP prisoners – a Lithuanian minster of war, an Italian naval officer and some other women. They drove north to Malchow where there was a small, hutted camp. Here they were kept for three days without water, but on the afternoon of 2 May she was hauled out to see Suhren. Suhren put her in a car with two Polish women, who used to work for him in the camp, and his children's nanny, and they drove off into the night followed by two cars with SS troops armed with machine guns. Around 10 p.m. they ran into the US Army and Odette asked to see an American officer. She explained briefly who she was, but when she returned to the car with some US troops, Suhren had disappeared.

THE AMERICAN RED CROSS

Meanwhile, Glen Whisler visited Malmöhus on behalf of the American Red Cross on 29 April, where he found several women who claimed American citizenship. The most talkative was a woman who had declared herself to the Swedish police to be Gabrielle Tritz, and who had arrived in a group of seventy-seven refugee Frenchwomen in Sweden on 27 April. When, next day, the women on Mary Lindell's list arrived in Malmö and joined her in quarantine at Malmöhus, Gabrielle promptly joined them.[1]

Gabrielle knew Mary from having fed evaders into the Marie-Claire escape line in 1943, and from having worked with her in the *Revier*. She had been born Marie Gabrielle Guldner on 29 December 1895 in the disputed territory of Alsace, a territory which changed hands several times between France and Germany in the nineteenth and twentieth centuries. It had suffered harsh, enforced Germanification under Imperial Germany and under the Nazis in the years 1871–1918 and 1940–45.

When the First World War broke out she was working as an au pair in Harrogate, Yorkshire. Officially she was an enemy alien, and in August 1915 she joined the general westward migration of the Guldner family to the USA where her brother was a doctor in Kansas. There, in 1917, Gabrielle took a course in first aid, which would later save her own life. In 1921 she married Herbert Powell, and two years later she had a daughter, Marie. That year, Gabrielle applied for and was granted American citizenship. However, the marriage did not last and Gabrielle returned to Europe where in 1928 she married Jean-Pierre Tritz, a lawyer also from Alsace.

Gaby and Jean-Pierre had homes in Paris and Poitiers, and during the occupation she became deeply involved in the Resistance, but on 6 January 1944 she was arrested by the Germans. She was deported from France on 16 March

1944 in a group of fifty-one Frenchwomen, all listed as *nacht und nebel* prisoners, to Germany.[2]

Besides Gabrielle, they were Toquette Jackson, Lucienne Dixon, Elsie Ragusin, Anna Bolyos, Olga and Frances (*sic*) Quastler and Berthe du Mont. Two American children, Ivan and Gladys Neumann, had travelled from Ravensbrück to Malmö in the company of Berthe du Mont and Virginia Oliver, but Virginia had been admitted to hospital. Whisler did not interview her, and she was therefore unable to tell him about the youngsters. None of the women had any identity cards or papers of any kind and they all needed help to put them in touch with relatives and to obtain funds.

The women's morale was good, but Whisler was incredulous that they had endured so much and yet their spirit was unbroken. Most were badly underweight, and Swedish doctors reckoned that they were less than half their normal weight but were rapidly recovering on a healthy diet. When Whisler first saw the women, the filthy rags in which they had arrived had been burned, but they were still dressed in overalls and coats issued by the Swedish authorities and had yet to be given the clothing that the women of Malmö had collected for them.

The account that the women gave Whisler of the sordid details of life in the camp was the first to reach the ears of anyone amongst the Allies. The facts were all the more chilling for being told in the cold-blooded prose in which Whisler reported them to the American embassy in Stockholm. The women were still very much under the leadership of Mary Lindell who, typically, added her voice to what the American women told Whisler.

A horrified Whisler was one of the first outsiders to hear the litany of how, on arrival at the camp, the women had been ordered to strip and stand under a cold shower then, watched by lounging and jeering soldiers, had been given a superficial medical check which included a vaginal examination. The instruments were not cleaned between patients and no treatment was available, not even for venereal disease. He learned from Gabrielle that only when Mary Lindell became responsible for some of these examinations was the sterilisation of instruments begun.

Whisler heard of frequent and arbitrary punishments, and more formal punishments including the stoppage of bread rations, and hard labour imposed on top of the twelve-hour day that had already been worked. There was also the peculiar punishment of being made to stand on the street corner in Fürstenberg where the villagers would jeer at them and abuse them. Mary Lindell and Toquette Jackson both vouched to Whisler that the hospital was well equipped but there were almost no medicines, that the palliasses were not changed and that new patients had to lie on the soiled mattresses of their predecessors. Nursing by fellow prisoners was sympathetic but often inept.

Prisoners tried to get work either in the *Revier* or in the kitchens, where conditions for them were slightly less terrible than elsewhere, and Gabrielle, on the strength of her first-aid course a quarter of a century before, succeeded in getting work in the tuberculosis block. There, she had seen patients selected, without regard to the seriousness of their cases, and taken to the gas chamber.

The head doctor, Trommer, had refused to enter the overcrowded ward, but another had passed through the ward pointing and saying, 'Give me that one and that one and that one.' The selected women were carried out by their hands and feet and dumped in carts. Mary told Whisler that these women were taken to the crematorium, where they were shot and thrown into the ovens. Lucienne Dixon told him of her distress that many prisoners whose mothers or sisters had disappeared did not know whose ashes they were carrying to the fields and roads, and Mary told Whisler her own estimate that between 1 December 1944 and 15 February 1945 some 5,000 women had been killed and cremated.

Amongst the Americans Whisler noted Anna Bolyos, born in Ohio in 1912, but he did not record what Anna was doing in Europe when the war overtook her. Her sister had been raped on the march from another camp to Ravensbrück and had died of her injuries, and her mother had been murdered in the camp. With this last, sad news, Whisler was satisfied that there were no more Americans (and only two British) left in the camp. He also recorded that the American women 'would not have gotten out at all if Mary had not insisted in telling the Swedish officers that they were there'.[3]

Whisler was appalled by what he had heard and concluded his ten-page report:

It is difficult to write such a report as this in a factual and objective way. The gross inhumanity of German cruelty practiced on these women makes one regret, at times, that United Nations principles and the future health of Europe make it inadvisable to enforce the Mosaic code of justice for a while. There is no need to comment further about the beatings with weighted rubber truncheons and wooden clubs, the slugging and slapping, the grinding hard work and the loss of sleep. Nor have I much information about the ugly rumour that there are women kept at Ravensbrück whose bodies have been distorted and deformed by sadistic operations in the name of pseudo-scientific research. Properly qualified intelligence officers might well check into that possible page in the German atrocity dossier.

One looks at the wispy bodies and the spindly arms and legs of these women with wonder that the human body and will to live can endure so much. And one is shocked to learn that only prisoners in the best condition are allowed to be evacuated from Ravensbrück. In one case described by Mrs Lindell, the head doctor ordered three Frenchwomen removed from an evacuation ambulance because they looked too bad. They, or their ashes, are still there.

* * *

The British authorities were rather slower to interview their nationals amongst the newly arrived refugees, though the consulate in Malmö was staffed by the British Secret Service, who reacted quickly to finding that there were at least two agents in Malmö Castle. It was a straightforward matter to bring Yvonne Baseden to Stockholm and put her on a plane to Scotland on 19 May, but Mary Lindell was found to be a carrier of diphtheria. The British consul, an older, corpulent man, wanted to send Mary home but the Swedish doctor, a tall, thin principled woman, wanted to keep Mary quarantined. There followed a finger-pointing row in which the doctor became white with rage and the consul red-faced. The row ended with the consul going off to get his ambassador to speak to higher Swedish authorities, but he did not return. Overnight, Karin understood, he had suffered a heart attack. However an official from the embassy arrived to claim Mary Lindell and she was released to go home, regardless of her medical condition. Ten days after Yvonne, Mary left Sweden too.[4]

Karin Blomqvist recalled that on the night before Mary left Malmö the British women had a celebration at Silver's Pension, thinking that they were all about to be repatriated. In fact, it was another ten days before the British women were moved to Gothenburg, where they were interviewed by officials from the British embassy on 8 June, and then they were repatriated.

TRIAL BY COURT MARTIAL

F or several months in early 1946 Mary Lindell was sent to tour the prison
camps of Germany which were newly filled with the defeated enemy. It was
not a happy experience. She had been asked for by Headquarters, British
Army of the Rhine, but there was resentment from the team led by Group
Captain Tony Somerhough, who were investigating war crimes.

In April, the judge advocate general (JAG) in London asked his deputy in
Germany for the results of Mary's investigation, since she had been sent to
Germany three months ago and the JAG complained that he was still 'in the
dark as to what, if any, progress had been made in the preparation of this case'
– i.e. war crimes at Ravensbrück. The JAG added, 'In view of the fact that some
60 of the staff of this camp are known to be in custody, it is highly desirable that
this case be brought to trial at the earliest possible moment.'

Somerhough replied tetchily that he was disappointed in Mary's visit: it is easy
to imagine that he was another authority figure who Mary would dismiss as a 'desk
wallah', and not surprising that Somerhough would complain that, 'as a witness',
Mary was 'considered highly unreliable and her attitude of mind is not objective.
No report was sent to you on her visit as no report had been demanded.'[1]

Eventually thirty-eight people were brought to trial in seven sessions of the
Hamburg War Crimes Tribunal between December 1946 and July 1948, and
Percy Treite was among the first to be tried. There was one charge for all the
defendants: that they were concerned in the ill-treatment and killing of Allied
nationals in violation of the laws and usages of war.[2]

The court heard that the camp was designed to hold 6,000 women, but
after 1943 there were never fewer than 12,000 interned there and by January
1945 there were 36,000. At least 50,000 women had been murdered there, and
many more of the total of 123,000 women who had passed through the camp
had been murdered too. Their deaths were from undernourishment, overwork,

exposure, overcrowding, lack of sanitation and systematic, brutal ill-treatment, and those who were too weak to work – or march – were killed by shooting or gassing. Pink cards, originally intended to grant temporary exemption from hard labour, became passports to death. Possessing grey hair was enough to be shot, and, after several hundred women had been shot, and after Fritz Suhren decided this was too slow, a gas chamber was built where the women were killed in batches of 150. From late 1944, the fires of the crematorium burned day and night. In February 1945, in anticipation of the Allied advance, Johan Schwarzhuber, the second-in-command at the camp, oversaw the killing of anyone considered incapable of being evacuated on foot.

The specific evidence against Treite – 'a brilliant, young surgeon of 34, half-British, perhaps the most complex of all the accused' – was that he had ordered the removal of mad women from the *Revier* to make room for others; in order to economise on medical supplies (which were in short supply) he had ordered that bandages were not to be changed more than once a week and women with 'incurable ulcers' were not to be treated; he had assisted in the selection of 800 women for another camp who were transported in such poor conditions that many died; he sent women with weak lungs to the TB ward; and he selected TB patients who were sent to the gas chamber.

Treite's defence was poor. He had attended beatings, but these were official beatings sanctioned under German law, and the orders were signed by Himmler in person. After he had refused to kill fifty Polish women by injection, he had been summoned late at night to attend their execution by shooting, but he had refused to do so again. He had also refused to take part in any selections for work, when he realised that those not selected were doomed to be gassed. He admitted knowing about the murder of women in the *Jugendlager*, and who had been made to stand at *Appel* for five or six hours a day in the winter air. However, he told the court, he had tried to adhere to the high standards of his profession, was disgusted by what he had seen and did what he could to improve the lot of the prisoners, but was powerless against the camp Kommandant, Suhren. When he realised that he could do no more, he had tried to be transferred from the camp.

Others were more eloquent on his behalf. Emmy Görlich, a German socialist and a political prisoner at Ravensbrück who had worked in the *Revier* from 1939–45, certified that Treite had tried to improve conditions and reduce overcrowding, to obtain better supplies of medicines and dressings, and to cleanse the wards of lice, and that he had protested about the lack of clean linen, the lengthy *Appels*, and the poor diet. Görlich also reported favourably on how

Treite had successfully operated on a group of Russian women who had been hurt when a vehicle overturned.

A dozen Dutch women certified that Treite did not perform any experimental operations or enforced sterilisations, nor selected women for the gas chamber. He had tried to save the newborn, and had generally done what he could to improve conditions in the hospital. Another group of Dutch women did write condemning Treite, not for any specific act, but as a member of the camp staff.

Yvonne Baseden also wrote from her mother's home in Arcachon to say that Treite had treated her well on the two occasions she had been admitted to the *Revier*. Treite's mother too wrote to the court: she had previously written from Switzerland to Albert Orsborn, General of the Salvation Army, asking for his intervention, but had received a cold reply. Others testified that Treite had performed a number of successful cancer operations and, tellingly, he had refused to accept stolen Red Cross parcels when these were shared out among the SS guards. Nevertheless, Treite was sentenced to be hanged.

Mary Lindell, who had given evidence in court, also wrote letters pleading for mercy for Treite. Far from being complicit in the death of Allied prisoners, she wrote, Treite had saved the lives of many, including her own, and inspired hope in all who received his care and attention, and rather than ill-treating prisoners he had given them all the care possible in the conditions prevailing in the camp. She added:

> Had Dr Treite left it would have been the biggest tragedy which could happen to the camp, because he was the only man who was human, the only man who looked after the sick people as a doctor should look after them, doing his duty as a doctor.

True to form Mary also criticised the judge advocate, who was 'partial and objectionable, had taken on the cross-examination of witnesses himself, and prevented other questions from being put which might have been [answered] in favour of the accused'. Others also questioned the impartial nature of Stirling's conduct of the tribunal: he had indeed badgered witnesses and counsel.[3]

Of the British women, only Barbara Chatenay wrote in favour of the death sentence, considering that anyone who spoke up for Treite must have belonged to a small clique who benefitted from his protection, 'I consider that anyone who acted and kept any official post in Ravensbrück well deserved death.'

Some of the issues before the court were finely judged. For example, there was not much difference in behaviour in the camp between two of the Kapos,

Eugenia von Skene and Julie Brichta, yet Eugenia was sentenced to ten years' imprisonment while Julie escaped trial. And the despicable dentist, Martin Hellinger, who robbed the dead and, worse, the dying, of their gold fillings, only received a sentence five years longer than Eugenia's. In Treite's case, Lord Russell, the Deputy JAG, had some difficulty in justifying the sentence of death and fell back on the New Testament and a moral judgement that Treite was a young man of decent birth and good education, not a low, brutal moron like some of his co-defendants, and that 'in so far as he sinned, he sinned against the light'.

* * *

With the end of the Hamburg War Crimes Tribunal, Mary returned to her self-imposed exile in France, only visiting London occasionally for ceremonies and the occasional reunion. She was awarded a second Croix de Guerre by the French, but her wartime services passed almost unnoticed by the British. In France she worked for the RAF Escaping Society, directing her energies and the society's attention to the French men and women, many of humble background, who had helped on the escape lines, and in 1967 she was awarded the OBE for this service. She continued to harangue visitors to Paris, the more senior the better, and she died at the age of 91 in 1986.

The citation for Mary's second Croix de Guerre read that she had been:

> [A] pioneer of the resistance, founder in the first days of the German occupation of an escape line for Allied personnel, a dedicated agent with a complete self-sacrificial devotion to the cause, arrested in 1941, she resumed her activity when released from prison serving the cause regardless of cost, always ready at her post until arrested and deported at the end of February 1944.

PATRIOTISM IS NOT ENOUGH

The history of the escape lines that sheltered thousands of Jews, Belgian, British, French and Polish soldiers after the fall of France, Allied airmen downed over western Europe, escaped prisoners of war, deserters who had been recruited from Lorraine into the German Army, and French wishing to avoid forced labour in Germany, focuses mainly upon the best-known lines – the Comet line, which started in Belgium, and the Pat line, which operated in Vichy France. However, as early as the summer of 1940 numerous escape lines had sprung spontaneously into being, many involving expatriate American and British residents in France. Historians have largely overlooked the role of the American embassy in Paris and American consular officials in Lyon and Marseilles in aiding these escape lines.

As is shown by a study of the 'Reports of Escape and Evasion' held at the British National Archives at Kew, and as the masterly analysis by Oliver Clutton-Brock reveals, thousands of French men and women from all walks of life took extraordinary risks to help in these escapes. Amongst these heroes and heroines, the complementary roles played by Mary Lindell and Pauline Barré de Saint-Venant deserve to be better known.

It was a tragedy that two such strong women as Mary and Pauline should find themselves unable to co-operate. Both were born in 1895, both were volunteer nurses in the First World War, both married into the French aristocracy and, in 1940, both began their personal resistance to the German occupation of France by organising escape lines independently of any higher organisation.[1]

Mary has been badly served by her first biographer, Barry Wynne, who listened to too much gossip from her without checking the facts: to be fair, there were no open archives in 1961, but if he had not been under the publisher's cosh he might have checked her story with other witnesses. Pauline has been badly served by French historians, who even confused her with a younger woman, Marie-Odile de Saint-Venant (born 9 March 1905), who may have been her sister-in-law. (Both Pauline and the real Marie-Odile were murdered at Ravensbrück.[2])

A brief record of Pauline's achievements was printed in 1957, but she was forgotten until revisionist historians tried to transfer the credit from the Englishwoman Mary to the Frenchwoman Pauline,[3] and it was only in 2011 that Pauline was honoured in her place of birth.[4]

It was inevitable that two such similar, strong women should clash. Each thought that the other was greedy for cash, and Mary thought that she had been betrayed by Pauline. At least Mary was forgiving and merciful to Pauline when they met in the *Revier* at Ravensbrück, and Mary did help to admit Pauline to the hospital.

Mary also clashed with the Romanian-born Vera Atkins. Mary and Vera first met in London in June 1945: the meeting between them must have been a very charged affair. Atkins was wearing her newly acquired RAF uniform. Some have seen her as the *éminence grise* of SOE's F Section, the section which had sent so many agents to their deaths. She did not know what role Mary had played in the war, and Mary, newly released from the horrors of Ravensbrück, made it very plain what she thought of people like Atkins who, as civilians, had stayed close to their desks while sending agents to their deaths at no risk to their own selves.

A particular point of disagreement was the manner of the death of the three agents, Lilian Rolfe, Denise Bloch and Violette Szabó. According to a report by Atkins, Mary did not know what had become of the three women agents, though this is at variance with Mary's evidence. Mary was adamant that the women agents had been hung, because their clothes (the clothes that she had smuggled in to them) were returned to the clothes store without bullet holes (her image of death by shooting was the image of Edith Cavell shot by a squad of soldiers, not by a small-calibre bullet fired to the back of the neck as was used at Ravensbrück).

Mary had another dispute, which was Vera's offhand treatment of Yvonne Baseden, and an enquiry that Atkins started into why, of all the woman agents, Yvonne had survived and the others had perished.[5] Thirty-five years later, Mary was still vehement enough about Atkins to dispute with Margaret Rossiter whether Atkins was head of intelligence for SOE's F Section, or whether she was just a civilian secretary. Her opinion was, 'She's a menace … isn't she dreadful? … the biggest big-mouthed bitch',[6] and when she had warmed to her argument Mary accused Maurice Buckmaster, the head of F Section, of being a murderer – or at best, 'an incompetent arse'.[7]

Mary's views of other women were often intemperate, yet accurate. She had met Odette Sansom in Ravensbrück and she doubted the portrayal of Odette Hallowes (as she had become) in Jerrard Tickell's 1949 biography[8] and in Herbert Wilcox's 1950 film of the book,[9] which created a stereotype image of the female SOE agent. Mary told Margaret Rossiter that the book was 'ridiculous' and the film 'no good'. In part, this was due to Buckmaster who, ever anxious to enhance the achievements of F Section, encouraged inflated claims of the success of his organisation – even to the extent of appearing on screen to play himself. Predictably, Buckmaster blamed the press. The problems about F Section, he said, would not have been publicised, 'if [the] press had not blown up the story of Odette Sansom'.[10] Equally predictably, while M.R.D. Foot was academic in his criticism of their meagre successes,[11] Mary Lindell went further and called Odette a murderess. Her accusation was that Odette had been too busy in bed with Churchill to make a rendezvous and that this had led to Germaine Tambour's arrest and ultimately her death with her sister in Ravensbrück. She repeated the accusation that Odette was ready to climb into bed with anyone.[12]

Statements like these shocked the American feminist historian Margaret Rossiter when she interviewed Mary Lindell towards the end of her life. She was expecting to meet a French aristocrat or an English lady. Certainly she found that Mary spoke with the self-confidence of an aristocrat, but she was no traditional lady. 'She was,' Margaret found, 'sometimes ungracious and abrupt, and if she thought people were phoney, she told them so.'

Of Mary herself, her early life is only partly revealed. She was one of the thousands of young British women who sought their emancipation by becoming nurses on the Western Front in the First World War, and she undoubtedly showed great personal bravery during the German advance in the spring of 1918. Soon after, in Warsaw she married a count who was not free under French law to do so – though this does not explain why she then exiled herself to France, where no one challenged her right to call herself the Comtesse de Milleville. By 1940 she had raised three teenage children and if, at the fall of France, she had chosen to flee, she could have done so with honour. Instead, affronted by the German occupation of her adopted city, she performed great acts of bravery. She was not blinded by the anger which might have inspired a few minutes of fame, but was blind to the danger of defying the enemy during five long years of stubborn, reckless resistance.

Like her role model of a quarter of century before, Edith Cavell, Mary was involved in running an escape line. She made it a family business, even while her family was breaking up around her. She survived nine months' imprisonment and when she made her own escape she would have been justified in staying in England to rest on her laurels. She chose to return to France and to set up the first War Office-sponsored escape line, having also chosen not to take a wireless operator (her choice was justified by events when her nominated operator, Tom Groom, made unwise, repeated use of the same safe house and was part of the cause of the collapse of another escape line, the Pat line). Mary's line, the Marie-Claire line remained open for a further six months.

The greatest achievement of the Marie-Claire line came in the aftermath of Operation Frankton, the Royal Marines' canoe raid on shipping at Bordeaux in December 1942. It is true that escape and evasion was also the work of other resistance organisations, but when Blondie Hasler and Bill Sparks, the survivors of Operation Frankton, arrived at Ruffec, all turned to Mary Lindell for leadership even though she was newly returned to France and was lying in hospital after a road accident – an accident which may have been an attempted assassination. Mary fed Hasler and Sparks into the Pat line and the coded report that she smuggled into Switzerland in February 1942 was the first news of their success and survival.

Some who worked for Mary on the Marie-Claire escape line also worked for other resistance agencies. For example, at Ruffec, Lise de Baissac had recruited Gaston Denivelle and Colonel de Gua into the Scientist circuit,[13] while others, like Gaby Tritz in Poitiers and the priests Andre Péan and Armand Blanchebarbe, worked as freelancers.

It was a pattern repeated throughout France. In the French Basque country, for example, there were at least ten resistance organisations that swam in an alphabetic sea – the AF, AS, CDL, CFLN, CFP, FTP(F), OMA, ORA, etc. – and whose loyalties ranged from neo-royalist and ultra-nationalist to communist, and whose hatred could be as anti-British as it was anti-German. There were, at least at first, as many pro-Pétain and pro-collaboration organisations,[14] and in French cities ruled by collaborators and riddled with informers the attrition among agents and wireless operators was horrific.[15]

Nationwide there were other organisations like the *Confrérie Notre-Dame* or CND, which was Catholic and right wing, but anti-Nazi; the *Francs-Tireurs et Partisans* or FTP, the armed wing of the French Communist Party; an *Armée Juive* (Jewish Army) and France's Polish minority and Spanish Communists who, in their turn, were refugees from the Spanish Civil War. French Socialists had their own resistance organisations, such as *Comité d'Action Socialiste* (CAS) and the Socialists dominated the *Organisation Civile et Militaire* (OCM).[16]

The British and French effort in London was also divided – SIS, SOE, MI9, BCRA (*Bureau Central de Renseignements et d'Action*). The German counter-offensive was barely more united, though nevertheless it had penetrated large areas of the SOE, the French Resistance and the escape lines. On this alphabetic sea of compromises, double-dealing, disassembly and dissimulation, Mary Lindell was a ship whose course never deviated from the moral compass of personal bravery and patriotism that she had set herself.

In Dijon she befriended Yvonne Baseden and, subsequently, at Ravensbrück she saved Yvonne's life. In the camp she made herself the self-appointed 'captain of the English' and of anyone outside the dominant national groups who she reckoned was sufficiently British (her concept of who was British stemmed from the nineteenth century and included Americans). Working from the camp hospital, Mary continued her resistance, stealing medicines, gathering intelligence, aiding other prisoners, smuggling food and clothes into the cell block, and finally producing her list, which enabled a score of American and British women to board the second to last White Bus to leave Ravensbrück as several thousand other women were being sent off on death marches and the raping Red Army closed in on the camp.

She endured blackguarding, principally by Julie Brichta and another French countess, Françoise de Lavernay. She was accused of collaboration in the camp, and of having been Percy Treite's lover. Undoubtedly Mary played upon Treite's English sentiments, but it is hard to imagine the circumstances in the camp where Mary and Treite, fifteen years her junior, might have conducted an affair. Suffice it to say that the matter was thoroughly investigated by British Intelligence in 1945 and the indictment was refuted.[17] Nevertheless, Mary would have been shocked if she had known what lay behind the prosecutor's questions to her at the Hamburg War Crimes Tribunal, 'Did you have a bed to yourself? Did you ever share a bed with anyone?' Just as the court must have been puzzled by her answer, 'Yes, when we first got to the hospital, with Yvonne Baseden.'[18]

At the Hamburg War Crimes tribunal Mary did organise a defence for Percy Treite: women of several nationalities gave witness or wrote to the court on Treite's behalf, amongst them Ann Sheridan and Ragna Fischer, but Mary was the star witness. When asked why she gave evidence in favour of Treite, 'What were the motives for your coming to this court?', she replied, 'I have got two reasons. The first is that I am a British subject and that I think that justice is justice, fair is fair, and that a great many things and suppositions have been made [that] because one is an SS one is necessarily a brute; and then secondly we British subjects and the Americans who were in that camp owe our lives to Dr Treite.'[19]

Several times in her life Mary Lindell summoned the image of her heroine Edith Cavell. Without doubt she took her inspiration from and consciously modelled herself on her heroine, as did thousands of other women in the early twentieth century in Britain and across Europe. Edith, who was motivated by her patriotism and her strong, Anglican belief, had written prior to her execution before a German firing squad, 'I realise that patriotism is not enough. I must have no hatred or bitterness towards anyone.' Mary had no overt religiosity, and was rarely given to any philosophising, except once when interviewed by Robert Morley. Her belief was, 'You either go with your enemy, or you go against your enemy. Well who is our enemy, they're all Jerries aren't they? You couldn't sit down and twiddle your thumbs and do nothing. It isn't my nature to do that.'

And in the end she was modest:

Oh, when they say I am a heroine, I am most embarrassed and I think it's ridiculous. After all is said and done, one does a job, it is a job. A lot of people say 'oh how courageous, how brave.' I say 'no': luck. I was lucky, I was wounded three times and they all said you can never recover. Luck. My number wasn't up. But the heroine is all twiddle-rot.

There was another difference between Edith Cavell and Mary Lindell: Edith had been shot, but however closely and recklessly she courted death, Mary missed her martyrdom.

Of Mary Lindell's career and character here are the opinions of two men who knew her best. The view of Donald Darling – the man who was 'Sunday' – was that her career was:

… one long run of misfortune and were it not for her remarkable patriotic spirit and willpower, she might understandably have given up the struggle … yet after further passages of arms with the Gestapo as well as lengthy spells in wretched prisons and seven months in Ravensbrück concentration camp, she emerged with her chin up, militant as ever. Even in her seventies, she would not be set aside by persons in authority whom she consider[ed] inefficient and unreasonable, as she imperiously inform[ed] them … I had to admire her determined fight against the malicious Fates.[20]

Airey Neave – the man who was 'Saturday' – was less equivocal. He thought that Mary Lindell was one of the most remarkable characters of the French Resistance and of British Military Intelligence during the war.

APPENDIX

Forename	Surname	Date of Birth	Place of Birth	Nationality	Agency	Murdered	Liberated	Landing card number in Malmö/ or name of other place
Francine	Johnston-Sebastien	?	?	French/ American			17/8/44	Fresnes
Gladys	Maublanc, de	12/2/1888	Canada	Canadian/ French	FR		12/9/44	Vittel
Virginia	D'Albert-Lake	4/6/1910	Dayton, Ohio	American/ French	FR		5/4/45	Libenau
Gemma	La Guardia Gluck	24/4/1881	New York	American/ Hungarian			15/4/45	Berlin
Pat(ricia)	Cheramy	21/3/1906	Aldbourne	British/ French	Pat		22/4/45	Swiss border
Agnes	Flanagan	16/5/1909		British			26/4/45	189800
Barbara Edith	Chatenay	3/06/1891	London	British/ French	FR		26/4/45	190158
Gabrielle	Tritz	29/12/1929	Alsace	French/ American	FR		27/4/45	190340

Name	Surname	Date of birth	Place	Nationality		Date	Number
Molly Burgess	Dessy	8/12/1907		Belgian/British		27/4/45	190859
Anne Marie	Roberts	10/11/1893	Belgium	British by marriage		27/4/45	191847
Virginia	Oliver	22/8/1906	Platte River	American		28/4/45	189110
Ivan (younger brother)	Neumann	6/6/1934		Hungarian/American		28/4/45	189111
Gladys (older sister)	Neumann	17/2/1931		Hungarian/American		28/4/45	189112
Berthe Madeline	Mont, du	?		German/American		28/4/45	189113
Julia	Barry	28/11/1895*	Makó, Hungary	Hungarian/British		28/4/45	190404
Marcelle Margarete	Rose	9/2/1910	Monte Carlo	British by marriage	MI9	28/4/45	191500 (Sjukvagn)
Charlotte Sylvia/e	Jackson	3/8/1889	Colombier, CH	Swiss/American	FR	28/4/45	191502
Lucienne Germaine	Dixon	22/12/1896	New York	French/American	FR	28/4/45	191503
Rachel (mother)	Krausz	5/2/1905		Hungarian by marriage		28/4/45	191504
Irene (daughter)	Krausz	1/10/1935		Hungarian by marriage		28/4/45	191506

Mary	Lindell	11/9/1895	Sutton, Surrey	British	MI9		28/4/45	191507
Mary	O'Shaughnessy	12/3/1898		British	FR		28/4/45	191508
Kate Anne	McCarthy	17/12/1895	Dromihage Eire	Irish/British	FR		28/4/45	191510
Elisabeth Mary Rose	Smith	22/11/1915*	Belgium	Canadian/British*	Hopper		28/4/45	191511
Elsie Anna Jeanette	Ragusyn	4/11/1921		American			28/4/45	191512
Yvonne	Baseden	20/1/1922	Paris	French/British	SOE		28/4/45	191513
Nadine	Hwang	9/3/1902	Chekiang, China	Belgium-Chinese			28/4/45	191514
Rosetta Marianna	Achmed	29/3/1912		Egyptian			28/4/45	191515
Magdalena (older sister)	Schimmel	28/7/1922	Hungary	Palestinian			28/4/45	191516
Franziska Marianna (daughter)	Quastler	27/2/1931		Argentine/American			28/4/45	191517
Edith (younger sister)	Schimmel	18/9/1929	Hungary	Palestinian			28/4/45	191518
Olga (mother)	Quastler	1/7/1905		Argentine/American			28/4/45	191519
Marie-Germaine Charlotte	Tonna-Barthet	16/11/1893		Maltese			28/4/45	191520
Anna	Bolyos	16/10/1913		American			28/4/45	191522

Ann Elizabeth Victoria Seymour de Beaufort	Sheridan	24/7/1917	Alexandria	British		28/4/45	192115
Doreen Ivy	Verani	5/5/1917		British/French		28/4/45	192116
Francoise Blemence Eleonore	Lavernay, de	18/1/1905		British		28/4/45	193268
Sadie	Loewenstein-Zdrojewski	21/11/1907	New York?	Canadian?	FR	28/4/45	
Sylvia Sophie	Rousselin	17/12/1900	Moseley	British/French		3/5/45	9175
Janine Alix	Dilley	30/9/1920	Paris	British	MI9	3/5/45	9880
Lotka	Jensen	17/5/1921		British		17/5/45	3239
Survived Ravensbrück but method and date of return not established							
Janet	Comert	16/3/1884	Chicago	American		11/5/45	Ravensbrück
Roberta	Mauduit, de	24/9/1899	Polwarth	British/French	MI9	?/5/1945	Leipzig
Odette	Sansom	28/4/1912		British	SOE	?	American zone
Eugenia	Skene, von	30/10/1906	Liverpool	British	[10 years @ Hamburg War Crimes Tribunal]		
Elisabeth	Winter, de	25/5/1919	New York	American	Red Orch	10/5/45	Frankfurt (Oder)
Josephine	Zborowsky	25/3/1894	Winnipeg	Canadian		?	?

Murdered at Ravensbrück or died shortly after liberation								
Denise Madeleine	Bloch	21/1/1916	Paris	French	SOE	m	5/2/45	-
Suzanne	Boitte	15/5/1919		French	BCRA	m	18/1/45	
Mary	Chevignard	3/11/1886	South Dakota	American/French		d	9/4/45	
Marie-Louise	Cloarec	10/5/1917		French	BCRA	m	18/1/45	
Cathleen	Crean	?	Ireland	British?		m	?	
Eugénie	Djendi	8/3/1923		French	BCRA	m	18/1/45	
Evelyne	Gore	13/3/1918		British		m	?	
Louise	Gould	?/?/1892	Jersey	British		m	??/2/45	
Rose-Marie	Jones	16/5/1916		French/British	(FR)	m	??/2/45	
Cicely	Lefort	30/4/1899	London	British/French	SOE	m	15/2/45	
Pierrette	Louin	6/4/1905		French	BCRA	m	18/1/45	
Renée	Noirtin	5/8/1879	Hoboken NJ	American		m	??/2/45	
Lilian	Rolfe	26/4/1914	Paris	British	SOE	m	5/2/45	
Yvonne Claire	Rudellat	11/1/1897	Paris	French/Italian	SOE	m	24/4/45	Belsen
Violette	Szabó	26/6/1921		French/British	SOE	m	5/2/45	
Mary-Helen	Young	5/6/1883	Aberdeen	British	FR	m	15/2/45	

Notes & Abbreviations

Also, from the Fondation pour la Mémoire de la Déportation, there were three British-born women on the transport of deportees from Compiègne on 28 April 1943:

> Edith Certhoux, born in Dartford, Kent, on 8 March 1891, prisoner No. 19366 at Ravensbrück, murdered in Auschwitz in July 1944.
>
> Suzanne Dubois, born in London, on 27 June 1915, prisoner No. 19323 at Ravensbrück, sent to forced labour in an aircraft factory at Neubrandenburg, fate unknown.
>
> Rosina Fournier, born in Wandsworth, London, on 7 July 1895, prisoner No. 19421 at Ravensbrück, sent to Neubrandenburg, murdered in February 1945.

In addition, TNA WO 311/819, an 'index to names of British subjects interned in enemy concentration camps', and annotated 'it is known that this list is incomplete', contains the names of five other women who were held at Ravensbrück, but who have not been identified by the author. They are:

> Miss M. Claire (probably a reference to Mary Lindell)
>
> Mrs G. aka Juliette Mathilde Gulley
>
> Miss Marie Oliver
>
> Mrs Marie Therese Phillips (possibly born 6 August 1905, deported from Paris in July 1944, prisoner No. 47171 at Ravensbrück, sent to forced labour at Neubrandenburg and Neu Rohlau, returned to France on 8 May 1945)
>
> Mrs Simone Piat (possibly born 7 March 1907, deported from Paris in October 1943, prisoner No. 24581 at Ravensbrück, liberated by the Red Cross at Mauthausen 22 April 1945)

Further information about these woman and anyone listed in the index would be welcomed.

*	Women who gave other dates of birth
BCRA	*Bureau Central de Renseignements et d'Action*
d	died shortly after release
FR	French Resistance
Hopper	A faux resistance group in northern France
m	murdered in captivity
MI9	British escape and evasion agency
Pat	Pat line
Red Orch	Red Orchestra (a pro-Soviet resistance group)
SOE	Special Operations Executive

NOTES

All references, FO, HS, WO, etc., are held in The National Archives (TNA), Kew unless otherwise stated.

Foreword

1   Margaret LaFoy Rossiter (1914–91) founded the Women's Studies Program and was a professor of modern European history at Eastern Michigan University. The bulk of her collection, which went into writing *Women in the Resistance*, covers approximately 7 linear feet of interview transcripts and audio recordings, government documents, correspondence, articles, excerpts, photographs, ephemera, questionnaires, personal accounts and drafts of chapters, as well as some research for and reprints and drafts of other works. The relevant taped interviews are: Rossiter (ROSSICA) 78 Side A, Henri Frenay Part II, Mme Geneviève Camcees, Paris, 26 October 1976 (part 1); Side B, Mme Camus, part II, first part of tape; Mary Lindell, beginning of interview I, 26 October 1976, Paris; Rossiter (ROSSICA) 77, Side A: Mary Lindell Part II; Side B: Mary Lindell Part III (Scotch C-90); Rossiter (ROSSICA) 67 Side A: Mary Lindell side 3, part IV; side B: part V, last of interview with Mary Lindell (Scotch C90).

2   Rossiter, pp.35–43, 209.

3   Rossiter, p.35.

4   *It Happened to Me – Mary Lindell: the Escapers*. This is a period piece made for BBC television around 1960 in which several wartime participants play themselves. No copy survives in the archives but a rare copy has been preserved by Scott Goodall in France.

5   *Women of Courage: My Number Wasn't Up* (Yorkshire Television: Peter Morley, 1976).

6   Sim, Kevin, *Women at War: Five Heroines who Defied the Nazis and Survived*.

7   Helm, Sarah, *A Life in Secrets: Vera Atkins and the Missing Agents of WWII*.

8   Roger Bryant in the parish magazine of St Faith, Havant, with St Nicholas, Langstone, January 2011.

9   Clutton-Brock, Oliver, *RAF Evaders: The Comprehensive Story of Thousands of Escapers and their Escape Lines, Western Europe, 1940–1945*.

10 Le Foulon, Marie-Laure, *Lady Mensonges: Mary Lindell, Fausse Heroine de la Résistance*.

11 Hastings, Max, *The Secret War: Spies, Codes and Guerrillas 1939–1945*.

Intro

1 The National Archives, Kew henceforth TNA RW 2/3 Letter from Carmen Mory to 'The Prosecutor, Major Stewart, Capt. da Cunha of the 23 Hussars R.C.'; and Caterina Abbati, *Ich, Carmen Mory: Das Leben einer BernerArzttochter und Gestapo-Agentin 1906–1947* (Chronos, Zürich, 1999).

2 Major General Victor John Eric Westropp (1897–1964): 1939, Commanding Officer 1st Divisional Signals; 1939–40, General Staff Officer 2, War Office; 1940, General Staff Officer 1, War Office; 1940–41, Assistant Adjutant General, War Office; 1941–42, Deputy Director of Personnel Services, War Office; 1944–46, Deputy Adjutant General, Army Headquarters India; 1947–51, Deputy Chief of Staff Allied Control Commission, Germany; 1948–51, British Commissioner, Military Security Board, Allied Control Commission Germany; 1951, retired.

3 Carl Ludwig Stirling CBE QC (1890–1973). See Imperial War Museum (IWM) 17014 Private Papers of C.L. Stirling CBE QC; http://www.josefjakobs.info/2015/01/the-rocky-road-to-josef-jakobs-court_12.html [accessed 1 March 2016].

4 His Honour John da Cunha (1922–2006) obituary in the *Daily Telegraph*, 19 July 2006: http://www.telegraph.co.uk/news/obituaries/1524267/His-Honour-John-da-Cunha.html [accessed 1 December 2015].

Chapter 1

1 *Women of Courage.*
2 *British Journal of Nursing*, 9 January 1915, p.27.
3 *British Journal of Nursing*, 2 January 1915, p.3.
4 Little, Helen D., *British Women's Work During the Great War.*
5 *British Journal of Nursing*, 6 March 1915, p.191.
6 *Daily Record*, 22 October 1915.
7 *Daily Record*, 30 October 1915.
8 Van Til, Jacqueline, *With Edith Cavell in Belgium.*
9 Hill, William Thomson, *The Martyrdom of Nurse Cavell: The Life Story of the Victim of Germany's Most Barbarous Crime* (London: Hutchinson & Co., 1915).
10 Souhami, Diana, *Edith Cavell* (London: Quercus, 2010).
11 *Reading Mercury*, 3 November 1917.
12 Wynne, p.14.
13 *Bucks Herald*, 27 July 1918.
14 *Daily Mirror*, 29 July 1918.
15 The French original reads: '*Les 28 at 29 mai, au moment de la poussée ennemie, s'est distinguée par son dévouement, son sang-froid et sa belle insouciance du danger. Apres le repli de la formation et malgré le bombardement, elle est encore restée sur place, aidant à sauver du matériel, signant les blessés et réussissant à faire évacuer des fermes, des enfants et des vieillards qui n'avaient pu fuir.*'
16 Sim, p.28.
17 Wynne, p.15.
18 *Daily Mail*, 24 May 1918.

19   *Western Mail*, 30 May 1918.
20   Rossiter, Audio 77, track 3.
21   WO 372/23/25121 – Medal card of Lindell, Gertrude. Corps: Young Women's Christian Association.
22   WO 372/23/25122 – Medal card of Lindell, Ghita. Corps: French Red Cross, rank, Anaesthetist.
23   See Rossiter, folder 3, f.4. 'MI9 Report on Marie-Claire'. These papers, marked 'Box 67', are believed to be copies of papers which originated in MI9 in London and were the draft of a report on the achievements in escape and evasion of the Marie-Claire and Marie-Odile escape lines. Margaret Rossiter obtained these papers in the mid 1970s when she was researching for her book *Women in the Resistance* (1986), and they are the earliest, independent assessment of Marie-Claire and her escape line. See National Archives & Records Administration, USA henceforth NARA RG 84 Vichy Embassy Confidential File 1942 820–820.02.

Chapter 2

1   Churchill, Winston, *Their Finest Hour Vol II* (Cassell: London, 1949), p.38.
2   *Ibid*, pp.42–49.
3   Chevrillon, p.10.
4   Wynne, pp.28 *et seq*.
5   Rossiter Audio 78, track 8.
6   *Ibid*.
7   Rossiter Audio 78, track 9.
8   Rossiter Audio 78, track 10.
9   Wynne, p.36.
10   Rossiter Audio 78, track 9.
11   Rossiter Audio 77, track 1.

Chapter 3

1   *Women of Courage*. Though Lindell's views of the French in June 1940 were outspoken, they were not exceptional: see Chevrillon, Claire, p.55. 'What I cannot stand, however (I wake at three in the morning tormented by it), is the spinelessness, the sloppiness, the stupidity, the laziness, and the selfishness of people who, up to 15 June, I believed morally superior to those who led them.'
2   WO 373/60/632 – War Office and Ministry of Defence: Military Secretary's Department: Recommendations for Honours and Awards for Gallant and Distinguished Service (Army). Combatant Gallantry and Meritorious Service Awards. Escape and Evasion and Special Operations. 29 November 1940–15 July 1941. Recommendation for award for Langley, James Maydon. Rank: Lieutenant (68294) Coldstream Guards.
3   *Women of Courage*.
4   Probably Michèle Cambards (1922–89) a natural child of Yves Mirande. She was abandoned by her mother in Paris in 1940 and took refuge with the de Millevilles.

After service as an ambulance driver with *Le Groupe Rochambeau*, a female ambulance corps created in 1943 in North Africa and incorporated into Leclerc's 1st Army and served in France, Germany and Indio-China, Cambards visited the home of the painter Vlaminck for a few days in the 1950s – and stayed for thirty years until her death. She wrote a score of novels, was popular at the village, and sometimes practised her nursing. She is buried in the cemetery of Rueil, close to the painter Maurice de Vlaminck and his family.

5   Wynne, p.46. This is what she told Wynne in 1961, but in 1980 Mary told a different version of this story, that it was British soil, for which she had, she implied, bribed a German guard to let her take it from the embassy garden.

6   Wynne, pp.48–49.

7   Sim, p.33.

8   *New York Times*, 24 April 1939.

9   WO 372/18 – Lieutenant Colonel C.A. Shaw (born Malaga 1871 – died Switzerland 1950) was awarded the DSO in 1901 during the Boer War. The *London Gazette* of 26 July 1901 reported: 'The King has been graciously pleased to give orders for the following appointments to the Distinguished Service Order, in recognition of the services of the undermentioned Officers during recent operations in South Africa: To be Companions of the Distinguished Service Order: Lieutenant Cecil Arthur Shaw, 7th Dragoon Guards, for good service in the capture of Steyn's following at Reitz.' He served in the 9th Lancers (1900–06), 7th Dragoon Guards (1906–12 and 1914–19) and the RAF (1919–22). The *London Gazette* of 22 June 1922 reported: 'Air Ministry … Stores Branch … Flight Lt Cecil Arthur Shaw, DSO, is placed on the retired list on account of ill health contracted in the Service, and is granted the rank of Maj. 28th June 1922.' He married, in London in 1915, Sylvia de Grasse Fox of Philadelphia.

10   West, Nigel, *MI6 …*, pp.68–73.

11   See Charles Glass, pp.157–58, and André Guillon, *Testimony of a French PoW on his Time in the American Hospital*: 'A very beautiful girl, she nonetheless did not win our sympathy because we were wounded and she knew absolutely nothing about the nursing profession.'

12   Say, Rosemary, p.71.

13   WO 208/3301/167 – Private A.A.L. Lang, service number 814935, Argyll and Sutherland Highlanders, escaped from Belgium and France and thence to Spain.

14   Etta Shiber, *Paris Underground*. In Shiber's book, Lieutenant C.D. Hunter (Cameron Highlanders) is given the name 'Jonathan Burke', and 'Corporal Meehan' is a fusion of the adventures Driver R. Dundas (RASC/51st Division) and Corporal G. Hood-Crees (5/The Buffs). For their escape reports see WO 208/3301. Catherine or Kate Bonnefous (née Robins) is rather poorly disguised as 'Kitty Beaurepos'. They lived at 2 rue Balny d'Avricourt, Paris 17. See also WO 208/3301/172 – Lieutenant C.D. Hunter (69673), Cameron Highlanders, escaped from occupied to unoccupied France and thence repatriated on medical grounds; WO 208/3301/192 – Driver R. Dundas (78491), Royal Army Service Corps, escaped from France to Spain. Appendix A Included: WO 208/3301/219 – Corporal G. Hood-Crees (6288221), the Buffs Regiment, repatriated from France; WO 308.3301/174 – Report of escape after

capture by Captain D.B. Lang, Adjutant 4th Btn Queens Own Cameron Highlanders, 51st (Highland) Division.

15 Shiber, p.170.

16 In the 1945 film, *Madame Pimpernel*, Kitty is played by Constance Bennett and Etta by Gracie Fields.

17 WO 208/3298/36 – Lance Corporal J. Lee-Warner (6088621), Queen's Royal West Kent Regiment, escaped from France to Spain. At the Salvation Army, Lee-Warner met Sergeant Major Fullerton of the Gordon Highlanders and six other British escapers. Lee-Warner and Fullerton cycled to the demarcation line, bluffed their way across, and returned to Britain via Marseilles and Lisbon on 1 August 1940.

Chapter 4

1 Diamond, Hanna, *Fleeing Hitler*, p.142.

2 Airey Neave, *Saturday at MI9* …, p.185. Also published in the USA as *Escape Room: the Fantastic Story of the Underground Escapelines in Nazi-Occupied Europe and of Room 900, London, the Secret Office from which the Escapelines Were Run* (Doubleday, 1969). This Bismarck was a son of Gottfried von Bismarck, who was a cousin to Otto von Bismarck, the first Chancellor of Germany.

3 Donald Caskie, *The Tartan Pimpernel*.

4 There are a number of people who the author has not identified and/or whose proper names the author has been unable to determine, and these are given in quotation marks, e.g. 'Trideau'.

5 WO 373/60/594 – Lewis, Captain James Charles Windsor, Welsh Guards, Escape and Evasion and Special Operations, Award of Military Cross, date of announcement in *London Gazette*, 21 March 1941.

6 Noël Riou (1898–1964) was a Breton farmer's son born in Plomelin in Finistère. He served in the army 1918–21, before joining the Paris police. By 1940 Riou was secretary general of the *Syndicat Général de la Police* (SGP), and when the SGP was disbanded, he helped to found two resistance movements, *l'Armée Volontaire* and *Patriam Recuperare*. He was also in touch with the British SIS via the American embassy and began to pass intelligence about the Germans and about the Vichy, and he helped to establish lines for many British and French men to escape to Spain. In October 1941 he fled Paris, but was arrested in May 1942 and deported to Germany, where he survived. Riou is celebrated as one of the first Paris policemen actively to resist the German occupation. See http://www.memoresist.org/resistant/noel-riou/ and http://www.ordredelaliberation.fr/fr/les-compagnons/827/noel-riou [accessed 1 December 2015].

7 Later Major General Horace Fuller (1886–1966) commanded American troops on the Western Front in 1918 and was later US military attaché in Paris until August 1940 when he left to command the US 3rd Infantry Division at Fort Lewis, WA.

8 This story and the following account rely entirely upon Wynne, but the book was published in Windsor Lewis' lifetime and he never challenged its accuracy.

Chapter 5

1   Maxime Delavergne, see Ashdown, end note chapter 31, n. 15.
2   Paddy Ashdown, p.86. Mary had visited Ruffec several times since 1940.
3   *New York Times*, 16 October 1940.
4   *New York Times*, 10 and 16 October, and 10 December 1940.
5   WO 208/3301/174 – Captain D.B. Lang, Queen's Own Cameron Highlanders, escaped from France to Syria and thence to Palestine. Lang and Second Lieutenant John Buckingham, his companion, were helped to cross into the unoccupied zone by Kitty Bonnefous.
6   FO 950/1757 Nazi persecution claim: Mr [E.] John Sutton. Sutton was arrested on 12 October 1940 and imprisoned without trial, first at Cherche-Midi and then in Germany, and was not liberated until 6 April 1945. His claim for compensation in 1960 was turned down by the British government on the grounds that he had been held by the German civil power and as a result of Nazi persecution party.
7   Glass, Charles, pp.157–58.
8   *New York Times*, 6 and 7 December 1940.
9   *New York Times*, 20 and 22 December 1940. Deegan was accused of having 'supported the unidentified British officer [presumably Windsor Lewis] and helped him to flee the country' and Cross was accused of having 'concealed a British secret agent [presumably Sutton] in the embassy for months. This man, it was stated, later was arrested outside the building and confessed to espionage.'
10   *New York Times*, 15 December 1940.
11   Sim, p.35. Sim records the date of warning as 3 February though this appears to be a mistake and it is more likely that Mary advised Michèle to disappear in early January 1941. How Michèle reached the USA or North Africa in order to join the *Le Groupe Rochambeau* ambulance corps is not known.

Chapter 6

1   Details of several thousand RAF and other E&E are contained in Clutton-Brock, Oliver. Other lists can be found at http://conscript-heroes.com.
2   WO 208/3301/213 – Lieutenant J.M. Langley MC, Coldstream Guards, escaped from Belgium to France and subsequently repatriated. Appendix A included.
3   WO 208/3301/176 – Captain A. Irvine-Robertson, Argyll and Sutherland Highlanders, and Lieutenant R.D.W. Griffin, 2/Dorsets escaped from France to Spain. Robertson gave papers to MI9 which had been entrusted to him at Lille and which 'appear to refer to soldiers hidden in North France, of which the number varied according to different people between 4,000 and 7,000'.
4   Shiber, p.80.
5   WO 208/3303 272 (F) – Gunner C. Hillier, service number 1509075 Royal Artillery, escaped from France to Spain.
6   WO 208/3301/320 – Lance Bombardier J.G. Enock (772473) Royal Horse Artillery, escaped from France to Spain.

7   Darling, Donald, *Secret Sunday*, p.17.
8   Sim, p.33.
9   Wynne, pp.50–51.
10 Wynne, pp.56–67.
11 WO 208/3300/159 – Major J.C. Windsor Lewis, Welsh Guards, escaped from Belgium to France and thence to Spain; and Wynne, pp.62–79.
12 Wynne, p.89.
13 Wynne, p.90.
14 Le Foulon, p.26 *et seq*.
15 WO 208/5568 – Directorate of Military Intelligence (DMI) war diary: organisation and establishments.
16 Shiber, p.195 *et seq*. Mary Lindell appears gently and ironically disguised as a beautiful and charming 20-year-old, a disguise sharply at contrast with Mary's own description of Etta and her friend Kitty as amateurish, money-grubbing and of having betrayed Cecil Shaw, see Wynne, pp.101–04.
17 *New York Times*, 16 March 1941.
18 The records of the *Fondation pour la Mémoire de la Déportation* show that 'Kate' Bonnefous was deported from Paris to Germany as a *Nacht und Nebel* prisoner on 19 June 1941 and spent time in several camps until she reached Jauer, in Lower Silesia (now Jower in south-west Poland), which was overrun by the Soviet Army in February 1945. See http://www.bddm.org/liv/details.php?id=I.7.#BONNEFOUS [accessed 19 July 2013].
19 TNA FO 371/50978 – Jauer was overrun by shock troops of the Russian Army who raped the young and old alike: '*Nous avons été libérées l1 12 février par les troupes de choc russes … et pendant 8 jours, les femmes âgées furent violées comme les jeunes.*'
20 Cowburn, Benjamin, *No Cloak, No Dagger*, p.50.
21 Diamond, pp.146 and 171.

Chapter 7

1   Wynne, pp.110–16.
2   Henri Honoré d'Estienne d'Orves (1901–41), French Navy officer, 'first martyr of Free France', and a major hero of the French Resistance, executed on 29 August 1941.
3   Octave de Milleville was arrested sometime in 1943 and deported to Germany to die at Mauthausen on 13 April 1945. Mary's lack of sentimentality about her children in her post-war memoirs appears to be remarkably cold-hearted.
4   Henri Gendreau and Michel Regeon, *Ruffec et les Ruffeçois dans la Guerre 1938 à 1945* (Editions la Péruse, Ruffec, nd), p.86.
5   Association for American Studies and Training, http://adst.org/oral-history/fascinating-figures/constance-ray-harvey-diplomat-and-world-war-ii-heroine/ [accessed 1 June 2015].
6   Air Commodore Ferdinand 'Freddy' Maurice Felix West VC (1896–1988) commanded No 50 Wing RAF in France during 1939, was briefly air attaché in Rome in early 1940, before moving to Berne where, inter alia, he assisted Allied airmen who had escaped into Switzerland. Learning of his underground activities, the Gestapo put a price on his head: he was awarded the CBE for this work.

7   Brigadier General Barnwell Rhett Legge (1891–1949) served briefly as assistant military
     attaché to France and then was the military attaché in Switzerland, based at the US
     embassy in Zurich, throughout the Second World War. As well as gathering intelligence,
     he helped arrange the escape of many aviators and for this he was awarded the Legion
     of Merit by the US government and the CBE by the British (see WO 373/152/206).

8   Virginia Hall (1906–82) was known as '*la dame qui boite*' ('the limping lady') and by other
     aliases; the Germans called her 'Artemis' and considered her 'the most dangerous of
     all Allied spies'. After the fall of France, Hall met and was talent-spotted by an SOE
     member while on a train out of France. Recruited and trained in England, she returned
     to Lyon under the cover of a reporter for the *New York Post* and from August 1941 to
     November 1942 she worked clandestinely in Vichy France. When the Germans occu-
     pied the south of France after the Allied landings in North Africa, she escaped through
     the Pyrenees, despite her artificial foot, only to return by sea as an OSS agent. (TNA HS
     9/647/4: Virginia HALL, aka Mary HALL – born 06.04.1906; see also Pearson, Judith
     L., *The Wolves at the Door* …; Binney, Marcus, chapter 4; and McIntosh, Elizabeth P.,
     pp.114–28.

9   Rossiter, 'MI9 Report on Marie-Claire'.

Chapter 8

1   Neave, p.183.
2   Neave, p.71.
3   Darling, p.106.
4   Rossiter 77, track 1.
5   *Women of Courage.*
6   M.R.D. Foot and J.M. Langley, *MI9* …, pp.80 and 86. See also Darling, *Secret Sunday*, p.105.
7   Lyman, Robert, *Operation Suicide: The True Story of the Cockleshell Heroes*, p.124.
8   Hastings, p.277; Langley, J.M., p.193.
9   Lyman, pp.125–26.
10   Darling, *Secret Sunday*, p.91.
11   Harrison, Michael Charles Cooper, and Henry Antrobus Cartwright, *Within Four Walls*.
     See also FO 383/381 – Germany: Prisoners, including, Return to the UK of British sol-
     diers escaped from Germany … 1918; FO 383/399 – Germany: Prisoners … Captain
     H.A. Cartwright, 4 Middlesex Regiment … Extract from letter by Captain Cartwright,
     Middlesex Regiment, on Fort Gorgast … 1918; FO 383/400 – Germany: Prisoners,
     including: reports on the treatment of British prisoners under the 10th (Hanover) Army
     Corps; FO 383/401 – Germany: Prisoners, including capture, trial and imprisonment
     of prisoners of war.
12   For the extent of British and German espionage activities in Switzerland during the
     Second World War see, for example, Read, Anthony, and David Fisher, *Operation Lucy:
     The Greatest Enigma of World War II.*

Chapter 9

1 *Women of Courage*.
2 Verity, Hugh, p.15.
3 Verity, pp.52–53.
4 See WO 373/186/124 – Recommendation for Award for Rodriguez, Ferdinand Edward.
5 Wynne, p.142.
6 Hôtel de France, Ruffec – http://gastronomeruffec.wifeo.com/rouillon-hoteliers.php [accessed 12 November 2015]. The Rouillons were arrested in May 1944 and deported to Germany, where Germaine was murdered at Ravensbrück on 9 March 1945. Roger survived and was liberated at Dachau on 29 April 1945.
7 L'Abbé Henri Péan is reckoned to have helped some 2,000 people, but on 13 February 1944 he was arrested and sadistically interrogated in the prison at Tours and died, aged 44, on 28 February. The Goupille family of seven, a visiting friend and their maid were arrested in February 1944 and deported in April 1944 to forced labour camps in Germany, but all survived (Rossiter, Box 3).
8 Oliver Clutton-Brock, pp.134–59.
9 WO 208/3312/1126 and 1127 – Sergeant H.O. Robertson, service number 1114418, & Sergeant H.J.B. Canter, service number 1319407, RAF, evasion from France.

Chapter 10

1 Foot, *SOE in France*, p.248.
2 Ashdown, p.93.
3 Lieutenant Colonel Herbert George 'Blondie' Hasler, DSO, OBE (1914–87) was a distinguished Royal Marines officer in the Second World War who, in December 1942, led a submarine- and canoe-borne commando raid against Axis shipping in Bordeaux. He was responsible for many of the concepts which ultimately led to the post-war formation of the Special Boat Service.
4 Operation Frankton: Mountbatten called it 'the most courageous and imaginative of all the raids ever carried out by the men of Combined Operations'.
5 *Daily Telegraph*, 3 December 2002, 'Marine Bill Sparks: last surviving Cockleshell hero'.
6 Ashdown, p.111.
7 Darling, *Secret Sunday*, pp.68–69.
8 Ashdown, pp.118–20.
9 Ashdown, p.362.
10 Neave, p.197.
11 Hitler issued the infamous Commando Order in October 1942 stating that all Allied commandos, even if in uniform or attempting to surrender, should be executed without trial. The order was issued in secret and made clear that failure by any German officer to carry it out would render him guilty of an act of negligence punishable under German military law.
12 Sparks, p.90.
13 Ashdown, pp.266–84.

14 It was not until 23 February 1943 that Combined Operations Headquarters heard that Hasler and Sparks were safe. Of the men who did not return, Sergeant Wallace and Marine Ewart were captured on 8 December and executed a few days later under Hitler's Commando Order; Lieutenant MacKinnon and Marines Conway, Laver and Mills were also captured and executed in Paris sometime in 1943. Corporal Sheard and Marine Moffatt were drowned on the first night.

15 Sparks, p.96.

16 Sim, p.55.

17 Sparks, p.106.

18 Sim, p.54.

Chapter 11

1 Brome, Vincent, and Albert Marie Guérisse, *The Way Back* … O'Leary was Major General Albert-Marie Edmond Guérisse, GC DSO (1911–89).

2 Rossiter, 'MI9 Report on Marie-Claire'.

3 *Ibid.*

4 Felucca *Seadog* landed six SOE F-Section agents (George Starr aka Hilaire, Marcus Bloom aka Urbain aka Bishop, Mary Katherine Herbert aka Claudine, Marie-Therese le Chêne aka Adèle, Odette Hallowes-Sansom aka Lise and Gracomino Galea) and one MI9 wireless operator, Tom Groome. The female agents were: Mary Katherine Herbert (1903–83), trained as courier, in the second group of SOE women agents which included Odette Sansom-Hallowes, Jacqueline Nearne and Lise de Baissac. She worked in Bordeaux for Lise's brother Claude de Baissac, bore his child who she named Claudine(!), was arrested on 18 February 1944 at a safe house run by Lise de Baissac in Poitiers, talked her way out of prison, and lay low in France for the rest of the war. Marie-Therese le Chêne (1890–), the oldest woman sent to France, arrived as courier to her husband Henri. Marie-Therese arrived on the south coast only a few days/weeks before her brother-in-law, Pierre, was arrested as he was operating his wireless in Lyon in November 1942. She returned to England by Hudson (Operation Dyer) in a party organised by Henri Déricourt on 19/20 August 1943. See HS 9/304/1. Odette Sansom occurs later in this story.

5 Darling, *Secret Sunday*, p.90. It seems extraordinarily stupid to have given Groome, whose passport had already been offered by the American George Whittinghill to Mary Lindell for use by her son Maurice de Milleville, a false identity which might link him to the de Millevilles.

6 This was Danielle Reddé. See HS 9/392/4 – Reddé Daniele or Daniel or Danielle aka Marocain, aka Edith Daniel, aka Danielle Reddé, aka Maria-Félicité Kermarec – born 07.10.1911. See also Darling, *Secret Sunday*, p.113.

7 Neave, *Saturday at MI9*, pp.117–18.

8 Sparks, pp.122–24.

9 See WO 208/3312/1140 – Major H.G. Hasler, OBE; WO 208/3313/1162 – Marine W.E. Sparks, PL/X 3664, Royal Marines; WO 208/3312/1131 – Flying Officer W.P.M.G. De Mérode and WO 208/3312/1160 – Sergeant J.G. Dawson. They were

the penultimate party to take the Pat line. In the last party were WO 2087/3312/1108
– Wing Commander J.R.A. Embling; WO 208/3313/1207 – Sergeant Robert Kidd
RNZAF; Sergeant M.B. Jones USAAF and 2nd Lieutenant Grady Wayne Roper
USAAF; some French and Belgian civilians; Edithe Reddé and HS 9/1545 – Nancy
Wake, aka 'the White Mouse'. See also Clutton-Brock, pp.197–98, and Russell Braddon,
pp.84–88.

10   Lyman, Robert, *Operation Suicide* …, p.277.
11   Ashdown, pp.297–301.
12   *Women of Courage.*

Chapter 12

1   Wynne, pp.190–93.
2   Aubrac, Lucie, *Outwitting the Gestapo* (Lincoln: University of Nebraska Press, 1993), p.94,
     published in French as *Ils partiront dans l'ivresse* (Editions du Seuil, 1997); Cordet, Francis
     Carnets de guerre en Charente [...], pp.164, 204; and Fondation pour la Mémoire de la
     Déportation, www.bddm.org/liv/recherche.php. Geneviève Fabvre, or Ginette Favre,
     was born 26 May 1923 in Egypt, celebrated her baccalaureate in Lyon on 13 July 1943,
     and immediately volunteered to join the Resistance. Deported from Paris on 15 August
     1944 on Transport list number I.264, her number at Ravensbrück was 57824. She
     worked at Torgau before returning to Ravensbrück, and is believed to have been one
     of the 300 who were entrained and marched to Switzerland. She was not among the
     Frenchwomen who were rescued by the Swedish Red Cross in April 1945.
3   Irénée Cros (1887–1943), code name Calmette, head of MUR from March 1943 until
     he was murdered in Foix by the Germans on 14 December 1943. Cros burned papers
     while the Germans were breaking down his door and he died under a fusillade of bullets
     when they burst in.
4   *Women of Courage.*
5   Darling, *Secret Sunday*, pp.98–99: 'At each extreme the mountains are easier to cross, and the
     time taken by a group of fit men is about ten hours, though many valleys have to be crossed
     from side to side to avoid police patrols on the roads below. To men not in good condition
     and perhaps ill-shod such a journey could become a nightmare of exhaustion and pain.'
6   Wynne, p.183.
7   Rossiter, 'MI9 Report on Marie-Claire', f.2. The girl was apparently called Simone
     Chouchon.
8   Wynne, pp.183–86, where Barbie is identified as 'Hauptmann Barber'. See also *Women
     of Courage.*
9   Wynne, p.184.
10   *Women of Courage.*
11   NARA RG 0226 Field Station Files, Paris-OSS-OP32-33, f.4.
12   Clutton-Brock, p.139.
13   Rossiter, p.42; Clutton-Brock, p.139.
14   NARA RG 0226, f.4. She was associated with the Committee for Secret Revolutionary
     Action or CSAR, an anti-Communist and anti-Semite organisation whose members

covered themselves with hoods at their secret meetings and were therefore called *cagoulards*, or hooded men. See also Simone, Andre, *J'accuse! The Men who Betrayed France*.

15 NARA RG 0226, f.20.
16 Rossiter Audio 77, track 3.
17 Darling, *Secret Sunday*, pp.118–20.
18 Rossiter Audio 77, track 3.
19 Rossiter, 'MI9 Report on Marie-Claire'.
20 The author has walked many of these routes. The route from Mauléon to the south and west through the Pyrenees is one of the lonelier but easier routes.
21 Darling, *Secret Sunday*, p.98.
22 Neave, p.20.
23 Clutton-Brock, p.xxv and Appendix 1, which lists 2,198 RAF evaders who were shot down over all of Western Europe in 1940–45.
24 Clutton-Brock, p.412.
25 *Daily Telegraph*, 18 October 2007. See http://www.telegraph.co.uk/news/obituaries/1566506/Andree-de-Jongh.html.
26 Broussine, Georges, *L'évadé De La France Libre : Le Réseau Bourgogne*.
27 Rossiter Audio 77, track 10.
28 Rossiter, 'MI9 Report on Marie-Claire'.
29 Darling, *Secret Sunday*, p.141.
30 Rossiter, 'MI9 Report on Marie-Claire'.

Chapter 13

1 WO 208/3315/25 – Sansoucy, Joseph Germoin Fabien. See also WO 208/3314/1393 – Pilot Officer R.G. Kirby, service number 134555.
2 Marie-Thérèse de Poix (1894–1970) was deported from Paris on 18 April 1944, freed by the Swedish Red Cross in April 1945 and reached Malmö on 27 April 1945.
3 WO 208/3315/1446 – Sparkes, James Norman.
4 WO 208/3315/1447-48 – Sheppard, Alan Henry, and Trott, Charles Frank. Their pilot, Brown, drowned when he fell into the Loire, three others of the crew were wounded and taken prisoners of war, and the gunner, King, was missing.
5 See http://media.nara.gov/nw/305270/EE-121.pdf; http://media.nara.gov/nw/305270/EE-122.pdf and http://media.nara.gov/nw/305270/EE-123.pdf.
6 WO 208/3315/1445 and WO 5582/1445 – Whitnall, Phillip.
7 Martelli, George, *The man who Saved London: the Story of Michel Hollard*. Michel Hollard (1898–1993) travelled widely in northern France using his cover as an engineer for the Maison Gazogène Autobloc (a manufacturer of wood gas generators). He led the AGIR réseau and reconnoitred German rocket launch sites. He made forty-nine trips to deliver his sketches and reports to Victor Farrell. Post-war he was awarded the DSO for having 'reconnoitred a number of heavily guarded V1 sites and reported on them'.
8 WO 208/3315/25 and WO 208 5582/1451 – Sansoucy, Joseph Germoin Fabien.
9 WO 208/3316/1570 and WO 208/5582/1570 – Sergeant Piotr Bakalarski. See also WO 373/94/439 and WO and WO 208/3316/1589 – Sergeant Witold Raginis.

10 WO 208/3317/1629 – Pilot Officer A.E. McSweyn RAAF. See also WO 373/95/11 and WO 208/5582/1629 – Driver E.G. 'Jeff' Williamson RNZASC.

11 WO 208/5582/1580 – Sergeant S.J.V. Philo.

12 Clutton-Brock, p.142.

13 WO 208/3317/1635 – Flying Officer M.H.F. Cooper; WO 208/3317/1636 – Flying Officer H.F.E. Smith RCAF; the appendix to these reports is at WO 208/5582/1635 & WO 208/5582/1636; see also WO 208/3318/1704 and WO 208/5582/1704 – Sergeant L.F. Martin RCAF.

14 The report by Sergeant L.F. Martin RCAF is missing from its place in the TNA at WO 208/3318/1704 but the 'most secret' appendix is at WO 208/5582/1704.

15 Cooper, Mike, *One of the Many*, p.37.

16 Rossiter Audio 77, track 7.

17 Cooper, pp.37–39.

Chapter 14

1 Sutherland, David, *He Who Dares* …, pp.74–92 and 121; Owen, James, *Commando* …, pp.203–08; and Van der Bijl, Nick, *Sharing the Secret* …, p.60.

2 WO 208/5583/1886 – Captain George Tsoucas; WO 208/3317/1628 and WO 208/5582/1628 – Captain 'Buck' Palm.

3 NARA RG 0226 f.51. This statement was probably made in early 1945 while Roger and Germaine Rouillon were in captivity in Germany and Lemétayer (Germaine's brother) was running the Hôtel de France.

4 Rossiter, 'MI9 Report on Marie-Claire'.

5 See http://www.bddm.org/liv/details.php?id=I.235.#REGEON. The Regeon sisters were arrested in early 1944 and transported from Paris on 30 June to Ravensbrück. Both survived, but of the 111 women in their transport twenty-six died.

6 The Comtesse Pauline Barré de Saint-Venant (1895–1945) would be deported from Paris on 15 August 1944 and was murdered at the end of March in Ravensbrück.

7 See WO 208/5582/1629 – Flight Lieutenant A.F. McSweyn. McSweyn's report, made in December 1943, is at variance with Cooper's recall, in 1997, that they left Mary Lindell at Pau, and so hurriedly that they had no time to say goodbye. See Cooper, pp.48–50.

Chapter 15

1 Rossiter, 'MI9 Report on Marie-Claire'.

2 The Englishman was Flying Officer John W. Brace, 76 Squadron RAF whose Halifax had been shot down over Bernay, Eure, and the Americans were Lieutenant Norman Eugene Toft, co-pilot, Sergeant Delbert William Klump, rear gunner, and Staff Sergeant Robert A. Vandegriff, wireless operator of a USAAF B17 shot down on 3 September 1943.

3 Mary told three slightly different versions of the arrest of Ginette and the four airmen. See Wynne, p.106, Sim, p.41, and *Women of Courage*.

4   Sim, p.66.
5   Wynne, pp.205–06.
6   *Ibid*.
7   *Women of Courage*.
8   McGeoch, Ian, *An Affair Of Chances* …, pp.167 *et seq*. Vice Admiral Sir Ian Lachlan Mackay McGeoch (1914–2007), a highly decorated submariner, may be considered a reliable witness.
9   Rossiter, 'MI9 Report in Marie-Claire'.
10   *Women of Courage*.

Chapter 16

1   Baseden, Yvonne, interview 6 August 2009.
2   See Stevenson, William, *Spymistress: The Life of Vera Atkins, the Greatest Female Secret Agent of World War II*. William Stevenson (1924–2013), author and journalist, is not to be confused with Sir William Stephenson (1897–1989), the millionaire Canadian soldier and businessman who, under the code name 'Intrepid', was Churchill's intelligence representative based in New York during the Second World War. See also Helm, Sarah, *A Life in Secrets*.
3   The other girls may have been Eileen Nearne and Denise Bloch.
4   Jean Pierre Charles Meunier, aka Mesnard, aka Pierre Mornet was Edouard or Moralist, leader of the Director circuit. See HS 9/1026/4 – Pierre Charles Meunier.
5   M.R.D. Foot, *Memories of an SOE Historian*, pp.86–87.
6   HS 9/576/2 – Marie Joseph Gonzagues de Saint-Geniès, aka Lucien, aka Georges Henri Hollenau.
7   HS 6/437 – Security files: repatriated prisoners of war; interrogations; war crimes; missing personnel; concentration camp lists. This file contains six folios of Yvonne Baseden's debrief made on 19 and 20 June 1945, soon after her return to London from Ravensbrück.
8   *Ibid*.

Chapter 17

1   Rossiter Audio 67, track 9.
2   'Reine' was possibly Reine le Tallec, born 21 January 1917 in Gouarec, Brittany. See '*Fondation Pour La Mémoire De La Déportation*', 2015 – http://www.bddm.org [accessed 23 November 2015]. Though the dates on the transport of men and women from Dijon and Besançon via the Belfort Gap seem unreliable.
3   Others were Elisabeth Smith's putative lover, Johnny Hopper, and Brian Stonehouse, all of whom passed through Saarbrücken in September 1943 on their way to Natzweiler-Struthof and Mauthausen. They were followed by Edward Zeff, who entered the camp on 16 November. While there, Zeff lost track of time but he was kept there for about a fortnight and afterwards he described the camp in graphic detail. See HS 6/584 – Zeff, and WO 311/263 – Neue Bremm Concentration Camp near Saarbrücken, Germany: ill-treatment of internees.

4   WO 311/263.

5   *Ibid.*

6   Pierrette Louin also used the name Pierrette Salinas.

7   Suzanne Boitte also used the name Suzy Lemesle; her married name was Mertzisen (different spellings occur).

8   Marie-Louise Cloarec also used the names Marie-Louise Le Clech and Marie-Louise Lesaint.

9   Helm, Sarah, p.106.

10   *Ibid.*

11   HS 6/437 – Security files: repatriated prisoners of war; interrogations; war crimes; missing personnel; concentration camp lists. This file contains six folios of Yvonne Baseden's debrief dated on 19 and 20 June 1945 soon after her return to London from Ravensbrück.

Chapter 18

1   Interview, 9 August 2009.

2   Wynne, p.240.

3   *Women of Courage.*

4   HS 6/437 – Security files: repatriated prisoners of war; interrogations; war crimes; missing personnel; concentration camp lists.

5   Wynne, p.245.

6   Wilfrid Noyce, pp.161–87.

7   Renault, Maisie, *passim.*

8   TNA LAB 2/2081/ETAR9919/1932 – Aliens Restriction Department: Correspondence with Mrs N.D. Rees concerning a blacklisted alien named Julia [i.e. Barry].

9   Bell, William M., *I Beg to Report …*, p.25 *et seq.*

10   Cohen, Frederick, *The Jews in the Occupied Channel Islands 1940–45* (Jersey Heritage Trust, 2000); http://www.bddm.org [accessed 23 November 2015]. *Transport Parti de Paris le 13 Mai 1944* (I.212), this list included Nadine Hwang and Marie-Germaine Barthet, aka Marie-Germaine Charlotte Tonna-Barthet née Ordobez.

11   Barry, Julia, *News of the World*, 31 March, 1946.

Chapter 19

1   Arch R. Wiggins, *The History of the Salvation Army: 1886–1904* (London: Thomas Nelson & Sons, 1964).

2   Frederick Coutts, *The Weapons of Goodwill: 1946–1977* (London: Hodder & Stoughton, 1978).

3   Frederick Coutts, *No Discharge in this War* (London: Hodder & Stoughton, 1975).

4   Frederick Coutts, *The Better Fight: 1914–1946* (London: Hodder & Stoughton, 1988).

5   Treite worked under Professor Walter Stoeckel, who had devised a treatment for cervical cancer by the removal of the uterus through the vagina, an operation named after him, the Schauta-Stoeckel operation. Stoeckel was also Martha Goebbels' personal

doctor, was awarded the Goethe Medal for Art and Science in 1941, and in 1944 was appointed to the Board of the General Commissioner for Health and Sanitation under Karl Brandt. Brandt was one of Hitler's inner circle. In the 1930s he had performed abortions in great numbers on women deemed genetically disordered, whose unborn children were thought likely to inherit such genetic defects, and, on the eve of the Second World War, he was appointed by Hitler to lead the so-called T-4 euthanasia programme. Under this programme, some 275,000 Germans who were judged incurably sick were exterminated, and some 360,000 women were sterilised. To prevent the victims being traced by their families, they were often sent to transit centres in major hospitals where they were supposedly assessed before being moved to special treatment centres – which was the Nazi name for their place of murder. What Treite knew about Stoeckel and Brandt's work, and the extent to which he may have honed his surgical skills in the sterilisation of women on the T-4 programme, is not known.

6   Wynne, p.251.

Chapter 20

1   Imperial War Museum (IWM) Documents 11860 – Private Papers of Dr E.A.S. Sheridan [who lived at 41 rue Michel Ange, Paris].
2   WO 235/307 – Hamburg War Crimes Tribunal. Defendants: Heinrich Peters; Johann Schwarzhuber; Gustav Binder; Fritz Suhren; Ludwig Ramdohr; Rolf Rosenthal; Adolf Winkelmann; Percy Treite; Hans Pflaum; Martin Hellinger; Gerhard Schidlausky; Eugenia von Skene; Dorothea Binz; Margaretha Mewes; Greta Boesel; Emma Raabe; Vera Salvequart; Elisabeth Marschall and Carmen Maria Mory: Proceedings: Days 28–38. Place of trial: Hamburg, Dec 1946–Feb 1947.
3   IWM 11860 – Sheridan.
4   RW 2/7/21 – Witness deposition: Hermine Salvini.
5   Ibid. See also Jack G. Morrison, Ravensbrück …, pp.224–38.
6   RW 2/7/28 – Witness deposition: Elisabeth Thury.
7   Ibid.
8   Morrison, pp.207–22. There were more than seventy sub camps, each with several hundred inmates.
9   Wynne, pp.255–56.
10   Åberg, Lars, Hoppets Hamn, pp.153–57. Different spellings of Nadine's surname appear, Hoang, Huang and Juan, but Nadine signed her name Hwang.
11   See Joan Schenkar, Truly Wilde: The Unsettling Story of Dolly Wilde, Oscar Wilde's Unusual Niece.
12   See Suzanne Rodriguez, Wild Heart: Natalie Clifford Barney and the Decadence of Literary Paris.
13   Åberg, pp.70–133.

Chapter 21

1   Virginia D'Albert-Lake and Judy Barret Litoff (ed.), An American Heroine …, pp.162–75.
2   Wrongly included on the 21 August list was Violette Szabó, who had already been deported from Paris a week earlier.

3   They included another woman who Virginia D'Albert-Lake referred to as 'Janette' and may have been Jeanine Alex Dilley, born 30 September 1920, who gave her next of kin as Walter Dilley c/o Mrs Llowns, 115 Bargery Road, Catford, London.

4   The author is grateful to Lucienne Caron Dixon's granddaughter, France Bertram, for much of the information in this chapter.

5   OCM was in turn the amalgamation of the Équipe Française d'Organisation du Redressement of the industrialist Jacques Arthuys, aka the Rue de Logenbach Group, and the *Confédération des Travailleurs Intellectuels* inspired by Maxime Blocq-Mascart. In early 1941 OCM was reinforced by employees of the Ministry of Public Works under the leadership of André Boulloche and the couple Georges and Raymonde Ricroch.

6   This was the occasion when Frank and his friends collected what they had from their Red Cross parcels for his grandmother to give to Lucienne.

7   For this particular act of bravery and for her prolonged intelligence work in occupied France and her example of courage and patriotism she was awarded the King's Medal for Courage in the Cause of Freedom.

8   Hal Vaughan, *Doctor to the Resistance*.

9   WO 208/3500 – J.F. Baron.

10   For this account, which differs from that given by Vaughan in *Doctor to the Resistance*, the author is grateful to Pete Jackson during an interview at L'Hôtel National des Invalides on 21 February 2013.

11   Interview with Pete Jackson, 21 February 2013.

12   Rossiter, p.204. See also Clutton-Brock, pp.276–80.

13   The Fréteval Forest is a thick woodland, 160km south of Paris. In the summer of 1944 scores of Allied airmen were corralled here rather than risk the escape lines, as the Allied armies advanced westwards. The operation was masterminded from London under the rather unimaginative name of Sherwood. The camp was liberated by the American 3rd Army on 11 August 1944 and 132 Allied airmen were rescued.

14   Raoul Nordling (1881–1962) was appointed Swedish Vice Consul in Paris in 1905, consul in 1917 and succeeded his father as Consul General in 1926. Raoul Nordling joined the board of Alfa-Laval in 1908 and became its chairman 1932–62.

15   Nordling, Raoul and Vinde, Victor Sauver, *Paris: Mémoires du Consul de Suède (1905–44)* (Paris: Complexe, 2002).

16   Hal Vaughan, pp.126–29.

17   Litoff, Judy Barret. *The Diary and Memoir of Virginia D'Albert-Lake* (New York: Fordham University Press, 2006), pp.141–54.

18   Bard, Mitchell G., p.14 *et seq*. Eighty-two American, forty-eight British, twenty-six Canadian, nine Australian, two New Zealanders and one Jamaican. Other sources say there were more, but not all the American and British men on this transport may have been airmen.

19   Ottaway, Susan, *Sisters, Secrets and Sacrifice …*, p.185.

20   *Daily Telegraph*, 'Alix d'Unienville SOE Courier in Wartime Paris', 20 November 2015 – http://www.telegraph.co.uk/news/obituaries/12005980/Alix-dUnienville-SOE-agent-obituary.html.

21 Members of the Royal Air Forces Ex-Prisoner of War Association, and Sir Francis Burt, *We Flew, We Fell, We Survived* (Royal Air Forces Ex-Prisoner of War Association (Western Australia Branch), 1990), see F/S R.W. Perry RAAF, p.70.

22 Nicole de Witasse, born 13 November 1911, murdered in Ravensbrück at the end of March 1945.

23 Elsewhere, D'Albert-Lake says that he was an American.

24 Some sources repeat that only seventeen women in this deportation returned, but analysis of the figures kept by the *Fondation pour la Mémoire de la Déportation* shows that of 542 women deportees from Romainville on 15 August 1944, 374 (69 per cent) returned, 121 (22 per cent) were murdered in Germany, and the fate of the remainder (9 per cent) is unknown.

Chapter 22

1   D'Albert-Lake, p.163.

2   D'Albert-Lake, p.165.

3   D'Albert-Lake, p.166.

4   Virginia D'Albert-Lake calls her 'Mme Le Bart'. She was Ernestine Labarthe, born 26 March 1903, transported from Paris on 15 August 1944, KZ number 57563, who died at Torgau in September 1944. Her daughter, Georgette, KZ number 57562, was also murdered by gassing at Ravensbrück, on or about 30 March 1945.

5   Ottaway, Susan, *Sisters, Secrets And Sacrifice*; and Jones, Liane, *A Quiet Courage*. See also: HS9/1089/2 – personal file of Eileen Mary Nearne, aka Alice Wood, aka Jacqueline Duterte; HS9/1089/4 – personal file of Jacqueline Françoise Mary Josephine Nearne, aka Josette Norville (bizarrely her field name was Jacqueline; not only was this her real name, and therefore of little security value, but it was also the field name of another agent, Yvonne Rudellat and her sister, Didi, had acquired false papers also in the name of Jacqueline); HS9/1089/3 – personal file of Francis Nearne – born 1916; see also HS 9/1318/3 – personal file of William Jean Savy.

6   Ottaway, *Sisters*, p.143.

7   Ottaway, *Sisters*, pp.196–98.

8   HS 9/1289/7 – Yvonne Claire Rudellat, née Cerneau, aka Jacqueline Vialliot; King, Stella, *'Jacqueline,' Pioneer Heroine of the Resistance*, an encyclopaedic biography of Yvonne Rudellat based on eyewitness accounts and first-hand interviews, but before many of the personal files of the participants were opened at Kew in 2003. Nevertheless, it is one of the first and best attempts to tell the story of the SOE in France as a coherent, narrative history. See also HS 9/522/5 – Raymond Henry Flower.

9   HS 9/183 – Andrée Raymonde Borrel; HS 9/379/8 Pierre Culioli.

10 HS 9/1186/2 – Frank Herbert Dedrich Pickersgill; HS 9/954/2 John Kenneth Macalister aka Jean Charles Mauinier. Both were hanged at Buchenwald on 14 September 1944. See also Vance, Jonathan F., *Unlikely Soldiers*.

11 Renée Rosier, born 4 June 1920, deported 15 August 1944, survived Ravensbrück and Bergen-Belsen and was liberated on 15 April 1945.

12 D'Albert-Lake, pp.173–74.

Chapter 23

1   Mary O'Shaughnessy, born 12 March 1898. See WO 208/3302/266 – Escape of Sgt E.G. Hillyard, service number 747947, 150 Bomber Squadron RAF, shot down in a Fairey Battle on 14 June 1940 and arrived in Gourock by sea on 23 February 1941. 'Miss S' has not been identified.

2   The transport of 552 women included Nadine Hwang. See WO 235/305 – First Hamburg War Crimes Tribunal sixth day, page 29, and WO 235/318. Post-war Mary O'Shaughnessy appeared as a witness at the Nuremburg War Crimes Trials. Later she returned to her work as governess, working in Kenya. She died on 11 September 1973 during a visit to the UK from Kenya to see an old friend from her days in Ravensbrück. In recognition for the work she had carried out, Mary was made an honorary member of the Royal Air Force Escaping Society.

3   Katherine Anne McCarthy, born in Ireland on 17 December 1895.

4   Murphy, David, 'Irish in the French Resistance and the SOE', pp.269–94 in Nathalie Genet-Rouffiac and David Murphy, *Franco-Irish Military Connections 1590–1945*.

5   Murphy, 'Irish in the French Resistance …', p.279. Agnes Flanagan, born in Offaly, Eire, on 16 May 1909.

6   FO 371/50982 – German War Criminals: crimes against Jews: atrocities in occupied territories.

7   Mary-Helen Young, born in Aberdeen on 5 June 1883, had been in France so long that she had become Marie-Hélène, *Aberdeen Press and Journal*, 27 September 1945.

8   Simone Leduc/Saint-Clair, born 25 February 1896 in Orléans, transported from Paris on 14 June 1944, prisoner number 43200 at Ravensbrück, liberated by the Red Cross on the German–Swiss border on 9 April 1945.

9   *The Courier and Advertiser*, 31 January 1948.

10   'Portraits de Deux Femmes Déportées Parcours et Témoignages Militants', 2015 – http://chsprod.hypotheses.org/portraits-deux-femmes-deportees [accessed 2 December 2015].

11   Barbara Chatenay was born on 3 June 1891. See Chatenay, Victor, *Mon Journal de Quatorze-Dix-huit*. See also http://fr.wikipedia.org/wiki/Victor_Chatenay [accessed 18 March 2014]. Antoine, Barbara and Victor's 17-year-old youngest son who had gone with his father to the café, was captured, tortured and sent to Buchenwald, which he survived. There were three older brothers: Louis-Pierre, known as 'Peter', who helped Allied flyers to escape to Switzerland and Spain until he crossed the Pyrenees himself in 1943, became a liaison officer in the American Army, landed in Normandy on D-Day 1944, and finished his war in Munich; Michel joined the British SAS, transferred to the Free French Army and was parachuted with his regiment into Holland in April 1945; and Jaques, a member of the 4th Free French Regiment of the SAS, who was killed in July 1944 during a parachute landing in Brittany. Their youngest child, Anne-Marie, carried messages for the Resistance.

12   FO 371/50977 – German War Criminals: crimes against Jews: atrocities in occupied territories.

13   FO 371/50982.

14   WO 208 3310/838 and WO 208/5582/838 – Sergeant J.E. Misseldine, service number 1291166, RAF, evasion from France.

15 There is an approximate version of events in Brome, Vincent, *The Way Back* …
16 FO 371/60512 – Claim by a Mr W. Koch of St Gallen for reimbursement of hospital expenses paid for a certain Madame E.C. Cheramy.

Chapter 24

1 Rossiter Audio 67, track 4.
2 FO 371/50982.
3 'Affidavit of Fritz Ernst Fischer, 21 November 1945' – http://www.phdn.org/archives/www.ess.uwe.ac.uk/genocide/Fischer.htm [accessed 5 December 2015].
4 Bles, Mark, *Child At War*, pp.257–91. See also Imperial War Museum, catalogue number 16483, interview with Hortense Augustine Daman Clews, 1996. Hortense worked for the Belgian Legion Resistance Organisation and Belgian Partisans Group 34 in Belgium, 1940–43, was arrested and imprisoned at Louvain Prison, February 1943 to June 1944, and held at Ravensbrück, June 1944 to April 1945. See also Malmöstadsarkiv SE-MSA-00453-10 Hortense (dob 12 August 1926) and her mother (dob 19 June 1894): they were rescued by the White Buses of the Swedish Red Cross and arrived in Malmö on 28 April 1945.
5 HS 6/437 – Security files: repatriated prisoners of war; interrogations; war crimes; missing personnel; concentration camp lists.
6 Jacqueline Bernard, born 16 June 1913, was deported from Paris on 15 August 1944 and was with the three English agents at Torgau and at Königsberg. Camp number 57774, she was liberated at Leitmeritz in May 1945.
7 Noyce, Wilfrid, pp.161–87.

Chapter 25

1 Verity, Hugh, p.94.
2 Yarnold, Patrick, *Wanborough Manor*, pp.94–101.
3 HS 9/908/1 – Cecily Margot Lefort, aka Cecile Marguerite Legrand aka Alice.
4 Verity, p.94.
5 Richards, Brooks, *Secret Flotillas: Clandestine Sea Lanes to France & French North Africa 1940–1944* (London: HMSO, 1996), p.218.
6 Escott, Beryl, *Heroines of SOE*; and Escott, Squadron Leader Beryl E., *Mission Improbable: a Salute to the RAF Women of SOE in Wartime France*.
7 Verity, p.197.
8 Fuller, Jean Overton, *The German Penetration of SOE* …, pp.64–67.
9 HS 9/258/5 – Francis Charles Albert Cammaerts, aka Charles Robert Laurent, aka Roger, aka Jockey. See also: HS 9/1235/6 – Pierre Jean Louis Raynaud, aka Pierre Francoise Roussel, aka Alain, aka Linkman, born 23 August 1921, and HS 9/908/1 – Raymond Louis Daujat, date of birth not known, died 31 December 1943.

Chapter 26

1   Eugénie Djendi, born 8 March 1923, aka Jenny Silvani, aka Jaqueline Dubreuil; Marie-Louise Cloarec, born 10 May 1917, aka Le Clech, aka Lesaint; Pierrette Louin, aka Pierrette Lasalina, born 6 April 1905; and Suzanne Mertzisen née Boitte (and mother of a little girl), born 15 May 1919, aka Lemesle, were commissioned into the *Corps Féminin de Transmissions d'Afrique du Nord*.

2   Danielle Williams, which was a code name, gave as her next of kin a Mrs Patterson of Portobello, Edinburgh. In fact, she was born on 21 January 1916 in Paris and her birth name was Denise Madeleine Bloch. She was described as 5ft 10in tall, Jewish, and her hair was variously said to be blonde, red-brown or black.

3   Lilian Rolfe and her identical twin sister, Helen, were born in Paris on 26 April 1914 and brought up in France, but enjoyed frequent visits to their grandparents in Camberwell, London, until in 1930 their father, an accountant, was offered a position in Brazil.

4   See also HS 9/55/7 – Jean Maxime Aaron, born 1 November 1901. Violette Szabó was born in Paris on 26 June 1921 to an English father and a French mother, Violette Reine Elizabeth Bushell, she was described on her SOE record cards as '1.64m tall, brown hair, brown eyes and mat [*sic*] complexion'.

5   Little Königsberg or Klein Königsberg was Königsberg in der Neumark, now known in Polish as Chojna, a border crossing on the River Oder and not Königsberg on the Baltic, now known as Kaliningrad.

6   HS 9/165/8 – Denise Madeleine Bloch. Letter dated 31 August 1945 from Marie-Thérèse Henry (born 7 June 1920) liberated at Königsberg on 5 February 1945.

7   RW 2/7/21 – Witness deposition: Hermine Salvini.

8   RW 2/7/28 – Witness deposition: Elisabeth Thury.

9   WO 235/317 – Johann Schwarzhuber statement dated 15 August 1946, witnessed by Waclaw Wierzbowski.

10 Sarah Helm, *A Life in Secrets* …, p.88.

11 Helm, pp.87–88.

Chapter 27

1   Lanckorońska, Countess Karolina, *Those Who Trespass Against Us* …

2   Tillion, Germaine, *Ravensbrück* …

3   Salvesen, Sylvia, *Forgive – But Do Not Forget*.

4   De Gaulle-Anthonioz, Geneviève, *The Dawn of Hope* …

Chapter 28

1   Lanckorońska, p.277.

2   *Ibid*.

3   Morrison, Jack G., *Ravensbruck: Everyday Life* …, pp.286–91.

4   Morrison, p.296.

Chapter 29

1 Burén, Göran. *Mordet på Folke Bernadotte* [*The Murder of Folke Bernadotte*], pp.26–37.
2 Bernadotte, Folke, *The Fall of the Curtain*, p.21. (Originally published in 1945 as *Slutet: mina humanitära förhandlingar i Tyskland våren 1945 och deras politiska följder* [*The End: my humanitarian actions in Germany in Spring 1945 and the political consequences*] and republished in 2009 as *Last Days of the Reich*, with a foreword by Sune Persson.)
3 Bernadotte, Folke, and Eric Lewenhaupt, *The Fall of the Curtain: Last Days of the Third Reich* (London: Cassel, 1945), p.20.
4 Tyas, Stephen and Witte, Peter, *Himmler's Diary 1945: A Calendar of Events Leading to Suicide* (Kindle edition). In *The Fall of the Curtain*, Bernadotte gives this date as 12 February.
5 Persson, Sune. *Escape from the Third Reich*, pp.87–88.
6 *Helsingsborgs Dagbald*, 2 April 2005, *Han var chaufför på Vita bussarna* [*He was a driver of the White Buses*].
7 Max Pauly, Kommandant of Stutthof concentration camp 1939–42 and Kommandant of Neuengamme and associated sub camps from September 1942 until May 1945, was found guilty of war crimes, including medical experimentation, sentenced to death and hanged in October 1946.
8 Persson, pp.208–12.
9 TNA PREM 3/197/6 – Surrender offer by Himmler through Sweden.
10 Bernadotte, Folke, and Sune Persson, *Last Days of the Reich*, pp.109–20.
11 Renault, Maisie, *La Grand Misère*; see also Noyce, p.183.
12 Renault, pp.149–57. See also FO 371/50982 – German war criminals: crimes against Jews: atrocities in occupied territories. For fulfilling this promise, the Bitish Foreign Office considered giving Frykman a gold watch.
13 Åke Svenson, *De Vita Bussarna* [*The White Buses*] (Quarnberget Förlag, 2007), p.159.
14 This dialogue is taken from Wynne's *No Drums … No Trumpets*, modified by other accounts that Mary gave of this story and what she gave in evidence to the Hamburg War Crimes Tribunal. See WO 235/307: Hamburg War Crimes Tribunal Proceedings: Days 28–38, Defendants … Johann Schwarzhuber … Percy Treite, etc.
15 Åberg, pp.70–133.

Chapter 30

1 Ragusin, Elsie A., *An American in Auschwitz*. All the information in this chapter is taken from Ragusin's book. Despite its alliterative title, she spent most of her imprisonment in Ravensbrück.
2 De Gaulle-Anthonioz, p.48. De Gaulle's description of her first interview with Suhren is similar to Elsie's.
3 Ragusin, pp.81.
4 Persson, pp.188–89 and 215–16 for details of RAF air attacks upon the White Buses.
5 Bernadotte and Persson, p.113.
6 Åberg, p.97.
7 Stadsarkiv Malmö, Kriminalpolisen i Malmö, Handlingar angående flytktingar, MSA Malmö 2009-05-11 BA F7:10. See also the appendix for list of American and British

women agents who were in Ravensbrück: the boxes indicate which women of the survivors travelled together to Sweden.

8 *Tisdagsklubben* was founded on 9 April 1940 – the day Germany invaded Norway – by the Swedish authoress and pacifist Amelie Posse-Brázdová (1884–1957). She married (1) Andreas Bjerre and (2) the Czech artist Oskar Brázda; she lived in the Vatican and in Czechoslovakia until she fled to Sweden in 1938 to avoid arrest by the Germans. Overtly *Tisdagsklubben* was a discussion club about culture, but its true purpose was to resist the spread of Nazism in Sweden.

9 Cruickshank, Charles, pp.61–65. This was a government-sponsored official history for which Cruickshank was given free access to offical documents.

10 Tennant, Peter, *Touchlines of War*, pp.76–80. Under the cover of press attaché at the British embassy in Stockholm for most of the war, Tennant was chief organiser for the SOE, running a wireless operator in Stockholm and countrywide branches which reconnoitred dropping zones, landing grounds and sabotage targets.

11 Fischer, Ernst, '*Glimptar fran ett Levande Museum* [Glimpses of a Living Museum]' talk to the Malmö Rotary Club, 24 May 1945.

12 Blomqvist, Karin Landergren, *Flyktingar på Malmö Museum 1945* [*Refugees at Malmö Museum*].

13 SE/LLA/11277 – Länsstyrelsen i Malmöhus län. IV Civilförsvarssektionens arkiv: Ö I a Registerkort över flyktingar inkomna till landet Lund [Registration cards of refugees arrived in the district of Lund].

14 FO 371/50977 – German War Criminals: crimes against Jews: atrocities in occupied territories, contains 'further notes,' by H.W. Border, 'regarding ex-internees from Ravensbrück who are to be repatriated by Swedish aircraft on 8 June', to M.E. Marrian, Ministry of Health, dated 5 June 1945.

15 FO 371/50982 – German War Criminals: crimes against Jews: atrocities in occupied territories, contains a lengthy report by George Clutton and six annexes from British refugees in Sweden to the British ambassador in Stockholm, dated 18 June 1945.

16 HS 9/908/1 – Cecily Margot Lefort, letter from V.M. Atkins to Major L. Dalton dated 5 February 1946.

17 Elisabeth Smith has been identified as the Belgian Renée Huyskens, and her wartime and post-war career is the subject of a separate work.

18 FO 371/50982 – this version of events was confirmed by Mary Lindell, Kate MacCarthy, Elizabeth Sheridan and Chatenay.

19 HS 9/648/4 – personal file of Odette Marie Celine Hallowes, née Brailly, aka Odette Sansom, aka Odette Churchill, born 28 April 1912.

20 Foot, M.R.D., *SOE In France*, p.252.

21 HS 6/439 – Security files: SPU 24 (Paris) vetting; interrogations of returned agents. According to a report dated 2 October 1944 by General Harold Redman, Deputy Commander of the French Forces of the Interior in 1944 and Deputy Head of SHAEF, Peter Churchill aka Pierre Chambrun 'was taken prisoner by the Germans in June 1943 and before capture he had been friendly with a German officer named Captain Johann Verbeck' (Verbeck was one of Bleicher's aliases).

22 RW 2/7/19 (2007) – Witness deposition: Odette Marie Seline Sansom.

Chapter 31

1   FO 371/51193 – Evacuation of women from concentration camp at Ravensbrück and refugees from Northern Germany.

2   See http://www.bddm.org/liv/details.php?id=I.189.#FRITZ [retrieved 1 October 2013]. All but four of this group of prisoners survived a year of concentration camp life at Ravensbrück or Mauthausen.

3   See also FO 371/51193.

4   Yvonne Baseden and Mary Lindell were flown by the same pilot, James Raeburn. For once the impeccable Swedish records are in conflict: Mary's record card (in Lund) shows that she stayed at Silver's Pension from 24 May to 23 June 1945, whereas the passenger lists (in Stockholm) show she left Sweden between 29 and 31 May.

Chapter 32

1   WO 309/417 – Ravensbrück Concentration Camp, Germany: killing and ill-treatment of allied nationals.

2   WO 235/315 – 'Defendant: Extracted papers' contains a summary of the trial by Brigadier Lord Russell of Liverpool, deputy judge advocate general.

3   WO 235/313 – Defendant: Petitions.

Chapter 33

1   Wynne, pp.258–61.

2   Pauline Gabrielle Barré de Saint-Venant, born 9 April 1895 at Villers-lès-Nancy, arrested 4 May 1944, murdered at Ravensbrück 23(?) March 1945, and 57807 (Ra) Marie-Odile de Saint-Venant, born 9 March 1905 murdered 23(?) March 1945.

3   Helluy, Joseph, and Jacqueline Helluy, *Mme Henry Barré De Saint-Venant …*

4   *L'Est Républicain*, 'Marie-Odile Laroche, Grande Résistante De Villers-Lès-Nancy', 5 May 2011. *L'Est* claimed that the Marie-Odile had sponsored more than 30,000 crossings of the demarcation line, and that more than eighty members of the escape had died and 200 had been deported.

5   Rossiter Audio 67, tracks 6 to 8.

6   *Ibid.*

7   Darling, *Secret Sunday*, p.107.

8   Tickell, Jerrard, *Odette: the Story of a British Agent*. Dublin-born novelist Tickell (1905–66) served in the British Army during the war on the fringes of the intelligence service and used the knowledge gained to write *Odette* and *Moon Squadron* (1956).

9   The film *Odette* (Herbert Wilcox, 1950) starred Anna Neagle as Odette, and Maurice Buckmaster as himself. Ironically Wilcox and Neagle had made the 1939 film of Edith Cavell which had so motivated Mary Lindell.

10   CAB 103/573 (released in 2003) *History of Special Operations Executive (SOE) in France* by Michael R.D. Foot. Upset by Foot's comments, Odette Sansom/Hallowes demanded a public apology and that offending passages relating to her and to Churchill should be removed from the second edition of *SOE in France*. Foot took revenge when he edited

the secret, in-house history of the SOE, first written in 1948, to describe the film *Odette* and Tickell's book as inaccurate, to classify Churchill's second mission in France as a wild goose chase and to imply that Odette only became a heroine after the appearance of the film. He suspected much worse of Churchill and of Sansom.

11   Mackenzie, W.J.M., *The Secret History of SOE*, pp.251–52.
12   Rossiter Audio 67, tracks 1 & 2.
13   HS9 77/1 – Lise Marie Jeanette de BAISSAC, aka ODILE, aka Irene BRISSE, née DAUNAT, aka Jeanette BOUVILLE, born 11 May 1905.
14   Ott, Sandra, *War, Judgment, and Memory*, pp.xxix–xxii, and for their competing histories see pp.174–80.
15   Hastings, p.273.
16   Hastings, p.276. All told, it is estimated that maybe 2 per cent and perhaps as many as 10 per cent of all Frenchmen worked for the Resistance at some time or other. By late 1944 many more, who had sat on the fence, and would be derisively called the RMA ('Resisters of the Month of August') and FFS (*'Forces Françaises de Septembre'*). There were also, of course, many individual French men and women, usually drawn from the humbler sections of society, who aided their country and the Allies, particularly in escape and evasion, and whose patriotic services have often been overlooked. See also Foot and Langley p.65, 'Escapers and evaders found almost uniformly … every sort of readiness to help among the poorer sorts of people and every sort of reserve among most of the rich.'
17   NARA RG 0226, f.7.
18   WO 235/307 – Hamburg War Crimes Tribunal, f.217. The name recorded by the court was 'Odette Baisden'.
19   *Ibid*, f.211.
20   Darling, *Secret Sunday*, p.107.

BIBLIOGRAPHY

Åberg, Lars, *Hoppets Hamn [Harbour Of Hope]* (Malmo: Roos & Tegner with Auto Images, 2011).

'Affidavit Of Fritz Ernst Fischer, 21 November 1945', *Phdn.org* (2015) – www.phdn.org/archives/www.ess.uwe.ac.uk/genocide/Fischer.htm [accessed 5 December 2015].

Allan, Stuart, *Commando Country* (Edinburgh: NMS, 2007).

Ashdown, Paddy, *A Brilliant Little Operation: The Cockleshell Heroes and the Most Courageous Raid of WW2* (London: Aurum Press, 2012).

Ashdown, Paddy, *The Cruel Victory: The French Resistance, D-Day and the Battle for the Vercors 1944* (London: William Collins, 2015).

Aubrac, Lucie, *Outwitting the Gestapo* (Lincoln: University of Nebraska Press, 1993).

Bailey, Roderick, *Forgotten Voices of the Secret War: An Inside History of Special Operations in the Second World War* (London: Ebury Press, 2009).

Bard, Mitchell G., *Forgotten Victims: the Abandonment of Americans in Hitler's Camps* (Boulder, Colorado: Westview Press, 1994).

Basu, Shrabani, *Spy Princess: The Life of Noor Inayat Khan* (Stroud: The History Press, 2008).

Bddm.org, 'Fondation pour la Mémoire de la Déportation' (2015) – www.bddm.org [accessed 23 November 2015].

Bell, William M., *I Beg to Report … Policing in Guernsey During the German Occupation* (Guernsey, Channel Islands: Guernsey Press, 1995).

Bernadotte, Folke, and Eric Lewenhaupt, *The Fall of the Curtain: Last Days of the Third Reich* (London: Cassel, 1945). Since republished as Bernadotte, Folke, and Sune Persson, *Last Days of the Reich: The Diary of Count Folke Bernadotte* (London: Frontline, 2009).

Binney, Marcus, *The Women Who Lived for Danger: The Women Agents of SOE in the Second World War* (London: Hodder & Stoughton, 2002).

Bleicher, Hugo, Erich Borchers and Ian Colvin (eds), *Colonel Henri's Story: The War Memoirs of Hugo Bleicher* (London: William Kimber, 1954).

Bles, Mark, *Child at War* (London: Hodder & Stoughton, 1989).

Blomqvist, Karin Landergren, *Flyktingar på Malmö Museum 1945 [Refugees at Malmö Museum 1945]* (Malmo: Malmo Museum, 2002).

Braddon, Russell, *Nancy Wake: The Story of a Very Brave Woman* (London: Cassell, 1956).

Bridgman, Jon, and Richard H. Jones, *The End of the Holocaust: The Liberation of the Camps* (Portland, Or: BT Batsford, 1990).

Brittain, Vera, *Testament of Youth* (London: Virago, 2014).

Brome, Vincent, and Albert Marie Guérisse, *The Way Back. The Story of Lieut-Commander Pat O'Leary* [nom de guerre of Albert M. Guérisse] (London: Cassell & Co., 1957).

Broussine, Georges, *L'évadé De La France Libre : Le Réseau Bourgogne* (Paris: Tallandier, 2000).

Brown, John, *In Durance Vile* (London: Robert Hale, 1981).

Brysac, Sharon Blair, *Resisting Hitler: Mildred Harnack and the Red Orchestra* (New York: Oxford University Press, 2000).

Buckmaster, Maurice J., *Specially Employed* (London: Batchworth Press, 1952).

Buckmaster, Maurice J., *They Fought Alone: The Story of British Agents in France* (London: Odhams, 1958).

Burén, Göran, *Mordet på Folke Bernadotte* [*The Murder of Folke Bernadotte*] (Stockholm: Leopard Förlag, 2012).

Caskie, Donald, *The Tartan Pimpernel* (Woodbourne Press, London, 1957).

Chatenay, Victor, *Mon Journal de Quatorze-Dix-huit* (Angers: Editons du Courrier de l'Ouest, 1968).

Chauveau-Veauvy, Yves, *Réseaux De Résistance SOE: Sologne, Berry, Rives De Loirs* (Saint-Avertin: A. Sutton, 2012).

Chevrillon, Claire, Jane Kielty Stott (trans.) and John F. Sweet (foreword), *Code Name Christine Clouet: A Woman in the French Resistance* (College Station: Texas A&M University Press, 1995).

Chsprod.hypotheses.org, 'Portraits de Deux Femmes Déportées| Parcours et Témoignages Militants', 2015 – http://chsprod.hypotheses.org/portraits-deux-femmes-deportees [accessed 2 December 2015].

Churchill, Peter, *Of their Own Choice* (London: Hodder and Stoughton, 1952).

Churchill, Peter, *Duel of Wits* (London: Hodder & Stoughton, 1953).

Churchill, Winston, *Their Finest Hour, Vol II* (Cassell: London, 1949).

Clutton-Brock, Oliver, *RAF Evaders: The Comprehensive Story of Thousands of Escapers and their Escape Lines, Western Europe, 1940–1945*, 2nd edn (London: Grub Street, 2012).

Cobb, Matthew, *The Resistance: The French Fight Against the Nazis* (London: Simon & Schuster, 2009).

Collins, Larry, and Dominique Lapierre, *Is Paris Burning? How Paris Miraculously Escaped Adolf Hitler's Sentence of Death in August 1944* (New York: Simon and Schuster, 1965).

Cooper, Mike, *One of the Many* (Hailsham, E. Sussex: J&KH Publishing, 1997).

Cordet, Francis, *Carnets De Guerre En Charente* (Romagnat: De Borée, 2004).

Cowburn, Benjamin, *No Cloak, No Dagger* (London: Jarrolds, 1960).

Cruickshank, Charles, *Special Operations Executive in Scandinavia* (Oxford: OUP, 1986).

Daily Telegraph, 'Alix D'Unienville SOE: Courier in Wartime Paris', 2015.

D'Albert-Lake, Virginia, and Judy Barrett Litoff (ed.), *An American Heroine in the French Resistance* (New York: Fordham University Press, 2006).

Darling, Donald, *Secret Sunday* (London: William Kimber, 1975).

Darling, Donald, *Sunday at Large: Assignments of a Secret Agent* (London: William Kimber, 1977).

De Gaulle-Anthonioz, Geneviève, *God Remained Outside* (London: Souvenir, 1999). Published in USA in slightly different translation as *The Dawn of Hope* (New York: Arcade Pub., 1999).

Delbo, Charlotte, Rosette L. Lamont (trans.) and Lawrence L. Langer (intro.), *Auschwitz and After* (New Haven: Yale University Press, 1995).

Diamond, Hanna, *Fleeing Hitler: France 1940* (Oxford: Oxford University Press, 2007).

Escott, Beryl E., *Mission Improbable* (Sparkford, Somerset: P. Stephens, 1991).

Escott, Beryl E., *Heroines of SOE* (Kindle Locations 1657-1660, The History Press, Kindle Edition).

Esteban, Mixel, *Regards sur la Seconde Guerre Mondial en Pays Basque* (Elkar, 2007).

Etherington, William, *A Quiet Woman's War: The Story of Elsie Bell* (Norwich: Mousehold Press, 2002).

Foot, M.R.D., *SOE in France* (London: HMSO, 1966).

Foot, M.R.D, and James Maydon Langley, *MI9: The British Secret Service that Fostered Escape and Evasion 1939–1945, and its American Counterpart* (London: Bodley Head, 1979).

Foot, M.R.D., *SOE: The Special Operations Executive 1940–46* (London: BBC, 1984).

Foot, M.R.D., *Memories of an SOE Historian* (Barnsley: Pen & Sword Military, 2008).

'Foreign Service List, 1940, Volume 1940, Page 5 | Document Viewer', *Mocavo* (2015) – www.mocavo.co.uk/Foreign-Service-List-1940-Volume-1940/108805/5?browse=true#20 [accessed 11 November 2015].

Fraser, David, *The Jews of the Channel Islands and the Rule of Law, 1940–1945: Quite Contrary to the Principles of British Justice* (Brighton: Sussex Academic Press, 2000).

Fuller, Jean Overton, *Déricourt: The Chequered Spy* (Salisbury: Michael Russell).

Fuller, Jean Overton, *Double Agent? Light on the Secret Agents' War in France*, 2nd edn (London: Pan Books Ltd, 1961). First published 1958, revised by the author.

Fuller, Jean Overton, *The German Penetration of SOE, France 1941–1944* (Maidstone: George Mann Books, 1996).

Garde, Pia-Kristina, *Mina Föräldrars Kärlek* (Strängnäs: Axplock, 2008).

Garlinski, Jozef, *The Swiss Corridor* (London: JM Dent, 1981).

Garnet, David, and Andrew Roberts (intro), *The Secret History of PWE: The Political Warfare Executive 1939–1945* (London: St Ermin's, 2002).

Gastronomeruffec.wifeo.com, 'Ruffec Hôtel De France Rouillon Foie Gras Pâtés' (2015) – gastronomeruffec.wifeo.com/rouillon-hoteliers.php [accessed 12 November 2015].

Gendreau, Henri and Michel Regeon, *Ruffec et les ruffécois dans la guerre de 1938 à 1945* (Ruffec: Editions La Péruse, 1990).

Gildea, Robert, *Fighters in the Shadows: A New History of the French Resistance* (London: Faber & Faber, 2015).

Glass, Charles, *Americans in Paris: Life and Death under Nazi Occupation 1940–1944* (London: Harper Press, 2009).

Gluck, Gemma La Guardia, and Rochelle G. Saidel, *Fiorello's Sister* (Syracuse, NY: Syracuse University Press, 2007).

'Gottfried Von Cramm', *Wikipedia* (2015) – en.wikipedia.org/wiki/Gottfried_von_Cramm [accessed 11 November 2015].

Haas, Albert, *The Doctor and the Damned: A Survivor's Account of the Nazi Concentration Camps* (London: Granada, 1984).

Hall, Roger, *You're Stepping on my Cloak and Dagger* (Annapolis, MD: Naval Institute Press, 2004).

Hamilton, Ragna, *Det Knuste Mig Aldrig [It Never Crushed Me]* (Copenhagen: Lademan, 1977).

Harrison, Michael Charles Cooper, and Henry Antrobus Cartwright, *Within Four Walls* (London: E. Arnold & Co., 1930).

Hart-Davis, Duff, *Man of War: Officer, Adventurer, Agent* (London: Arrow Books, 2013).

Harvey, Winifred, *The Battle of Newlands* (Guernsey: Ladies' College, 1995).

Hass, Albert, *The Doctor and the Damned: A Survivor's Account of the Nazi Concentration Camps* (London: Granada, 1984).

Hastings, Max, *The Secret War: Spies, Codes and Guerillas 1939–1945* (London: William Collins, 2015).

Helluy, Joseph, and Jacqueline Helluy, *Mme Henry Barré De Saint-Venant, Qui Prit Le Nom De Marie-Odile Laroche, Commandant Des Forces Françaises Combattantes, Chef Du Réseau Marie-Odile: Mort Pour La France À Ravensbrück, Le 23 Mars 1945* (Nancy: J. Helluy, 1957).

Helm, Sarah, *A Life in Secrets: Vera Atkins and the Missing Agents of WWII* (New York: Nan A. Talese/ Doubleday, 2005).

Helm, Sarah, *If This is a Woman* (Little Brown, 2015).

Hemingway-Douglass, Reanne, and Don Douglass, *The Shelburne Escape Line: Secret Rescues of Allied Aviators by the French Underground and the British Royal Navy and London's MI9* (Anacortes, WA: Cave Art Press, 2014).

Hill, William Thomson, *The Martyrdom of Nurse Cavell: The Life Story of the Victim of Germany's Most Barbarous Crime* (London: Hutchinson & Co., 1915).

Hobam, Nicolas, *Quatre Années de Lutte Clandestine en Lorraine* (Nancy: Berger-Levault, 1946).

Hue, André, and Ewen Southby-Tailyour, *The Next Moon* (London: Penguin, 2005).

Humbert, Agnès, tr. Barbara Mellor, and afterword Julien Blanc, *Résistance: A Woman's Journal of Struggle and Defiance in Occupied France* (New York: Bloomsbury, 2008).

Hunt, Antonia, *Little Resistance* (New York: St Martin's Press, 1982).

Irwin, Will, *The Jedburghs* (New York: Public Affairs, 2005).

Is Paris Burning? (Paris brûle-t-il?) (Paris: René Clément, contains archive film, 1966).

Jeffery, Keith, *MI6: The History of the Secret Intelligence Service* (London: Bloomsbury, 2010).

Jones, Liane, *A Quiet Courage* (London: Corgi, 1998).

Karski, Jan, *Story of a Secret State: My Report to the World* (London: Penguin Classics, 2011). First published in Polish in the USA in 1944.

Kershaw, Alex, *Avenue of Spies* (New York: Crown Publishers, 2015).

King, Stella, *'Jacqueline', Pioneer Heroine of the Resistance* (London: Arms and Armour, 1989).

Lanckorońska, Karolina, Noel Clark, and Norman Davies, *Those Who Trespass Against Us* (London: Pimlico, 2005).

Langley, J.M., *Fight Another Day* (London: Collins, 1974).

Le Foulon, Marie-Laure, *Lady Mensonges: Mary Lindell, Fausse Heroine de la Résistance* (Paris: Alma, 2015).

L'Est Républicain, 'Marie-Odile Laroche, Grande Résistante De Villers-Lès-Nancy', 2011.

Lester, Elenore, *Wallenberg: The Man in the Iron Web* (Eaglewood Cliffs, NJ: A Reward Book, 1982).

Lewis, Alfred Allan, and Constance Woodworth, *Miss Elizabeth Arden* (New York: Coward, McCann & Geoghegan Inc., 1972).

Lexikon-der-wehrmacht.de, 'Lexikon Der Wehrmacht', 2015 – http://www.lexikon-der-wehrmacht.de/Personenregister/B/BismarckKv.htm [accessed 11 November 2015].

Little, Helen D., *British Women's Work During the Great War* (Naval & Military Press and Imperial War Museum).

Long, Helen, *Safe Houses are Dangerous* (Abson, Bristol, England: Abson Books, 1989).

Lorain, Pierre, *Secret Warfare: The Arms and Techniques of the Resistance* (London: Orbis Pub., 1984).

Lougarot, Giselle, and Bob Edme, *Dans L'ombre des Passeurs* (Donostia, Spain: Elkar, 2004).

Lyman, Robert, *Operation Suicide: The True Story of the Cockleshell Heroes* (London: Quercus, 2012).

Mackenzie, W.J.M., *The Secret History of SOE* (London: St Ermin's Press, 2000).

Marshall, Robert, *All the King's Men: They Betrayed their Own* (Glasgow: William Collins & Sons, 1988).

Martelli, George, *The Man Who Saved London: the Story of Michel Hollard* (London: Odhams Press, 1961).

Masson, Madeleine, *Christine: SOE Agent & Churchill's Favourite Spy* (London: Virago, 2005).

McGeoch, Ian, *An Affair of Chances: A Submariner's Odyssey 1939–44* (London: Imperial War Museum, 1991).

McIntosh, Elizabeth P., *Sisterhood of Spies: Women of the OSS* (Annapolis, MD: Naval Institute Press, 1998).

Members of the Royal Air Forces Ex Prisoner of War Association, and Francis Burt, *We Flew, We Fell, We Survived* (Royal Air Forces Ex Prisoner of War Association (Western Australia Branch), 1990).

'Michèle Cambards', *Rueil.la.gadeliere.pagesperso-orange.fr*, 2015 – rueil.la.gadeliere.pagesperso-orange.fr/pages/michele_cambards.htm [accessed 11 November 2015].

Millar, George, *Maquis: Personal Record Of Sabotage, Escape & Guerilla Warfare In Occupied France* (London: Pan Books, 1956). First published 1945 and revised by the author.

Millar, George Reid, *Horned Pigeon* (London: Wm Heinemann Ltd, 1947).

Miller, Joan, *One Girl's War* (Dingle, Co. Derry: Brandon Book Publishers Ltd, 1986).

Miller, Russell, *Behind Enemy Lines: The Oral History of Special Operations in World War II* (London: Pimlico, 2003).

Mocavo, 'Foreign Service List, 1940, Volume 1940, Page 5 | Document Viewer', 2015 – http://www.mocavo.co.uk/Foreign-Service-List-1940-Volume-1940/108805/5?browse=true#20 [accessed 11 November 2015].

Moorehead, Caroline, *A Train in Winter: A Story of Resistance, Friendship, and Survival in Auschwitz* (London: Vintage, 2012).

Morrison, Jack G., *Ravensbrück: Everyday Life in a Women's Concentration Camp 1939–45* (Princeton, NJ: Wiener, 2000).

Mueller, Michael, *Canaris: The Life and Death of Hitler's Spymaster* (London: Chatham, 2007).

Mulley, Clare, *The Spy who Loved: The Secrets and Lives of Christine Granville, Britain's First Female Special Agent of World War II* (London: Macmillan, 2012).

Murphy, David, "'I Was Terribly Frightened At Times": Irish Men And Women in the French Resistance and F Section of SOE, 1940–5', in *Franco-Irish Military Connections, 1590–1945*, 1st edn (Dublin: Four Courts Press, 2009).

Neave, Airey, *Saturday at MI9: A History of Underground Escape Lines in North-West Europe in 1940–5* (London: Hodder & Stoughton, 1969). Published in USA as *The Escape Room: The Fantastic Story of the Underground Escape Lines in Nazi-Occupied Europe* (Garden City, NY: Doubleday, 1970).

Nicholas, Elizabeth, *Death be not Proud: The True and Poignant Story of Seven Brave Women of the SOE who were Betrayed to the Germans and Cruelly Murdered in the Second World War* (London: White Lion Publishers, 1958).

Nicolson, David Aristide, *Warlord of the Resistance: The Story of Roger Landes* (Havertown: Pen and Sword, 1994).

Night and Fog [*Nuit et Brouillard*] (Documentary. France: Alain Resnais, 1955).

'Noël Riou, 1038 Compagnons, Compagnons, Musée de L'ordre de la Libération', *Ordredelaliberation.fr* (2015) – www.ordredelaliberation.fr/fr/les-compagnons/827/ noel-riou [accessed 11 November 2015].

Noyce, Wilfrid, *They Survived: A Study of the Will to Live* (New York: EP Dutton, 1963).

Odette (Film. Herbert Wilcox, 1950).

One Against the Wind (Film. USA: Larry Elikann, starring Judy David as Mary Lindell and Kate Beckinsale as her daughter, 1991).

Ott, Sandra, *War, Judgment, and Memory in the Basque Borderlands, 1914–1945* (Reno: University of Nevada Press, 2008).

Ottaway, Susan, *Violette Szabó: 'The Life that I Have …'* (Barnsley: Leo Cooper, 2002).

Ottaway, Susan, *Sisters, Secrets and Sacrifice: Two Sisters, Two Special Agents, Two Lives Risked for our Freedom* (London: Harper Collins, 2013).

Owen, Frank, *The Eddie Chapman Story* (London: Allan Wingate, 1953).

Owen, James, *Commando: Winning World War II Behind Enemy Lines* (London: Abacus, 2013).

Padfield, Peter, *Himmler, Reichsfuhrer SS* (New York: Holt, 1991).

Parker, Geoffrey, *The Black Scalpel: A Surgeon with SOE* (London: William Kimber, 1968).

Pattinson, Juliette, *Behind Enemy Lines: Gender, Passing and the Special Operations Executive in the Second World War* (Manchester: Manchester University Press, 2007).

Pearson, Judith L., *The Wolves at the Door: The True Story of America's Greatest Female Spy* (Guilford, Conn: Lyons Press, 2005).

Perrault, Gilles, and Peter Wiles (trans.), *The Red Orchestra* (New York: Schocken Books, 1969).

Perrin, Nigel, *Spirit of Resistance: The Life of SOE Agent Harry Peuleve* (Barnsley: Pen & Sword Military, 2008).

Persson, Sune, *Escape from the Third Reich: Folke Bernadotte and the White Buses* (Barnsley: Frontline, 2009) First published in Swedish as *Vi Åker Till Sverige: De Vita Bussarna 1945* [*We're Going to Sweden: The White Buses 1945*] (Rimbo: Fischer & Co., 2002).

Pitchfork, Graham, *True Stories of the RAF and Commonwealth Aircrews of WWII* (The National Archives, 2007).

'Portraits De Deux Femmes Déportées | Parcours Et Témoignages Militants', *Chsprod.hypotheses.org* (2015) – chsprod.hypotheses.org/portraits-deux-femmes-deportees> [accessed 2 December 2015].

Phdn.org, 'Affidavit Of Fritz Ernst Fischer, 21 November 1945', 2015 – http://www.phdn.org/archives/www.ess.uwe.ac.uk/genocide/Fischer.htm [accessed 5 December 2015].

Quétel, Claude, *Femmes Dans La Guerre 1939–1945* (Paris: Larousse, 2006).

Ragusin, Elsie A., *An American in Auschwitz: An Inspirational Biography of Faith, Tenacity and Patriotism*, 2nd edn (Winter Park FL: Legacy Book Publishing, 2010).

Read, Anthony, and David Fisher, *Operation Lucy: The Greatest Enigma of World War II* (London: Hodder & Stoughton, 1980).

Read, Anthony, and David Fisher, *Colonel Z: The Secret Life of a Master Spy* (London: Hodder & Stoughton, 1984).

Renault, Maisie, Louis Francois (intro.), and 'Remy' (foreword), *La Grand Misère* (Paris: Éditions Chavane, 1949).

Rigden, Denis, *SOE Syllabus: Lessons in Ungentlemanly Warfare* (London: National Archives, 2001).

Rodriguez, Suzanne, *Wild Heart: Natalie Clifford Barney and the Decadence of Literary Paris* (New York: Ecco, 2003).

Rossiter, Margaret L., *Women in the Resistance* (New York: Praeger, 1986).

'Les Rouillon et l'Hôtel de France', *Gastronomeruffec.wifeo.com* (2015) – gastronomeruffec.wifeo.com/rouillon-hoteliers.php [accessed 12 November 2015].

Routledge, Paul, *Public Servant, Secret Agent: The Elusive Life and Violent Death of Airey Neave* (London: Fourth Estate, 2003).

Rueil la Gadeliere, 2015 – http://rueil.la.gadeliere.pagesperso-orange.fr/pages/michele_cambards.htm [accessed 11 November 2015].

Salveson, Sylvia, *Forgive but do not Forget* (London: Hutchinson, 1958).

Say, Rosemary, and Noel Holland, *Rosie's War: An Englishwoman's Escape from Occupied France*, 2nd edn (London: Michael O'Mara Books, 2011).

Schenkar, Joan, *Truly Wilde: The Unsettling Story of Dolly Wilde, Oscar's Unusual Niece* (London: Virago, 2000).

Schneider, Helga, *Let Me Go: My Mother and the SS* (London: Vintage, 2005).

Seymour-Jones, Carole, *She Landed by Moonlight: The Story of Secret Agent Pearl Witherington, the 'Real Charlotte Gray'* (London: Hodder & Stoughton, 2013).

Shiber, Etta, *Paris – Underground* (London: George G. Harrap, 1944).

Shuker, Nancy, *Elizabeth Arden: Beauty Empire Builder* (Woodbridge, Conn: Blackbirch Press, 2001).

Sim, Kevin, *Women at War: Five Heroines who Defied the Nazis and Survived* (New York: William Morrow and Co., 1982).

Simone, Andre, *J'accuse! The Men who Betrayed France* (London: George G. Harrap, 1941).

Souhami, Diana, *Edith Cavell* (London: Quercus, 2010).

Southby-Tailyour, Ewen, *Blondie: A Biography of Lieutenant Colonel H.G. Hasler* (Barnsley, South Yorkshire: Pen & Sword, 2003).

Sparks, William, with Michael Munn, *The Last of the Cockleshell Heroes* (Leo Cooper, London, 1992).

Stafford, David, *Secret Agent: The True Story of the Special Operations Executive* (London: BBC, 2000).

Starns, Penny, *Odette: World War Two's Darling Spy* (Stroud: History Press, 2009).

Stevenson, William, *Spymistress: The Life of Vera Atkins, the Greatest Female Secret Agent of World War II* (New York: Arcade Publishing, 2007).

Sugarman, Martin, *Fighting Back: British Jewry's Military Contribution to the Second World War* (London: Vallentine Mitchell, 2010).

Sutherland, David, *He Who Dares: Recollections of Service in the SAS, SBS and MI5* (London: Leo Cooper, 1998).

Suttill, Francis J., *Shadows in the Fog: The True Story of Major Suttill and the Prosper French Resistance Network* (Stroud: The History Press, 2014).

Svenson, Åke, *De Vita Bussarna [The White Buses]* (Quarnberget Förlag, 2007).

Sweet, Matthew, *The West End Front: The Wartime Secrets of London's Grand Hotels* (London: Faber, 2012).

Szabó, Tania, *Young, Brave and Beautiful: The Missions of Special Operations Executive Agent Lieutenant Violette Szabó, George Cross, Croix de Guerre avec Étoile de Bronze* (Stroud: The History Press, 2015).

Tennant, Peter, *Touchlines of War* (Hull: Hull University Press, 1992).

Thurman, Judith, *Secrets of the Flesh: A Life of Colette* (London: Bloomsbury, 2000).

Tickell, Jerrard, *Odette: The Story of British Agent* (London: Chapman & Hall, 1949).

Tickell, Jerrard, *Moon Squadron* (London: Allan Wingate, 1956).

Tillion, Germaine, and Gerald Satterwhite (trans.), *Ravensbrück: an Eyewitness Account of a Women's Concentration Camp* (New York: Doubleday, 1973).

Tillotson, Michael, *SOE and the Resistance* (London: Continuum, 2011).

Tucker-Jones, Anthony, *Operation Dragoon: The Liberation of Southern France 1944* (Barnsley: Pen & Sword Military, 2009).

Van der Bijl, Nick, *Sharing The Secret: The History of the Intelligence Corps 1940–2010* (Barnsley: Pen & Sword Military, 2013).

Van Til, Jacqueline, *With Edith Cavell in Belgium* (New York: HW Bridges, 1922).

Vance, Jonathan F., *Unlikely Soldiers: How Two Canadians Fought the Secret War Against Nazi Occupation* (Toronto: Harper Collins, 2008).

Vaughan, Hal, *Doctor to the Resistance* (Washington DC: Brassey's, 2004).

Verity, Hugh, *We Landed by Moonlight: The Secret RAF Landings in France 1940–1944*, 3rd edn (Wilmslow: Crecy, 1998).

Vomécourt, Philippe de, *An Army of Amateurs* (Garden City, NY: Doubleday, 1961).

Vomécourt, Philippe de, *Who Lived to See the Day* (London: Hutchinson, 1961).

Wake, Nancy, *The White Mouse* (Macmillan: Melbourne, 1985).

Walters, Anne-Marie, *Moondrop to Gascony* (Wiltshire: Moho Books, 2009).

West, Nigel, *MI6: British Secret Intelligence Service Operations 1909–45* (London: Weidenfeld & Nicolson, 1983).

Wikipedia, 'Gottfried Von Cramm', 2015 – https://en.wikipedia.org/wiki/Gottfried_von_Cramm [accessed 11 November 2015].

Women of Courage: My Number Wasn't Up (Yorkshire Television: Peter Morley, 1976).

Woodhead, Lindy, *War Paint: Helena Rubinstein and Elizabeth Arden* (London: Virago, 2003).

Wynne, Barry, *No Drums – No Trumpets: The Story of Mary Lindell* (London: A. Barker, 1961).

Yarnold, Patrick, *Wanborough Manor: School for Secret Agents* (Puttenham: Hopfield Publications, 2009).

Young, Gordon, *In Trust and Treason* (London: Studio Vista, 1959).

INDEX

LINDELL'S LIST

The History Press

The destination for history
www.thehistorypress.co.uk